HTML and JavaScript

BASICS

FOU

Karl Barksdale
Utah County Academy of Sciences
Orem, Utah

Shane Turner
Software Engineering Consultant

COURSE TECHNOLOGY
CENGAGE Learning™

Australia • Brazil • Japan • Korea • Mexico • Singapore • Spain • United Kingdom • United States

COURSE TECHNOLOGY
CENGAGE Learning™

HTML and JavaScript BASICS, Fourth Edition
Karl Barksdale, Shane Turner

Executive Editor: Donna Gridley

Product Manager: Allison O'Meara McDonald

Development Editor: Rachel Biheller Bunin

Associate Product Manager: Amanda Lyons

Editorial Assistant: Kim Klasner

Senior Content Project Manager: Jill Braiewa

Associate Marketing Manager: Julie Schuster

Director of Manufacturing: Denise Powers

Text Designer: Shawn Girsberger

Manuscript Quality Assurance Lead: Jeff Schwartz

Manuscript Quality Assurance Reviewers: John Freitas, Serge Palladino, Danielle Shaw

Copy Editor: Karen Annett

Proofreader: John Bosco, Green Pen Quality Assurance

Indexer: Elizabeth Cunningham

Art Director: Faith Brosnan

Cover Designer: Hanh L. Luu

Cover Images: Influx Productions/Getty Images, Dieter Spannknebel/Getty Images

Compositor: GEX Publishing Services

For product information and technology assistance, contact us at
Cengage Learning Customer & Sales Support, 1-800-354-9706

For permission to use material from this text or product, submit all requests online at **www.cengage.com/permissions**
Further permissions questions can be emailed to
permissionrequest@cengage.com

Library of Congress Control Number: 2009942458

ISBN-13: 978-0-538-74235-1

ISBN-10: 0-538-74235-6

Course Technology
20 Channel Center Street
Boston, Massachusetts 02210
USA

Cengage Learning is a leading provider of customized learning solutions with office locations around the globe, including Singapore, the United Kingdom, Australia, Mexico, Brazil, and Japan. Locate your local office at:
www.cengage.com/global

Cengage Learning products are represented in Canada by Nelson Education, Ltd.

To learn more about Course Technology, visit **www.cengage.com/coursetechnology**

Visit our company website at **www.cengage.com**

Printed in the United States of America
1 2 3 4 5 6 7 16 15 14 13 12 11 10

ABOUT THIS BOOK

HTML and JavaScript BASICS is specifically intended for novice computer users who have no experience in software development or Web page design. The lessons in this book encourage the use of simple text editors that are available to virtually every computer user, and Web browsers that are available free of charge to anyone who has access to the Internet. The HTML and CSS material presented in this book will prove useful to any student who has an interest in creating functional Web sites. Likewise, the JavaScript lessons will not only provide useful information in and of themselves, but will also introduce students to sound programming principles that can be applied to many other popular programming languages including Java, C++, and C#.

To complete all lessons and End-of-Lesson material, this book will require approximately 20-24 hours.

Start-up Checklist

- Text editing software such as Notepad or SimpleText
- JavaScript-enabled Web browser such as Internet Explorer 8

INSIDE THE BASICS SERIES

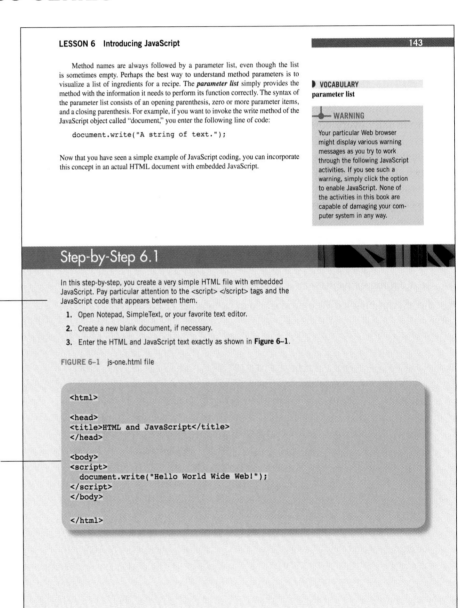

LESSON 6 Introducing JavaScript

Method names are always followed by a parameter list, even though the list is sometimes empty. Perhaps the best way to understand method parameters is to visualize a list of ingredients for a recipe. The *parameter list* simply provides the method with the information it needs to perform its function correctly. The syntax of the parameter list consists of an opening parenthesis, zero or more parameter items, and a closing parenthesis. For example, if you want to invoke the write method of the JavaScript object called "document," you enter the following line of code:

```
document.write("A string of text.");
```

Now that you have seen a simple example of JavaScript coding, you can incorporate this concept in an actual HTML document with embedded JavaScript.

▶ VOCABULARY
parameter list

◆—WARNING

Your particular Web browser might display various warning messages as you try to work through the following JavaScript activities. If you see such a warning, simply click the option to enable JavaScript. None of the activities in this book are capable of damaging your computer system in any way.

Step-by-Step 6.1

In this step-by-step, you create a very simple HTML file with embedded JavaScript. Pay particular attention to the <script> </script> tags and the JavaScript code that appears between them.

1. Open Notepad, SimpleText, or your favorite text editor.
2. Create a new blank document, if necessary.
3. Enter the HTML and JavaScript text exactly as shown in **Figure 6–1**.

FIGURE 6–1 js-one.html file

```
<html>

<head>
<title>HTML and JavaScript</title>
</head>

<body>
<script>
  document.write("Hello World Wide Web!");
</script>
</body>

</html>
```

Step-by-Step Exercises offer "hands-on practice" of the material just learned. Each exercise uses a data file or requires you to create a file from scratch.

HTML Figures show the script used in step-by-steps. Text to type appears in bold.

Lesson opener elements include the **Objectives** and **Suggested Completion Time**.

End of Lesson elements include the **Summary**, **Vocabulary Review**, **Review Questions**, **Lesson Projects**, and **Critical Thinking Activities**.

Instructor Resources Disk

ISBN-13: 9780538742368
ISBN-10: 0538742364

The Instructor Resources CD or DVD contains the following teaching resources:

The Data and Solution files for this course.

ExamView® tests for each lesson.

Instructor's Manual that includes lecture notes for each lesson and references to the end-of-lesson activities and Unit Review projects.

Answer Keys that include solutions to the lesson and unit review questions.

Copies of the figures that appear in the student text.

Suggested Syllabus with block, two quarter, and 18-week schedule.

PowerPoint presentations for each lesson.

ExamView®

This textbook is accompanied by ExamView, a powerful testing software package that allows instructors to create and administer printed, computer (LAN-based), and Internet exams. ExamView includes hundreds of questions that correspond to the topics covered in this text, enabling students to generate detailed study guides that include page references for further review. The computer-based and Internet testing components allow students to take exams at their computers, and save the instructor time by grading each exam automatically.

ABOUT THE AUTHORS

Karl Barksdale was a former Development Manager for the Training and Certification team at WordPerfect Corporation and a marketing Manager in the Consumer Products division for WordPerfect/Novell after their corporate merger. He was also the External Training Manager for Google's Online Sales and Operations division. He is best known for authoring and co-authoring over 62 business and computer education textbooks. Albeit, the job he enjoys most is teaching at the Utah County Academy of Sciences, an early college high school on the Utah Valley University Campus. (www.karlbarksdale.com)

E. Shane Turner completed a B.S. degree in Computer Science at Brigham Young University in 1987. He then spent nearly two decades working as a software engineer with many well-known companies including WordPerfect Corporation, Novell, Microsoft, and MCI. He has spent the last four years working as a software engineering consultant specializing in many Internet technologies, such as HTML, CSS, JavaScript, XML, Java, and PHP.

ACKNOWLEDGMENTS

Typical acknowledgements here to everyone who worked on the book, especially Rachel, Allison, and Donna. Thanks to my wife Stephani and our nine children Laura, Anthony, Diana, Katie, Afton, Evan, Roman, Emma, and Andrew for their support.

–Shane Turner

Bring Your Course Back To the BASICS

Developed with the needs of new learners in mind, the **BASICS** series is ideal for lower-level courses covering basic computer concepts, Microsoft Office, programming, and more. Introductory in nature, these texts are comprehensive enough to cover the most important features of each application.

Windows Movie Maker BASICS
ISBN-13: 978-0-324-78940-9
ISBN-10: 0-324-78940-8

This new text in the *BASICS* series explores Windows® Movie Maker 6.0 using Windows Vista and offers the essential skills for mastering this video-editing program. Topics include importing media, organizing elements, editing movies, adding sounds and texts, and publishing movies. Whether used in an introductory course or in conjunction with software tutorial instruction, this text proves to be the best solution for movie-making education.

Computer Literacy BASICS, 3rd Edition
Hardcover
ISBN-13: 978-1-4390-7853-2
ISBN-10: 1-4390-7853-X

Softcover
ISBN-13: 978-1-4390-7861-7
ISBN-10: 1-4390-7861-0

This revised third edition of *Computer Literacy BASICS* provides complete coverage of the new 2009 Internet and Computing Core Certification (IC3) standards. This Certiport-approved courseware is perfect for those preparing for IC3 certification and is appropriate for any introductory computer literacy course where the goal is to provide an overview of the most up-to-date computer topics of today.

CONTENTS

UNIT I   HTML BASICS

UNIT II JAVASCRIPT BASICS

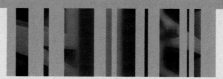

Estimated Time for
Unit 1: 7.5 hours

UNIT I

HTML BASICS

LESSON 1

Quick HTML Know-How

■ OBJECTIVES

Upon completion of this lesson, you should be able to:

- View HTML tags.
- Enter starting tags.
- Save correctly.
- Integrate levels of headings into Web pages.
- Create unordered, ordered, and embedded lists.

Creating Web pages has never been difficult, as you will see in this text. Designing dynamic Web pages is made even easier by a host of software tools designed for this creative task. At the root of every Web page, you'll find a series of tags and codes. This lesson will help you understand the mystery of the tags and codes beneath all the Web pages you visit online.

■ VOCABULARY

angle brackets

apps

Cascading Style Sheets (CSS)

Flash

gadgets

home page

HTML page

Hypertext Markup Language
(HTML)

Java

JavaScript

landing page

tags

Web browser

Web page

Web site

welcome page

XHTML

XML

▶ VOCABULARY
Web page
Web site
Web browers
Hypertext Markup Language
   (HTML)

Communicating on the Web

Web pages present a cascading explosion of multimedia. One *Web page* after another shares text, images, gadgets, maps, video, sound, and multimedia effects with a simple click or finger tap on any laptop or smartphone. *Web sites* are collections of related Web pages. Web pages are displayed by *Web browsers* whose job it is to locate and display Web information.

The dominant Web browser for the past two decades has been Microsoft's Internet Explorer. Internet Explorer's early forerunners and innovative competitors, National Supercomputing Center's freeware browser Mosaic and Netscape Navigator, have all but evaporated from common use. Fortunately, a recent renaissance in browser development has produced some challenging mainstream competitors to Internet Explorer, including Mozilla's Firefox, Apple's Safari, and Google's Chrome. Other interesting niche browsers include Opera, Avant, and Flock. Refer to **Figure 1–1** for common browser icons.

Our guess is that—if you are reading this book—you're already comfortable using at least one browser to go online. We suggest that you download three or four of these innovative browsers that you have not yet used to view Web pages. Give these new browsers a spin. Get a feel of the creativity behind today's browsing capacities. In this text, we give instructions for the two most widely used browsers, Internet Explorer and Firefox. However, browsers share many features, so the instructions for other browsers are very similar and you should easily be able to figure out how to use them.

FIGURE 1–1   Several of the popular browsers

Interfacing HTML and Other Tools

What do all of these browsers have in common? They all read and understand the various languages of the Internet explored in this text, starting with the foundation of all Web pages, *Hypertext Markup Language* or *HTML*. HTML is the original Web page creation tool. It allows you to create dynamic Web pages. HTML tells Web browsers how Web pages should look on a computer or handheld smartphone screen. HTML tags work everywhere on the Web and display Web pages on Macintosh, Linux, and Windows computers. They even work on Web-enabled cell phones, palm-sized devices, and Web-enabled television.

Powerful HTML-companion tools like *Cascading Style Sheets (CSS)* create convenient ways to determine the style (the look and feel of the fonts, colors, and spacing) on multiple Web site pages. Amazing additions to HTML, like *Extensible Markup Language (XML)* and *Extensible Hypertext Markup Language (XHTML)*, give new power to an old medium.

There are many other languages used online, such as *Java*, a programming language used widely with Internet applications; *Flash*, a high-impact multimedia creation tool; and *JavaScript*, a Java-like scripting language used to create miniapplications called alternatively *apps* and *gadgets*.

Nevertheless, HTML is the unifying language of the World Wide Web. HTML creates the foundation upon which these other programming languages can build. It is the starting point for any online developer, and it's where you should start, too. With a few simple HTML *tags*, you can determine the placement of colors, pictures, apps, gadgets, and backgrounds on Web pages. If you enter your tags correctly, Web browsers can display your pages properly the world over.

▶ VOCABULARY
Cascading Style Sheets (CSS)
XML
XHTML
Java
Flash
Javascript
apps
gadgets
tags

Uncovering the Page Beneath the Page

Figures 1–2A and **1–2B** show the same page viewed in two different ways. **Figure 1–2A** shows how visitors see the page in Internet Explorer, and **Figure 1–2B** shows the tags and code underneath the hood that create the visual display. All of the words, pictures, gadgets, and colors that you see in **Figure 1–2A** are organized by the tags you see in **Figure 1–2B**. The page is taken from a Web site created using Google Sites, a CSS-like development tool that allows the rapid creation of content sites. Three Google Gadgets have been added to the page, including Google's Calendar app.

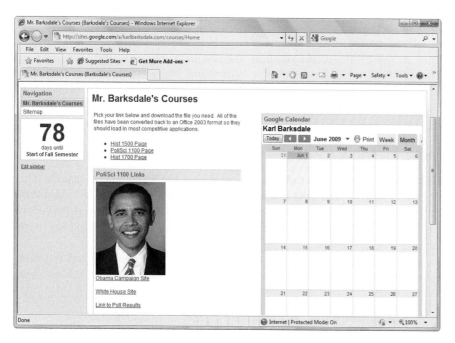

FIGURE 1–2A   A Google Sites CSS-style Web page (*sites.google.com*)

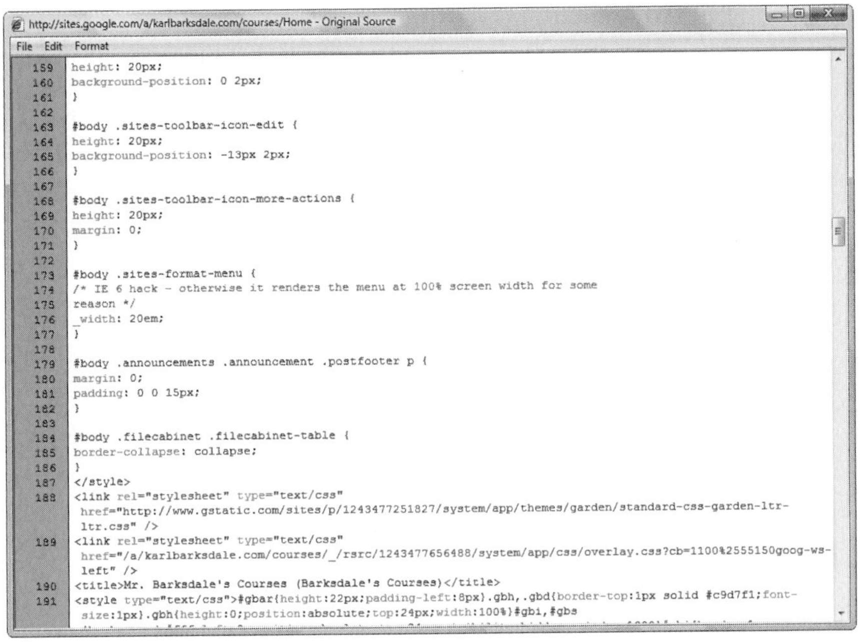


```
height: 20px;
background-position: 0 2px;
}

#body .sites-toolbar-icon-edit {
height: 20px;
background-position: -13px 2px;
}

#body .sites-toolbar-icon-more-actions {
height: 20px;
margin: 0;
}

#body .sites-format-menu {
/* IE 6 hack - otherwise it renders the menu at 100% screen width for some
reason */
_width: 20em;
}

#body .announcements .announcement .postfooter p {
margin: 0;
padding: 0 0 15px;
}

#body .filecabinet .filecabinet-table {
border-collapse: collapse;
}
</style>
<link rel="stylesheet" type="text/css"
 href="http://www.gstatic.com/sites/p/1243477251827/system/app/themes/garden/standard-css-garden-ltr-
 ltr.css" />
<link rel="stylesheet" type="text/css"
 href="/a/karlbarksdale.com/courses/_/rsrc/1243477656488/system/app/css/overlay.css?cb=1100%2555150goog-ws-
 left" />
<title>Mr. Barksdale's Courses (Barksdale's Courses)</title>
<style type="text/css">#gbar{height:22px;padding-left:8px}.gbh,.gbd{border-top:1px solid #c9d7f1;font-
 size:1px}.gbh{height:0;position:absolute;top:24px;width:100%}#gbi,#gbs
```

FIGURE 1–2B HTML tags for the Google Sites-created page shown in Figure 1–2A

Notice that **Figure 1–2B** isn't pretty or easy to understand. It shows the HTML tags and other code that creates the colorful and understandable Web page shown in **Figure 1–2A**. A Web browser interprets the tags and generates the Web page that the Web user sees.

There are lots of tags and many ways to use them. This hint should keep you from getting confused: **HTML tags are just instructions to the Web browser**. They tell the browser how to display information. Many times, you can look at the final Web page and guess what tags created the effect. If you remember this hint, learning HTML will be much easier.

How HTML Works

> **VOCABULARY**
> **angle brackets**

HTML tags are so simple that anyone can learn a few essential tags quickly. They usually appear in pairs enclosed in ***<angle brackets>***. These brackets are on the comma and period keys on your keyboard. Hold the Shift key and press the comma key to create a left angle bracket. Hold the Shift key and press the period key to create a right angle bracket.

To more clearly understand how HTML tags work, analyze the following example. If you want to center the title of this book on a Web page, all you need to do is enter:

```
<center>HTML and JavaScript BASICS</center>
```

Notice that there is a starting tag, <center>, and a closing tag, </center>. The only difference between the two tags is a slash (/) following the left angle bracket in the closing tag. <center></center> form a pair of tags, and if you haven't guessed already, anything between these tags will be centered on the page. Anything outside of these tags will not be affected by the command.

> **EXTRA FOR EXPERTS**
>
> If you are using Internet Explorer 7 or Internet Explorer 8, make your life easier and display the menu bar. For Internet Explorer 7, click the Tools button, and then click Menu Bar from the list. For Internet Explorer 8, click the Tools button, point to Toolbars, and then click Menu Bar. This allows you to use the View menu for opening and closing Web pages.

Step-by-Step 1.1

Now it's your turn. The following steps allow you to open a Web page of your choosing. Viewing the page behind the page is as easy as selecting View Source or the similar command, such as Page Source, from the View menu in your browser (see **Figures 1–3A** and **1–3B**).

1. Open your Web browser by clicking its icon on the Start menu or by double-clicking its icon on the desktop.

2. (Internet Explorer users, read *Extra for Experts* and display the menu bar.) When a page appears, use your mouse to click the **View** menu (Internet Explorer and Firefox) or click the **Page** button on the toolbar (Internet Explorer), as shown in **Figures 1–3A** and **1–3B**.

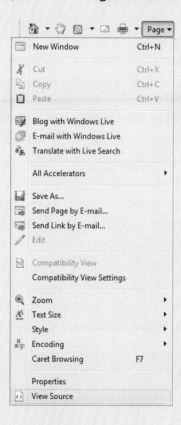

FIGURE 1–3A
The Page (Alternatively: View), View Source command in Internet Explorer

FIGURE 1–3B
The View, Page Source command in Mozilla Firefox

3. If you are using Internet Explorer, click the **Page** button on the toolbar, and then click **View Source** (see **Figure 1–3A**), or if you have unlocked the menu bar, click **View** on the menu bar, and then click **Source**.

   If you are using Firefox, click **View** on the menu bar and then click **Page Source**. (See **Figure 1–3B**.)

   A new window opens displaying the page beneath the page.

4. Examine the tags that appear on the page beneath the Web page. The tags will look similar to the tags you saw in **Figure 1–2B**.

5. Use your browser to view three or four other Web pages and view the source page for each of these pages. List seven tags that you find repeatedly in these pages. Guess and record what you think they do in **Table 1–1**.

TABLE 1–1   Common tags

NUMBER	TAG	EFFECT IT CREATES ON THE WEB PAGE
Sample		Centers text on a Web page
1		
2		
3		
4		
5		
6		
7		

NET BUSINESS

Business Discovers the Web

The World Wide Web (WWW) was created in the late 1980s in Europe. It was used limitedly in academic circles for about the next five years. However, it didn't capture the public's imagination until 1994 when a Web browser called Mosaic came on the scene. It was the first Web browser that allowed both pictures and text to accompany Web pages.

Excitement grew around this new way to present and share information. Then, Netscape Communications Corporation released its browser called Netscape Navigator. Netscape caught the imagination of businesses in 1995, and everything was different from that point on.

In just a few short years, the World Wide Web became the new advertising and commercial medium that we see today. Billions and billions of dollars were invested by companies and corporations hoping to cash in on this new, golden, information-sharing system. Suddenly, hundreds of thousands of corporate Web page creators began to learn HTML so they could put their business Web pages online.

Entering Your Mystery Tags the Old-Fashioned Way

Before you start entering tags, you need to be aware of the many terms used to describe pages created with HTML tags. The truth is that these names are used so interchangeably that most people are totally unaware that there are slight but important distinctions in their meanings.

- *Web page*: Also referred to as a Web document or HTML document, includes any page created in HTML that can be placed on the World Wide Web.
- *Home page*: The main or primary Web page for a corporation, organization, or individual. A personal home page is the first page you see as you start up your Web browser. When you click the Home icon in the browser, you will go directly to your starting home page.
- *Welcome page*: Designed especially for new visitors to a Web site.
- *Landing page*: A targeted "welcome" page used by Web advertisers. This is the page that appears after someone clicks on a Web ad, as seen in a Google Search or AdWords campaign or on an AdSense advertiser's page.
- *Web site*: Can include a collection of many interconnected Web pages organized by a specific company, organization, college or university, government agency, or individual. Web sites are stored on Web servers. CSS are often used to create a standard look and feel for a site.

Is it all clear now? Understanding these terms will help you learn how the Web works.

> **VOCABULARY**
>
> **Web page**
>
> **home page**
>
> **welcome page**
>
> **landing page**
>
> **Web site**

Creating a Powerful Advantage with Tags

There are many ways to create HTML tags. You can use specialized software, such as Expression Web 2 by Microsoft or Dreamweaver by Adobe, to create exciting Web pages. You can also go online and use free tools such as Sites from Google (*sites.google.com*). These programs help organize your HTML pages, enter text, move elements around, and create superior Web page effects without ever entering an HTML tag. You can create Web pages based on documents created with applications, for example Microsoft Office Word, Excel, or PowerPoint and Google Docs (*docs.google.com*). In fact, Google Docs creates Web-based documents, spreadsheets, and presentations, which all reside online in the Internet cloud and can be shared around the world as Web pages.

You will want to use one of these programs to create most of your Web pages. For the following activity in this lesson, however, you enter HTML tags at the core level using a simple text editor.

Why Learn HTML?

There are several reasons why it is important for you to learn HTML. Here is a list of five good reasons.

- First, by entering a few tags, you will develop a deeper understanding of how HTML really works.
- Second, you'll be able to troubleshoot Web pages when picky little errors occur.

- Third, you'll be able to view other pages and learn how others achieved certain effects.

- Fourth, you'll be able to better understand the file and folder structures found on Web servers.

- Fifth, and most important, you'll understand how HTML and other tools like XHTML, JavaScript, CSS, and XML work together.

What to Use

Any text editor will work for creating both HTML tags and JavaScript code. This is one of the reasons HTML and JavaScript are so popular. You do not need any specialized software tools to create exciting Web pages. Our recommendation is to use the simplest, most basic tools available. In Windows, you can use Notepad. On a Macintosh, you can use SimpleText. These text editors are easy to use and available on nearly every computer.

WARNING

Ask your instructor for advice on the text editor you should use before you jump in and waste a lot of time entering tags into the wrong text-editing tool.

Step-by-Step 1.2

Learning to enter a few HTML tags the old-fashioned way will give you a big advantage as you start to learn XHTML, JavaScript, XML, or CSS skills. Let's quickly cover the basics.

1. Open Notepad, SimpleText, or your favorite text editor.

2. Create a new document, if necessary.

3. Enter the tags shown in **Figure 1–4** in this exact order. Don't leave out a single angle bracket (<) or slash (/). Every character and letter is important.

FIGURE 1–4   Enter these tags exactly as shown here

```
<html>
<title></title>
<body>
<center></center>
<p></p>
<p></p>
<p></p>
<p></p>
<p></p>
</body>
</html>
```

4. The tags you just entered are called the basic tags. They include a standard set of tags that appear in most Web pages. But your page will look very sad and boring without a little text. Enter text between the tags, as shown in **Figure 1–5**. (Notice that the new text to be entered is shown in bold as a visual cue to help you as you work to create the HTML files in this book.)

FIGURE 1–5   Enter the text between the tags exactly as shown here

```
<html>
<title>HTML and JavaScript</title>
<body>
<center>Creating HTML and JavaScript</center>
<p>Learning to create HTML tags can help you in many ways: </p>
<p>You will develop a deeper understanding of how HTML really works. </p>
<p>You will be able to troubleshoot Web pages when errors occur. </p>
<p>You will be able to view other pages and learn how certain effects
were created. </p>
<p>You will understand how HTML and JavaScript work together. </p>
</body>
</html>
```

5. Leave your text editor open and go on to Step-by-Step 1.3 where you will learn how to save HTML files.

WARNING

In the past, HTML wasn't case sensitive. You could use uppercase <TAGS>, lowercase <tags>, or mixed <TagS>. With HTML 4.01 and XHTML 1.0 standards, new and stricter methods are now being implemented. It is now considered good form to only use lowercase <tags>.

Saving and Viewing Your HTML Page

HTML documents are text files. This means that they are saved in the simplest way possible. For the most part, text files only save the characters you see on your keyboard. All of the sophisticated word-processing commands are erased, leaving just the characters.

Saving as text allows HTML files to move quickly over the Web. However, the problem with text files is that most people don't know how to save them. Before you save, there are a few things you need to know first.

To tell one type of file from another, for example a photograph from a document, computers add file extensions to filenames. Sometimes you can see these extensions on your computer and sometimes you can't. Depending on your computer's operating system settings, the extensions might or might not be visible, but the software on your computer knows the kinds of file types it can open.

Extensions identify file types. **Table 1–2** lists some of these common file extensions.

TABLE 1–2   Common File Extensions

EXTENSION	FILE TYPE
.doc and .docx	Microsoft Word 2003 or 2007 document
.rtf	Microsoft's Rich Text Format
.txt	Text file
.html	HTML file on some computer systems
.htm	HTML file on some computer systems
.jpg or .jpeg	A popular image format used on the Web

⊢— WARNING

Ask your instructor if you need help saving an HTML/text file on your unique server setup or with your specific text editor.

HTML files are text files with an .html or .htm extension. Although the format that you need for HTML is text, the ending or extension must be .html (or .htm if you're using some Windows-based software). The .html or .htm extensions signal to the Web browser that this is an HTML text file. The .html extension is like putting up a sign saying, "Hey, browser, read me. I'm an HTML document."

Step-by-Step 1.3

The following steps show you how to save an HTML/text file in Notepad. Saving in other text editors, such as SimpleText, is very similar so you'll be able to use these directions to save your file.

1. Click **File** on the menu bar, and then click **Save As**.

2. Navigate to the folder where you save your documents, and then click the **New Folder** button in the Save As dialog box to create a new folder in which to save your HTML and JavaScript work.

3. Name the folder as you want or as directed by your instructor, and then open the folder into which you want to save your files.

4. Click the **Save as type** arrow, click **All Files (*.*)**, and then type **one.html** to name your file, as shown in **Figure 1–6**. Then click **Save**. If everything saves properly, go on to Step 5. Check with your instructor to make sure you save your file properly.

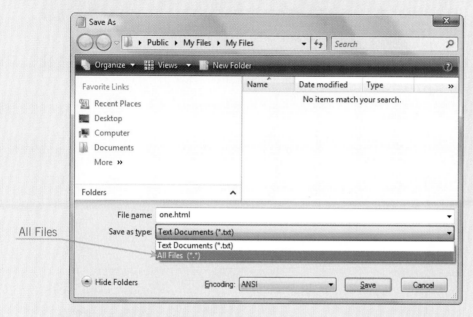

FIGURE 1–6
Name a text file with an .html extension

5. Viewing your HTML page in a Web browser is easy. These steps show you how to do this in Internet Explorer and Firefox.

    If you are an ***Internet Explorer*** user, perform the following steps (the steps for Firefox are listed after these steps):

    a. Start the Internet Explorer Web browser.

    b. Click **Tools** on the toolbar, point to **Toolbars**, and then click **Menu Bar**, as shown in **Figure 1–7**.

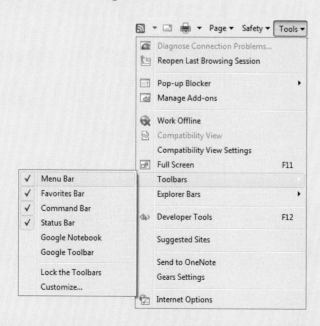

FIGURE 1–7
Open the menu bar to make it easier to use

c. Click **File** on the menu bar, and then click **Open**.

d. Click the **Browse** button, and then navigate to the folder where you saved your one.html file.

e. Click **one.html** in the Open text box, and then click **Open**, as shown in **Figure 1–8**.

f. In the Open dialog box, click **OK**.

FIGURE 1–8
Find your file in IE

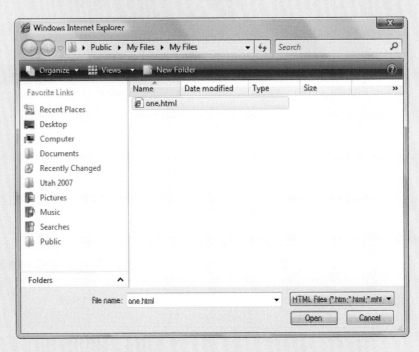

If you are a *Firefox* user, perform the following steps:

a. Start the Firefox Web browser.

b. Click **File** on the menu bar, and then click **Open File**, as shown in **Figure 1–9**.

FIGURE 1–9
Open File command in Firefox

c. Click the **Files of type** arrow, and then click **All Files**, if it is not already selected.

d. Browse to the folder where you saved the one.html file.

e. Click the **one.html** file, and then click **Open**, as shown in **Figure 1–10**.

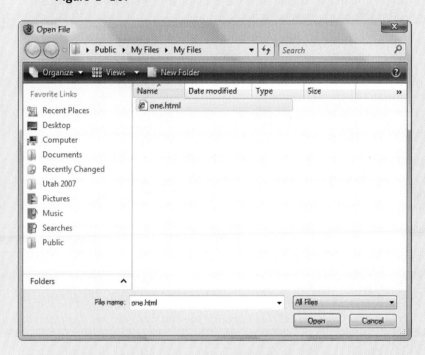

FIGURE 1–10
Find your file in Firefox

6. View your file. It should look like **Figure 1–11**.

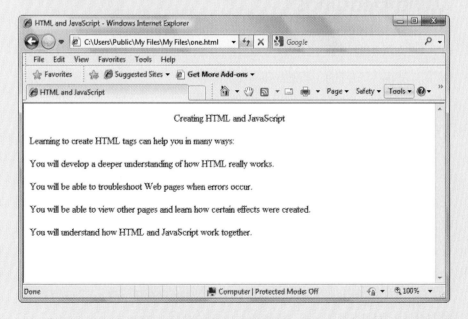

FIGURE 1–11
Congratulations! Your Web page probably looks like this sample

7. How does your Web page look? Make any corrections necessary, save the text file again, return to your browser, and then click the browser **Reload** or **Refresh** button to see the changes you have made.

NET BUSINESS

The Browser Wars

In 1994, the dominant browser was called Mosaic. It was freeware out of the National Supercomputing Center at the University of Illinois in Champaign-Urbana. At the time Netscape came on the scene, Mosaic was adding 600,000 new users a month. But things changed in a hurry.

In the first three months of 1995, Netscape's Navigator browser gained a reputation for being a faster browser. By midyear, it had captured 50 percent of browser users, and by the end of the year, it commanded a whopping 80 percent of the browser market.

Netscape's dominance was quickly challenged by rival Microsoft, which came out with its Internet Explorer browser. Microsoft gave away copies of its browser in hopes of cutting into Netscape's lead. Microsoft also had an advantage in that its Windows operating system ran on over 90 percent of personal computers. By bundling Windows and Internet Explorer together, Microsoft created a unique marketing advantage.

However, Microsoft's advantage led to many legal battles. Several antitrust lawsuits argued that Microsoft was using its dominance in Windows to crush Netscape and to eliminate its competition unfairly. Microsoft claimed it was simply adding more value for its customers by making its Internet Explorer browser easier to access by its Windows customers.

The browser wars continue today. Microsoft's Internet Explorer is still the dominant player in most markets; Netscape's Navigator has all but disappeared from use. Fortunately, for the sake of competition, Mozilla's Firefox took Netscape's place and has made a charge at Internet Explorer's dominance. By 2009, Internet Explorer's market share dropped to 65 percent. Other browsers have also been developed to further challenge the dominance of Internet Explorer, including Apple's Safari and Google's Chrome, which by 2009 occupied the third and fourth positions, respectively.

Using Headings

Most printed documents use headings to help the reader find important portions of text. Think of a report you have written. The main heading usually appears at the top and in the center of the page. Subheadings or secondary headings usually appear at the side of the paper and are often shown in bold.

HTML gives you six standard headings, or title sizes, from which to choose. In later step-by-steps, you'll learn of more sophisticated ways to manipulate the size and appearance of text. Nevertheless, the heading tags provide an easy way to control the size of your text, making it stand out so your reader can view the headings clearly.

The heading tags are easy to remember. They use the letter H with a number from 1 to 6 to indicate the level of the heading. Heading numbers indicate the level of importance for marked headings, with 1 being the most prominent and 6 being the least prominent. Look for:

```
<h1></h1>
<h2></h2>
<h3></h3>
<h4></h4>
<h5></h5>
<h6></h6>
```

Anything inside the heading tags will be made larger or smaller, depending on the number. For example:

```
<h1>Very Big</h1>
<h3>In the Middle</h3>
<h6>Very Small</h6>
```

Step-by-Step 1.4

In this step-by-step, you open the HTML file you have been working on and add the heading or title tags.

1. Open your text editor.

2. Open your **one.html** or **one.htm** file, if it is not still open.

   If you are using Notepad, click **File** on the menu bar, click **Open**, click the **Files of type** arrow, and then click **All Files**, as shown in **Figure 1–12**. Otherwise, you will not be able to view your .html or .htm file.

FIGURE 1–12
Open a file in Notepad

Select to display
All File types

3. Enter the heading tags shown in bold in **Figure 1–13**.

FIGURE 1–13   Add the heading tags

```
<html>
<title>HTML and JavaScript</title>
<body>
<center><h1>Creating HTML and JavaScript</h1></center>
<p><h2>Learning to create HTML tags can help you in many ways:<h2></p>
<p><h3>You will develop a deeper understanding of how HTML really
works.<h3>
</p>
<p><h4>You will be able to troubleshoot Web pages when errors occur.<h4>
</p>
<p><h5>You will be able to view other pages and learn how certain effects
were created.<h5></p>
<p><h6>You will understand how HTML and JavaScript work together.<h6></p>
</body>
</html>
```

4. Save your new HTML file as **two.html** or **two.htm** to the same folder that you saved the previous file.

5. Start your Web browser, and then open your **two.html** or **two.htm** file to view it in the browser window. It should look like **Figure 1–14**.

FIGURE 1–14
Various size headings in a
Web page

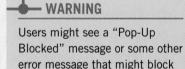

WARNING

Users might see a "Pop-Up Blocked" message or some other error message that might block the opening of the page. Simply click the option to allow the content to be viewed. If you need help, ask your instructor or read the Help files for your specific browser.

Heading tags really change the look of a page. In our example in **Figure 1–14**, there should be only three levels of information:

```
<h1></h1> The title at the top
<h2></h2> The introductory line followed by a
colon ( : )
<h3></h3> The list of the reasons to learn HTML
tags
```

6. Return to your text editor and change the heading tags. Use no more than three <h></h> tags for this Web page. Think about your tag choices, and then make your Web page comfortable to read, emphasizing the three levels this document dictates. Resave your file to make your changes become effective.

Using Numbered and Bulleted Lists

In the previous step-by-step, you were asked to reorganize your two.html file and use the <h> tags in a more consistent manner. In this step-by-step, we are going to improve the Web page document even further.

One of the most powerful ways to organize information on a Web page is by the use of lists. There are several kinds of lists, including the following:

```
<ul></ul> Unordered (or bulleted) lists
<ol></ol> Ordered (or numbered) lists
```

Step-by-Step 1.5

The unordered lists tags <ul></ul> create bulleted lists. Start your list with the opening <ul> unordered lists tag, mark the items to be listed with the list <li></li> tags, and place an </ul> tag at the end of your list. Try it!

1. Open your **two.html** or **two.htm** file for text editing.

2. Enter the **<ul></ul>** tags at the start and at the end of the list to create an unordered list, as shown in **Figure 1--15**.

3. Replace the **<p>** and **</p>** tags with **<li>** and **</li>** tags for each sentence in the list, as shown in **Figure 1–15**.

FIGURE 1–15   Enter the unordered list tags

```
<html>
<title>HTML and JavaScript</title>
<body>
<center><h1>Creating HTML and JavaScript</h1></center>
<p><h2>Learning to create HTML tags can help you in many ways:</h2></p>

<ul>
<li><h3>You will develop a deeper understanding of how HTML really works.
</h3></li>
<li><h3>You will be able to troubleshoot Web pages when errors occur.
</h3></li>
<li><h3>You will be able to view other pages and learn how certain
effects were created.</h3></li>
<li><h3>You will understand how HTML and JavaScript work together.
</h3></li>
</ul>

</body>
</html>
```

4. Save your file as **three.html** or **three.htm** to the folder where you saved the other HTML files for this lesson.

5. View your three.html or three.htm Web page in a browser to see how it looks. It should be similar to **Figure 1–16**.

FIGURE 1–16
An unordered list

6. Open your **three.html** or **three.htm** file for text editing, if it is not already open.

7. Change the pair of **<ul></ul>** tags to **<ol></ol>** tags to change your list from an unordered list to an ordered list, as shown in **Figure 1–17**. No other changes are necessary.

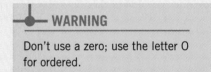

WARNING

Don't use a zero; use the letter O for ordered.

FIGURE 1–17 Enter the ordered lists tags

```
<html>
<title>HTML and JavaScript</title>
<body>
<center><h1>Creating HTML and JavaScript</h1></center>
<p><h2>Learning to create HTML tags can help you in many ways: </h2></p>

<ol>
<li><h3>You will develop a deeper understanding of how HTML really works.
</h3></li>
<li><h3>You will be able to troubleshoot Web pages when errors occur.
</h3></li>
<li><h3>You will be able to view other pages and learn how certain
effects were created.
```

Continued on next page 〉〉

FIGURE 1–17   Enter the ordered lists tags

《 *Continued from previous page*

```
</h3></li>
<li><h3>You will understand how HTML and JavaScript work together.
</h3></li>
</ol>

</body>
</html>
```

8. Save your file as **four.html** or **four.htm**.

9. View your four.html or four.htm page in a browser to see how it looks. It should look similar to **Figure 1–18**.

FIGURE 1–18
An ordered or numbered list

10. Open your **four.html** or **four.htm** file for text editing, if it is not already open.

11. Add two pairs of **<ul></ul>** tags in the middle of the list, as shown in **Figure 1–19**.

FIGURE 1–19   Enter additional unordered lists tags

```
<html>
<title>HTML and JavaScript</title>
<body>
<center><h1>Creating HTML and JavaScript</h1></center>
<p><h2>Learning to create HTML tags can help you in many ways: </h2></p>

<ol>
<li><h3>You will develop a deeper understanding of how HTML really works.
</h3></li>

<ul>
<li><h3>You will be able to troubleshoot Web pages when errors occur. </
h3></li>
<ul>

<li><h3>You will be able to view other pages and learn how certain
effects were created.
</h3></li>
</ul>
</ul>

<li><h3>You will understand how HTML and JavaScript work together.
</h3></li>
</ol>
</body>
</html>
```

12. Save your file as **five.html** or **five.htm**.

13. View your five.html or five.htm Web page in a browser to see how it looks. It should look similar to **Figure 1–20**.

FIGURE 1–20
Embedded and indented lists

14. Exit your browser and text editor and shut down your computer if you are finished for today. Otherwise, continue to the Summary section.

SUMMARY

In this lesson, you learned:

- How to identify HTML tags.
- How to enter your starting tags.
- How to save your HTML file correctly.

- How to integrate levels of headings into Web pages.
- How to create unordered, ordered, and embedded lists.

 VOCABULARY REVIEW

Define the following terms:

angle brackets	HTML page	Web browser
apps	Hypertext Markup Language (HTML)	Web page
Cascading Style Sheets	Java	Web site
Flash	JavaScript	welcome page
gadgets	landing page	XHTML
home page	tags	XML

■ REVIEW QUESTIONS

TRUE / FALSE

Circle T if the statement is true or F if the statement is false.

T   F   **1.**   The <li> tag defines a list item.

T   F   **2.**   The <ol> tag creates a bulleted list.

T   F   **3.**   The <center> tag formats text so that it is centered on the page.

T   F   **4.**   The opening tag is marked by a / or slash.

T   F   **5.**   The <ul> tag creates a list with no particular order.

T   F   **6.**   You can use both uppercase and lowercase text inside your tags.

T   F   **7.**   <h5> creates the largest heading; <h1> creates the smallest heading.

T   F   **8.**   HTML files must be saved with an .html or .htm extension.

T   F   **9.**   If you happen to leave out a / or a <, the browser will still be able to figure out what you want to display.

T   F   **10.**   Learning HTML is very, very difficult and impossible to learn by mere mortals.

FILL IN THE BLANK

Complete the following sentences by writing the correct word or words in the blanks provided.

1. A(n) _____ list shows items in no particular order.

2. A(n) _____ list shows items in a numerical order.

3. File _____ are three-letter suffixes that tell what type of file a file is.

4. _____ was the first Web browser that Netscape competed against.

5. HTML is made up of _____, which are commands enclosed in angle brackets (< >).

6. An HTML file usually begins with the _____ tag.

7. The text seen by viewers in a browser window is written between the _____ tags.

8. A(n) _____ page is designed to be the first page a visitor sees after clicking on a Web ad.

WRITTEN QUESTIONS

Write a short answer to each of the following questions:

1. Think of a way to explain how HTML tags work to people who have never created a Web page before in their lives. How can you explain how HTML works to a novice?

2. Explain the process of viewing the HTML source code for an HTML Web page.

3. Explain how you must save HTML text pages.

4. What are filename extensions? Give examples.

5. After trying three or four different browsers, which do you like best and why?

■ PROJECTS

PROJECT 1–1: GUIDE YOURSELF THROUGH HTML, XHTML, AND CSS

You have just been hired as the Webmaster for GreatApplications, Inc., a major software and Web site developer, but your HTML/XHTML skills are limited. You need to find some good HTML or XHTML information fast! What do you do?

The answer is obvious. Hit the Web. Pick a search tool like Google, MSN, or Yahoo! or some other site like Wikipedia, and enter the search words:

HTML

HTML Guides

Learning HTML

XHTML

XHTML Guides

Learning XHTML

Use the following table to record the titles and URLs or Web addresses and write a brief summary of the helpful HTML and XHTML Web pages you find:

TABLE 1–3   Helpful Web pages

TITLE THAT APPEARS IN THE TITLE BAR	WEB ADDRESS OR URL	DESCRIPTION

PROJECT 1–2: PICK SEVEN SUPER PAGES

GreatApplications, Inc., is looking for design ideas for their new Web site welcome page. In a team of three or four, create a list of your favorite Web pages. Find seven great Web pages and discuss what makes them so cool. Vote, and make your vote count as you rank the seven welcome pages from Number 1 to Number 7. List your team's choices below for future reference.

TABLE 1–4   Well-Designed Web Pages

RANKING	TITLE AS IT APPEARS IN THE TITLE BAR	WEB ADDRESS OR URL
1.		
2.		
3.		
4.		
5.		
6.		
7.		

PROJECT 1–3: SITE, SITE, WHO NEEDS A SITE?

Web sites are important for many companies, groups, and individuals. We all know that many corporations would go out of business without their quality Web sites. But just how important are great-looking Web sites for noncommercial organizations and government agencies?

List reasons why these organizations need Web sites:

Government agencies:

Nonprofit organizations:

Universities:

 # CRITICAL THINKING

ACTIVITY 1–1

Prepare a 100- to 250-word answer to the following question. The World Wide Web is a large web of computer networks that share HTML files. You can visit a new Web page every minute of every day for the rest of your life and never come close to reading a fraction of the available Web pages. There are billions of Web pages. While HTML has allowed people to share Web pages easily, has HTML also contributed to information overload? If so, how and what can be done about it?

ACTIVITY 1–2

There is an error in the following set of tags, and you are to find it and fix it. What will the current tags do to your page? What does it look like after you make the correction?

```
<ol>
<li>Item A</li>
<ul>
<li>Item A1</li>
<li>Item A2</li>
</ul>
<li>Item B</li>
<ul>
<li>Item B1</li>
<li>Item B2</li>
</ul>
</ul>
```

ACTIVITY 1–3

Diagram the tags that will allow you to create a sophisticated outline in HTML (you know, the kind you had to do for your last research paper). In what ways can your research paper be enhanced online in HTML?

◼ CAPSTONE SIMULATION

All good authors know that before starting a big writing project, it is often a good idea to create an outline of the information they want to present. Outlines can be very effective in helping writers to organize their thoughts and to make sure their writing follows a logical flow of ideas. Use the HTML skills you have learned in this lesson to create an outline for a book that is composed of units, chapters, and sections.

Project Requirements:

- Your outline must have a title that is centered at the top of the page.

- Your outline must contain at least two units in an ordered list.

- Your outline must contain at least three chapters per unit, also ordered.

- Your outline must contain at least three sections per chapter—not ordered.

LESSON 2

Basic Organization Techniques

■ OBJECTIVES

Upon completion of this lesson, you should be able to:

- Format page information with single and double spacing.
- Organize page information with lines.
- Implement attributes and values.
- Change Web page color defaults by altering attributes and values with both HTML and CSS.
- Create a hyperlink to another location within a Web page.
- Make a hyperlink to a URL or Web page on the Web.
- Link to another Web page on your own computer.

The World Wide Web is the creation of hundreds of thousands of people who are constantly developing, improving, posting, and publishing amazing online Web pages. The Web is a community where you can be totally creative. All you need to join in is a little knowledge of HTML, XHTML, CSS, and JavaScript. With these development tools in your bag of tricks, you will be limited only by your imagination as you build your own online world.

■ VOCABULARY

attribute

deprecated

hexadecimal

hyperlinks

hypertext links

Hypertext Transfer Protocol (HTTP)

standards

Uniform Resource Locator (URL)

value

▶ VOCABULARY

hypertext links

hyperlinks

deprecated

Building Better Web Pages

As you have traveled the Web, you have seen creative and exciting Web pages, and you have seen other Web pages that are unimaginative. The main difference between a great and a dull page comes down to the little things—the choice of lettering, colors, and pictures and the selection of elements that help with the overall organization of the pages.

You can use many HTML/XHTML techniques to make your pages perfectly presentable. These are single- and double-spacing techniques and other specialized organizing tags that can make any Web page easier to read. Web pages can be made more appealing by adding space between paragraphs or by placing lines between different sections of the Web page. Centered and bold titles can certainly aid readers. Color choices are extremely important. Changing the colors of your text and page background can make a document not only more appealing, but also easier to follow. Use the right colors, and your page will be fabulous.

Hypertext links help make Web pages interesting and easy to navigate. *Hyperlinks*, as they are often called, can be clicked to allow users to navigate to another Web site, to another Web page at the current Web site, or to a specific location within the current document. If you have a lot of information on a single page, creating an index can help your reader jump to the exact information for which they are looking.

Deprecation

HTML is changing, and with new XHTML standards emerging, it is becoming a much stricter development environment. Many tried-and-true tags are now unappreciated. More to the point, they are being *deprecated*, which means they are being downgraded, devalued, or even becoming obsolete! Sad as it might seem, the simple <center></center> tag introduced in Lesson 1 might be moved to the scrap heap sometime in the future. Don't worry much about it—it's not going away anytime soon. Nevertheless, although all browsers still recognize the old <center> tag and others like it, the way you should center a title today is to include it as a style inside an appreciated tag such as <h></h>, such as the following:

```
<h1 style="text-align:center">Organizing Tags</h1>
```

Single and Double Spacing

As you learn the new HTML elements taught in this lesson, you will be introduced to new ideas on how to organize your Web pages. Most early Web pages were long, boring collections of words. All that has changed, as you will see in this next step-by-step activity. There is no longer any reason to create tedious, hard-to-read Web pages. You can easily organize text with the help of a few new tags: <p></p> for paragraph and <br /> for break.

Step-by-Step 2.1

In the following step-by-step, you see firsthand how to improve the readability and organization of your page.

1. Open Notepad, SimpleText, or your text editor.

2. Start a new blank document, and then enter the HTML Web page information exactly as shown in **Figure 2–1**.

FIGURE 2–1 Enter these tags and words exactly as shown

```
<html>
<head>
<title>HTML and JavaScript</title>
</head>

<body>
<h1 style="text-align:center">Organizing Tags</h1>

There are many ways to organize a Web page. This Web page will organize
text, hypertext links, colors and fonts. You'll also demonstrate single
spacing, double spacing, and the use of line breaks.

This Web page will display how to organize Web pages in a number of
ways using:

Powerful Lines
Hyperlinks to HTML, XHTML and JavaScript Sources
Hyperlinks to Previously Created Web Pages
Fancy Fonts
Perfect Pictures
Orderly Tables
Extraordinary Extras

</body>
</html>
```

3. Click **File** on the menu bar, click **Save**, and then save the file with the name **six.html** or **six.htm** using the same method that you learned in Step-by-Step 1.3.

4. Open your Web browser and view the six.html page. It should look like a single block of text, as shown in **Figure 2–2**. (Refer back to Step-by-Step 1.3 if you need a reminder on how to view an HTML file in your Web browser.)

Notice that although the page might have looked organized when you entered it as HTML tags in the text editor, without a few organizing tags, the organization of the page falls apart when viewed in a Web browser. The use of a few selected tags can help clean up and create order on a page. The two easiest tags you can use to organize a page are the <p></p>, or paragraph, tags and the <br />, or break, tag. The <p></p> tags create a double space around the text. The <br /> tag creates a single-spaced break.

WARNING

The br tag does not need a pair or a separate closing tag but should still be closed. To create the tag and close it at the same time, enter a space after the letters br and enter a slash / before the right angle bracket like this: <br />. The space isn't essential. For that matter, you still don't really need to close this tag, but it's good form to do so.

FIGURE 2–2
An unorganized Web page

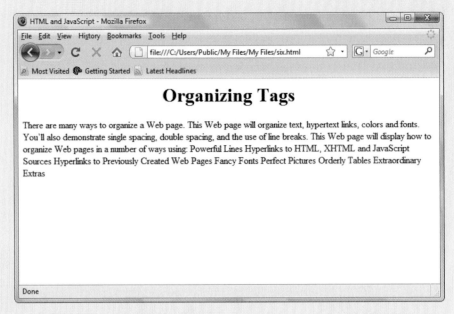

5. Open your **six.html** or **six.htm** file in Notepad, SimpleText, or your text editor.

6. Add the <p></p> and <br /> tags to the document, as shown in bold in **Figure 2–3**.

FIGURE 2–3   Enter the <p></p> and <br /> tags

```
<html>
<head>
<title>HTML and JavaScript</title>
</head>

<body>
<h1 style="text-align:center">Organizing Tags</h1>

<p>There are many ways to organize a Web page. This Web page will
organize text, hypertext links, colors and fonts. You'll also demonstrate
single spacing, double spacing, and the use of line breaks. </p>

<p>This Web page will display how to organize Web pages in a number of
ways using: </p>

Powerful Lines <br />
Hyperlinks to HTML, XHTML and JavaScript Sources <br />
```

Continued on next page 〉〉

FIGURE 2–3 Enter the <p></p> and <br /> tags

《 *Continued from previous page*

```
Hyperlinks to Previously Created Web Pages <br />
Fancy Fonts <br />
Perfect Pictures <br />
Orderly Tables <br />
Extraordinary Extras <br />

</body>
</html>
```

7. Use the **Save As** command to save your updated file as **seven.html** or **seven.htm**.

8. Review your work, and then open the **seven.html** file in your Web browser. The page should look much better this time, with text organized on your screen, similar to **Figure 2–4**.

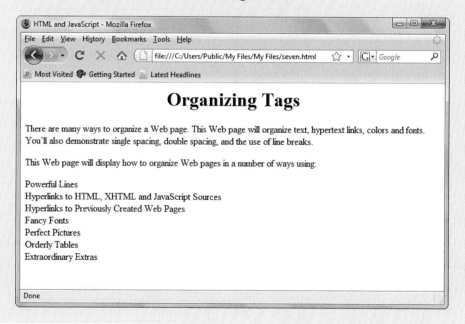

FIGURE 2–4
The <p></p> and <br /> tags clean up a Web page

Adding Lines and Background Colors

HTML and XHTML tags can be enhanced. For example, to change the background color of your page, you can add the background *attribute* (or special quality) and give the tag a color *value* (or a definition of the attribute), as shown in **Figure 2–5**. Attributes and values are powerful tools to help you organize and change the look of

▶ VOCABULARY
attribute

value

your Web pages. For example, you've already used attributes and values when you inserted this code into the file six.html:

```
<h1 style="text-align:center">Organizing Tags</h1>
```

In this example, h1 the style attribute is defined by an attribute specification, and the center value is written as follows: "text-align:center". You can also add attributes and values to the <body> tag, as shown in **Figure 2–5**. In this example, the style value has an attribute set, namely "background-color:blue". Values are always placed in quotation marks.

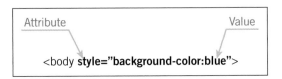

FIGURE 2–5   Changing background colors

Named Colors

You can enter color names as text values. Red, blue, green, black, white, and yellow are common colors. But there are many variations. For example, here are just a few examples of named shades of blue:

- aliceblue
- cornflowerblue
- darkblue
- deepskyblue
- dodgerblue
- lightskyblue

You can look up HTML color names and all the variations online.

Color by Number in Hexadecimal

Although you can enter color names as text values, computers understand codes and numbers. Therefore, values must be converted into code that the computer understands, so the word *yellow* will be converted by the browser into the appropriate color value in numerical terms (which is #FFFF00 for yellow).

Using the common names of colors is somewhat limiting. Color values can be carefully controlled and changed to match virtually every color in the rainbow by using special numerical or **_hexadecimal_** values. The invention of hexadecimal coding is one of the greatest advances in computing. Hexadecimal digits operate on a base-16 number system rather than the base-10 number system we normally use. Hexadecimal numbers use the letters A, B, C, D, E, and F along with the numbers 0 to 9 to create 16 different digits. For example, look at the following color values expressed as hexadecimal numbers in **Table 2–1**.

▶ **VOCABULARY**
hexadecimal

TABLE 2–1 Color values expressed as hexadecimal numbers

COLOR	HEXADECIMAL NUMBER
White	#FFFFFF
Green	#00FF00
Black	#000000
Blue	#0000FF
Red	#FF0000
Yellow	#FFFF00

Shades of these colors are created by changing the hexadecimal numbers. For example, a really great sky blue can be created on your HTML page with the hexadecimal number 00CCFF. Do you want a nice light purple? Try FF95FF. An alternate green can be created with AAFF00. Substitute text color values with numbers in your Web page and see what happens. For example, try this in the <body> tag and see what happens:

```
<body style="background-color:#AAFF00">
```

Horizontal Rules Rule

Another widely used tag is the <hr />, or horizontal, rule. This tag simply creates a horizontal line across the page. Just as you can with other tags, you can add attributes and values to the <hr /> tag to change the size and shape of the horizontal rule. It must also be closed, just like the <br /> tag, with a space and a slash.

NET BUSINESS

Bad Color Choices

Some Web page builders select clashing backgrounds and colors that make Web pages difficult to read. It is considered bad form to create hard-to-read Web pages. Before you publish your Web page to the Web, test your pages and make sure that all the text appears clearly on the page and that your color choices don't detract from what you are trying to say.

Also, when making your selections, it is a good idea to think about the needs of visually impaired persons and those who suffer from color blindness. Mixing red and green color shades in an incorrect way can cause color-blind people to struggle with the text. Making your font sizes too small can cause trouble for those who have poor vision. Using a dark background with dark letters can make a page difficult for anyone to read.

Step-by-Step 2.2

In this section, you change color values, first using words and then experimenting with hexadecimal numerical values.

1. Open your **seven.html** or **seven.htm** file for text editing, if it is not already open.

2. Enter **style="background-color:yellow"** inside the body tag near the top of your Web page, as shown here and in bold in **Figure 2–6**.

   <body **style="background-color:yellow"**>

3. Save your work in a file named **eight.html** or **eight.htm**.

4. View the **eight.html** file to see the changes to the page in your Web browser. Your page should turn yellow.

5. Experiment. Switch back to the **eight.html** file, and then change the background color value to **blue**, **green**, **red**, **white**, or another color of your choice. View the color changes in your browser, and then change the background color back to yellow.

6. Switch back to your **eight.html** or **eight.htm** file. Enter the various <hr /> tags, attributes, and values as marked in bold in **Figure 2–6** near the bottom of the page before the </body> tag. Don't leave out a single : or ; or ".

FIGURE 2–6   Adding background colors and lines

```
<html>
<head>
<title>HTML and JavaScript</title>
</head>

<body style="background-color:yellow">

<h1 style="text-align:center">Organizing Tags</h1>

<p>There are many ways to organize a Web page. This Web page will
organize text, hypertext links, colors and fonts. You'll also demonstrate
single spacing, double spacing, and the use of line breaks. </p>

<p>This Web page will display how to organize Web pages in a number of
ways using: </p>
```

Continued on next page »

FIGURE 2–6 Adding background colors and lines

《 Continued from previous page

```
Powerful Lines <br />
Hyperlinks to HTML, XHTML and JavaScript Sources <br />
Hyperlinks to Previously Created Web Pages <br />
Fancy Fonts <br />
Perfect Pictures <br />
Orderly Tables <br />
Extraordinary Extras <br />
<hr />
<h2>Powerful Lines</h2>

A Horizontal Rule that is 10 pixels high.
<hr style="height:10px" />

A Horizontal Rule 30 pixels high.
<hr style="height:30px" />

A Horizontal Rule width set at 50%.
<hr style="width:50%" />

A Horizontal Rule width set at 25% and height set at 20 pixels.
<hr style="width:25%;height:20px" />

A Horizontal Rule without attributes and values.
<hr />

</body>
</html>
```

7. Save your file as **nine.html** or **nine.htm**.

8. View the file **nine.html** in your browser so you can see the horizontal lines in your Web browser. Your page should look like **Figure 2–7**.

9. For fun and to see how color affects a Web page, change the color value in the nine.html file from a word for the color (such as "yellow") to a numerical value preceded by the pound sign (#), such as:

```
<body style= "background-color:#E6E6FA ">
```

10. Resave your **nine.html** or **nine.htm** file. Open the file in your browser and view the change.

FIGURE 2–7
Powerful lines

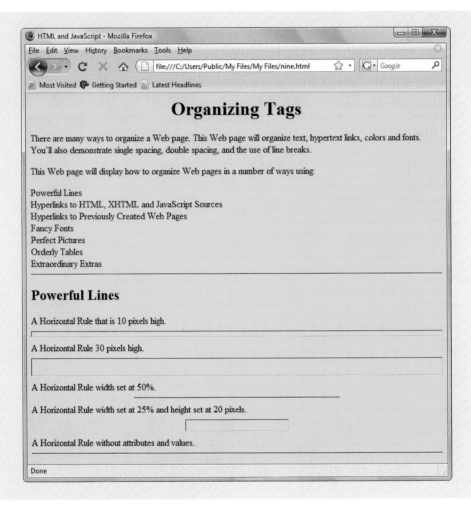

FIGURE 2–7
Powerful lines

EXTRA FOR EXPERTS

The term *pixel* is short for picture element, which is the smallest single dot of color your monitor is capable of producing on the screen as determined by its resolution settings. You would need a magnifying glass to see one.

Placing Hyperlinks Inside Your Document

Web pages became popular because they made it possible for a person to link easily and quickly to other Web pages or to various sections inside a Web page with a simple click. Hyperlinks are easy to use but a little difficult to understand at first.

To use a hyperlink, just click the link. Links can be graphics or words. Text links are easily identified because they are often underlined and appear in a different color. Links change color after they have been clicked, as shown in **Figure 2–8**. And, if you are unsure if a graphic or word is a link, you can simply place your mouse pointer over the word or picture. If it is a link, the pointer changes to a hand pointer.

Hyperlinks are created with special tags called anchor tags. The tag has several parts and looks like this:

```
<a href="insert location of file"></a>
```

Link or anchor tags are fairly useless unless you define the place to which you are linking. There are several ways to use anchor tags. You can:

- Link to another place within your own document
- Link to a Web page anywhere on the Web
- Link to another Web page on your own computer

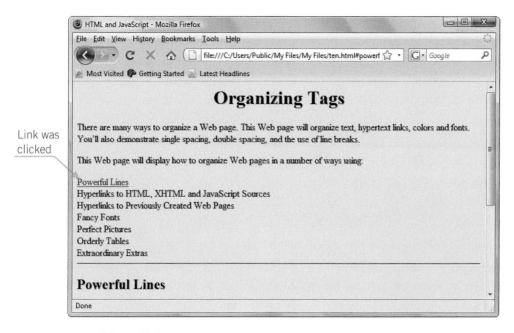

Link was clicked

FIGURE 2–8 A hyperlink text

Creating a link within a document requires a two-step process. The first <a> tag you insert creates a hypertext link to a location within your document. The attribute is href= and the value is "#powerful". The quotation marks are necessary, as is the #, sometimes referred to as a pound sign.

The second anchor tag identifies the exact location in your Web page to which you want to link. You will create a tag with the attribute name= and a value called "powerful" with quotation marks.

Step-by-Step 2.3

In this step-by-step section, you learn to insert links in an HTML document, a vital and useful skill.

1. Open your **nine.html** or **nine.htm** file for text editing, if necessary.

2. Add the following anchor **<a></a>** tags before and after the first Powerful Lines list item, as shown here and marked in bold in **Figure 2–9**.

   ```
   <a href="#powerful">Powerful Lines</a><br />
   ```

4. Insert the following anchor **<a></a>** tags around the second Powerful Lines list item, as shown here and marked in bold in **Figure 2–9**.

   ```
   <h2><a name="powerful">Powerful Lines</a></h2>
   ```

5. Save your new file as **ten.html** or **ten.htm**.

6. View the changes in your Web browser. When you click the Powerful Lines link, as seen in **Figure 2–8**, it will change color and you should jump down the page to the Powerful Lines heading in your document.

> **WARNING**
>
> The pound sign # can be created by holding the Shift key down and pressing the number 3. The quotation marks (") are created by holding down the Shift key and pressing the apostrophe (') key.

FIGURE 2–9   Insert internal linking tags

```
<html>
<head>
<title>HTML and JavaScript</title>
</head>

<body style="background-color:#E6E6FA">

<h1 style="text-align:center">Organizing Tags</h1>

<p>There are many ways to organize a Web page. This Web page will
organize text, hypertext links, colors and fonts. You'll also demonstrate
single spacing, double spacing, and the use of line breaks. </p>

<p>This Web page will display how to organize Web pages in a number of
ways using: </p>

<a href="#powerful">Powerful Lines</a><br />
Hyperlinks to HTML, XHTML and JavaScript Sources <br />
Hyperlinks to Previously Created Web Pages <br />
Fancy Fonts <br />
Perfect Pictures <br />
Orderly Tables <br />
Extraordinary Extras <br />
<hr />

<h2><a name="powerful">Powerful Lines</a></h2>
A Horizontal Rule that is 10 pixels high.
<hr style="height:10px" />

A Horizontal Rule 30 pixels high.
<hr style="height:30px" />

A Horizontal Rule width set at 50%.
<hr style="width:50%" />

A Horizontal Rule width set at 25% and height set at 20 pixels.
<hr style="width:25%;height:20px" />

A Horizontal Rule without attributes and values.
<hr />

</body>
</html>
```

ETHICS IN TECHNOLOGY

Respect the WWW

A Web page shouldn't be offensive. You're responsible for what you create and post or publish online. RESPECT the Web. When creating your Web pages, consider these guidelines:

R = Responsible: Assume personal responsibility and create only principled and appropriate pages.

E = Everybody: Try to create Web pages that everybody can enjoy, appreciate, and consider of value.

S = Simple: Make your Web pages easy to navigate. Make information simple to find.

P = Purposeful: Have a clear purpose for every Web page you put on the Web. Don't post or upload unnecessary pages.

E = Ethical: Make sure all the content of every Web page you post corresponds to your values and has a beneficial purpose.

C = Correct: Make sure all the words on your page are spelled correctly, all the sentences are grammatically correct, and all the hyperlinks work.

T = Totally worth visiting: Try to create pages that others will think are totally worth their time to visit.

Creating Hypertext Links to the Web

The feature that first made the Web popular was the ability to jump from one page to another. With people publishing pages around the world, being able to view a page on your computer that originated anywhere in the world with a single click was incredible. Before you can do this, however, you must know all about URLs. *URL* stands for *Uniform Resource Locator*. URLs allow a Web browser to pinpoint an exact file on a Web server, or computer, on the Web. The concept is really quite simple. Have you ever seen a URL similar to this sample?

http://www.cengage.com/webpagefolder/anotherfolder/afile.html

▶ **VOCABULARY**
Uniform Resource Locator (URL)

Hypertext Transfer Protocol (HTTP)

When you enter a URL into your HTML Web page, you're identifying a path to a specific HTML file. This file might be on your local computer or on a computer on the Web.

You often can see the name of the file at the end of the URL. Look at the end of our sample URL. The filename *afile.html* is the name of a file (afile). The .html extension identifies the file as an HTML document that your Web browser can display.

However, before you can open and view the file *afile.html*, you need to know the path or the way to this file. The key to finding the filename's path is by looking at its URL or Web address. Let's see what this means by breaking down the sample URL into its various parts.

In some URLs, you might see the letters http followed by a colon and two slashes. The *http://* tells your computer network how to transfer or move the files you are requesting. *HTTP* stands for *Hypertext Transfer Protocol*. (You might also see *https://*. The *s* stands for secure.) A protocol is a communication system that is used to transfer data over computer networks. It is a digital language that Web servers use to communicate with Web browsers.

The second part of the address, *www.cengage.com*, is the actual name of the Web server (or computer on the Web) that hosts (where the Web page is posted or published) the Web page for which you are looking. The *www* stands for World Wide Web and directs the search to a specific Web server. This *www* prefix can be dropped altogether if so designed by the site owner. For example, *google.com* and *www.google.com* direct you to the same location. However, changing the prefix can take the user to different services, such as *sites.google.com*, *gmail.google.com*, or *docs.google.com*.

The *.cengage* part of the URL is the name of the company that maintains the Web server. The *.com* says that this is a commercial or business site. You might see other addresses that are marked as *.edu* for education, *.gov* for government Web sites, *.org* for a nonprofit or cooperative organization, or *.biz* for business sites.

The slashes and names in the rest of the URL (*/webpagefolder/anotherfolder/*) represent folders on the Web server. These are also called subdirectories. You have subdirectories on your computer. **Figure 2–10** shows how folders are organized on a Windows computer. All computers use some sort of folder system to organize files. If you want to find a file on a computer, you need to know the path through the many possible folders in which the file is stored. Knowing the path is the key to finding the Web page you want on a computer.

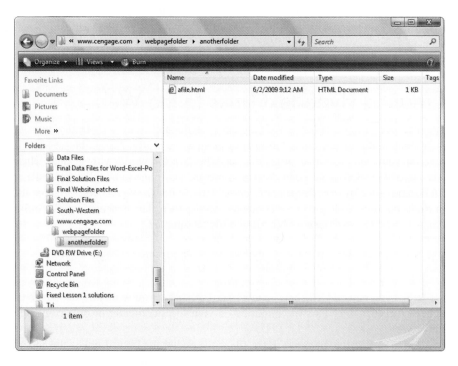

FIGURE 2–10   A Windows folder or directory organization

Before you can find a Web site's welcome page, you need to know the URL. In this step-by-step, you enter URLs for some companies that have been working to create a better, more exciting Web. Many of the sites have information on HTML, JavaScript, and other important Web tools. They include the following:

- *http://www.microsoft.com*
- *http://sites.google.com*
- *http://www.mozilla.org*
- *http://www.facebook.com*
- *http://www.w3.org*
- *http://www.wikipedia.org*

Step-by-Step 2.4

This is a critical step-by-step section in which you apply links to Web sites and Web pages anywhere in the world.

1. Open your **ten.html** or **ten.htm** file for text editing, if it is not already open.

2. Enter the tags for the second item in the list, as shown in this step in bold (as well as in **Figure 2–11**) to create a hypertext link from that entry in the list near the top of the page to the new section you will create.

   ```
   <a href="#hyperlinks">Hyperlinks to HTML, XHTML
   and JavaScript Sources</a><br />
   ```

3. Enter the tags to create a new level 2 heading with the words **Hyperlinks to HTML, XHTML and JavaScript Sources** just below the last <hr /> tag in your Web page and just before the </body> tag as shown in this step in bold and in bold in **Figure 2–11**. The <a name> tag is used to create an internal hypertext link from the link you created in Step 2.

   ```
   <h2><a name="hyperlinks">Hyperlinks to HTML,
   XHTML and JavaScript Sources </a></h2>
   ```

4. Below the new level 2 heading and before the </body> tag, enter the following hypertext links exactly as shown in this step and in bold in **Figure 2–11**.

   ```
   <a href="http://www.microsoft.com">Microsoft</a><br />
   <a href="http://sites.google.com">Google</a><br />
   <a href="http://www.mozilla.org">Mozilla</a><br />
   <a href="http://www.facebook.com">Facebook</a><br />
   <a href="http://www.w3.org">W3</a><br />
   <a href="http://www.wikipedia.org">Wikipedia</a><br />
   <hr />
   ```

5. Your entire page of tags should appear like those in **Figure 2–11**. Save your work as **eleven.html** or **eleven.htm**.

FIGURE 2–11   Hypertext linking tags

```
<html>
<head>
<title>HTML and JavaScript</title>
</head>

<body style="background-color:#E6E6FA">
```

Continued on next page »

FIGURE 2–11   Hypertext linking tags

« Continued from previous page

```
<h1 style="text-align:center">Organizing Tags</h1>

<p>There are many ways to organize a Web page. This Web page will
organize text, hypertext links, colors and fonts. You'll also demonstrate
single spacing, double spacing, and the use of line breaks. </p>

<p>This Web page will display how to organize Web pages in a number of
ways using: </p>

<a href="#powerful">Powerful Lines</a><br />
<a href="#hyperlinks">Hyperlinks to HTML, XHTML and JavaScript Sources</a>
<br />

Hyperlinks to Previously Created Web Pages <br />
Fancy Fonts <br />
Perfect Pictures <br />
Orderly Tables <br />
Extraordinary Extras <br />
<hr />

<h2><a name="powerful">Powerful Lines</a></h2>
A Horizontal Rule that is 10 pixels high.
<hr style="height:10px" />

A Horizontal Rule 30 pixels high.
<hr style="height:30px" />

A Horizontal Rule width set at 50%.
<hr style="width:50%" />

A Horizontal Rule width set at 25% and height set at 20 pixels.
<hr style="width:25%;height:20px" />

A Horizontal Rule without attributes and values.
<hr />

<h2><a name="hyperlinks">Hyperlinks to HTML, XHTML and JavaScript Sources
</a></h2>
<a href="http://www.microsoft.com">Microsoft</a><br />
<a href="http://sites.google.com">Google</a><br />
<a href="http://www.mozilla.org">Mozilla</a><br />
```

Continued on next page »

FIGURE 2–11   Hypertext linking tags

《 *Continued from previous page*

```
<a href="http://www.facebook.com">Facebook</a><br />
<a href="http://www.w3.org">W3</a><br />
<a href="http://www.wikipedia.org">Wikipedia</a><br />
<hr />

</body>
</html>
```

6. View your work in your Web browser. Your new links should look like **Figure 2–12**. Notice that links change color when clicked.

7. If your computer is connected to the Web, click the links in your Web page and see if they work. If your links don't work properly, carefully review your tags and make any necessary corrections. Save your work again. Then reload or refresh your page in your Web browser to view the page and test the links.

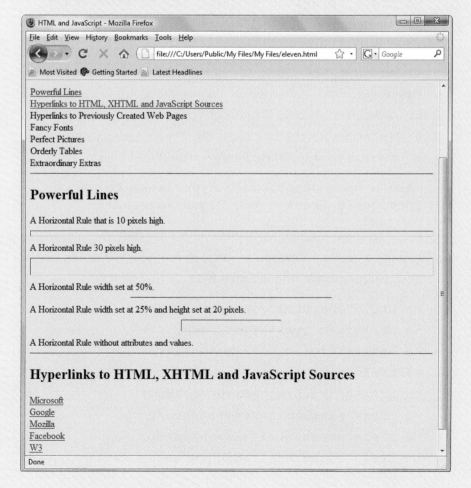

FIGURE 2–12
Hyperlinks in your Web browser

> **WARNING**
>
> Even though you saved the changes to the HTML file you are creating, your browser won't automatically update the Web page with the changes you made to the file. To view the changes you made to the Web page, you have to let the browser know there's an updated file. There are several ways to do this. You can open the page again, you can press the F5 function key on a Windows computer, or you can click the Reload or Refresh button on the browser toolbar. This loads an updated copy of your Web page into your browser.

Linking to Your Work

In this step-by-step, you link to the first 11 HTML pages you have created in this book. Keeping track of all your pages in this way will help you quickly review the progress you have made. A list of pages is helpful if you need to create an online portfolio page demonstrating all of the Web pages you have created.

Step-by-Step 2.5

In this step-by-step, you learn to link all of your work from a single master table of contents or index-style page to show off and organize all of your Web pages.

1. Open your **eleven.html** or **eleven.htm** file in your text editor, if it is not already open.

2. Create a hypertext link from the top of your page to the new section you will create in this exercise. Enter the tag as the third item in the list below the Powerful Lines and Hyperlinks to HTML, XHTML and JavaScript Sources links you've already created. The text to be entered is shown in bold here and in **Figure 2–13**.

```
<a href="#previous">Hyperlinks to Previously
Created Web Pages</a><br />
```

3. As shown in Figure 2–13, add a new level 2 heading that includes the <a name> tag. The heading text is **Hyperlinks to Previously Created Web Pages**. Enter it just below the <a href="http://www.wikipedia.org">Wikipedia</a>
  <hr />tags you added in the previous step-by-step, and just before the </body> tag. The <a name> tag allows you to link to this exact spot from the tag you created in Step 2.

```
<h2><a name="previous"> Hyperlinks to
Previously Created Web Pages</a></h2>
```

4. Below the new heading, above the </body> tag near the end of your document, create the hypertext links to each of your HTML files exactly as shown here and in bold in **Figure 2–13**.

```
<a href="one.html">One</a><br />
<a href="two.html">Two</a><br />
<a href="three.html">Three</a><br />
<a href="four.html">Four</a><br />
<a href="five.html">Five</a><br />
<a href="six.html">Six</a><br />
<a href="seven.html">Seven</a><br />
<a href="eight.html">Eight</a><br />
```

```
<a href="nine.html">Nine</a><br />
<a href="ten.html">Ten</a><br />
<a href="eleven.html">Eleven</a><br />
<hr />
```

5. Your entire page of tags should now appear like those shown in **Figure 2–13**. Save your work as **twelve.html** or **twelve.htm**.

FIGURE 2–13   Creating links to Web pages you have created

```
<html>
<head>
<title>HTML and JavaScript</title>
</head>

<body style="background-color:#E6E6FA">

<h1 style="text-align:center">Organizing Tags</h1>

<p>There are many ways to organize a Web page. This Web page will
organize text, hypertext links, colors and fonts. You'll also demonstrate
single spacing, double spacing, and the use of line breaks. </p>

<p>This Web page will display how to organize Web pages in a number of
ways using: </p>

<a href="#powerful">Powerful Lines</a><br />
<a href="#hyperlinks">Hyperlinks to HTML, XHTML and JavaScript Sources
</a><br />
<a href="#previous">Hyperlinks to Previously Created Web Pages</a><br />

Fancy Fonts <br />
Perfect Pictures <br />
Orderly Tables <br />
Extraordinary Extras <br />
<hr />

<h2><a name="powerful">Powerful Lines</a></h2>
A Horizontal Rule that is 10 pixels high.
<hr style="height:10px" />

A Horizontal Rule 30 pixels high.
<hr style="height:30px" />

A Horizontal Rule width set at 50%.
<hr style="width:50%" />
```

Continued on next page 〉〉

FIGURE 2–13   Creating links to Web pages you have created

《 *Continued from previous page*

```
A Horizontal Rule width set at 25% and height set at 20 pixels.
<hr style="width:25%;height:20px" />

A Horizontal Rule without attributes and values.
<hr />

<h2><a name="hyperlinks">Hyperlinks to HTML, XHTML and JavaScript Sources
</a></h2>
<a href="http://www.microsoft.com">Microsoft</a><br />
<a href="http://sites.google.com">Google</a><br />
<a href="http://www.mozilla.org">Mozilla</a><br />
<a href="http://www.facebook.com">Facebook</a><br />
<a href="http://www.w3.org">W3</a><br />
<a href="http://www.wikipedia.org">Wikipedia</a><br />
<hr />

<h2><a name="previous"> Hyperlinks to Previously Created Web Pages</a>
</h2>
<a href="one.html">One</a><br />
<a href="two.html">Two</a><br />
<a href="three.html">Three</a><br />
<a href="four.html">Four</a><br />
<a href="five.html">Five</a><br />
<a href="six.html">Six</a><br />
<a href="seven.html">Seven</a><br />
<a href="eight.html">Eight</a><br />
<a href="nine.html">Nine</a><br />
<a href="ten.html">Ten</a><br />
<a href="eleven.html">Eleven</a><br />

<hr />

</body>
</html>
```

6. Open the **twelve.html** file in your Web browser.

7. Click the **Hyperlinks to Previously Created Web Pages** link to get to the index of Web page files. Click the **One** link to open the One.html file in the Web browser. If it does not work, review **Figure 2–13** and make any corrections that are necessary.

8. Click the **Back** button on the browser toolbar to return to your twelve.html page. Click each new link to the files to make sure they work and open each of the files in your browser. The new links will change color and should look like **Figure 2–14**.

9. Fix any errors that you might find. If you make an error, review your code against the sample in **Figure 2–13**.

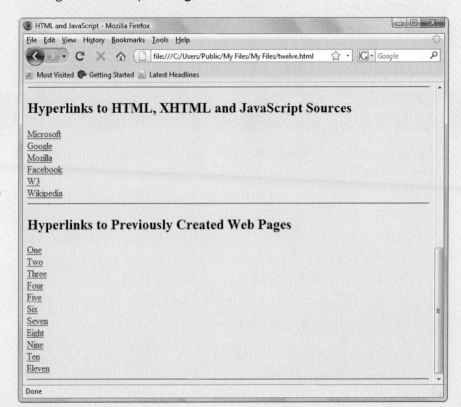

FIGURE 2–14
Links to previously created Web pages

WARNING

The way this code is written, all of your HTML files must be located in the same folder for the hyperlinks to work correctly.

Coloring Text

While online viewing Web pages, have you noticed that the text colors often change from Web site to Web site? In Step-by-Step 2.2, you changed the background color of your Web page by inserting the "yellow" value. Now, you are going to take your first small step into CSS, or Cascading Style Sheets. You will learn a lot more about CSS in Lesson 5. With CSS, you define your styles in advance between the <style> tags. CSS allows you to define colors for the entire page without having to change specific lines of code. This will save you from having to set the styles for each line in the code. You have to define the CSS default style with the following: <style type="text/css">. Your style definitions must appear between the <head></head> tags. This way, you define all of the chosen styles for the entire page. The values will appear between curly brackets { }, which are entered by holding the Shift key and pressing the bracket keys [ ].

Table 2–2 shows you three parts of a document you can change with CSS.

TABLE 2–2   Text color

TAG TO MODIFY	CHANGING VALUES
1. Change the color of the h1 text	h1 {color:red}
2. Change the color of the h2 text	h2 {color:blue}
3. Change the color of text between the <p></p> tags	p {color:darkblue}

Step-by-Step 2.6

In this step-by-step, you learn how to change color attributes and values with a few simple CSS commands in the next set of steps.

1. Open your **twelve.html** or **twelve.htm** file for text editing, if it is not already open.

2. Between the <head></head> tags at the beginning of the Web page, enter the style definitions using the <style type=> tag and attributes with the value definition "text/css". Then add the color definitions for the segments of text marked by the h1, h2, and p tags as seen in this step and as shown in bold in **Figure 2–15**.

```
<style type="text/css">
h1 {color:Red}
h2 {color:Blue}
p {color:Green}
</style>
```

FIGURE 2–15   Changing the text color on a Web page

```
<html>
<head>
<title>HTML and JavaScript</title>
<style type="text/css">
h1 {color:Red}
h2 {color:Blue}
p {color:Green}
</style>
</head>
```

3. Save your work as **thirteen.html** or **thirteen.htm**.

4. View the thirteen.html file in your Web browser. Your page should appear as shown in **Figure 2–16**.

5. Switch back to the thirteen.html file in the text editor. Change the colors using commonly named colors for your h1, h2, and p color values. Resave your document and take a look to see if you like your new color choices.

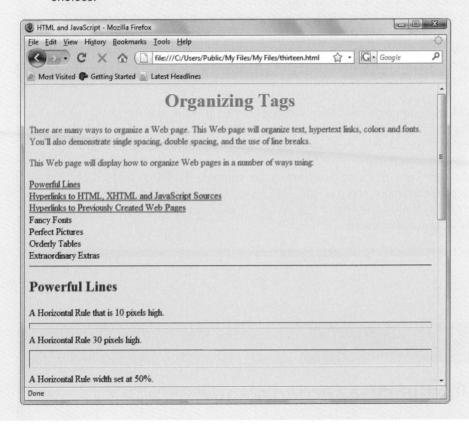

FIGURE 2–16
Text colors changed using CSS definitions

TECHNOLOGY CAREERS

Changing Standards

If you choose a career in Web design, you'll need to learn all you can about HTML, XHTML, XML, and CSS standards. *Standards* are powerful because they inform Web browser developers and programmers of the rules they need to meet to develop and display Web pages properly.

When Web standards are applied properly by browser developers, it doesn't matter if the person viewing the Web page is running a Macintosh or a Windows machine or even a Linux workstation. The reason HTML Web pages can be viewed by people all over the world on different platforms is that everyone must stick to the same standards.

New standards, new tags, and new commands are being added all the time. After enough changes have been proposed and approved, a standards committee will certify a new version of the standards that all browsers must understand. New sets of standards are published every few years. If you want to enter this industry, it is important to keep up with the changes.

Newly approved versions of standards are indicated by numbers, for example, HTML 1, HTML 2, HTML 3, HTML 4, and so on. You can learn more about HTML, CSS, and XHTML standards online. In fact, there is a project that has you do exactly that at the end of this lesson. If you are considering a career in this field, this will be a critical activity for you to complete.

NET BUSINESS

Perfect Proofreading Tips

Proofreading HTML tags can be difficult. Even the slightest error can drastically change the look of a Web page. Here are some common errors to look for:

- Make sure all your angle brackets < > are facing in the proper direction.
- Often, Web page writers misuse the Shift key when making angle brackets or creating a slash. This results in a comma, a period, or a question mark where the slash or angle brackets should appear.
- If all the defined text doesn't change, make sure your CSS definitions appear between the <head> </head> tags.
- If you want a double space instead of a single space, use a <p></p> tag instead of a <br /> tag.
- Check all of your tags to make sure they are closed properly, like <hr />. If bullets appear long after a list, perhaps you forgot to close the unordered list tag </ul>.

SUMMARY

In this lesson, you learned:

- How to organize page information with single and double spacing.
- How to organize page information with lines.
- How to use attributes and values to improve Web page design.
- How to change color style defaults, attributes, and values with CSS styles.

- How to create hypertext links to a spot in a Web document.
- How to create hypertext links to another page on the World Wide Web.
- How to create hypertext links to Web pages on your own computer.

■ VOCABULARY REVIEW

Define the following terms:

attribute	hyperlinks	standards
deprecated	hypertext links	Uniform Resource Locator (URL)
hexadecimal	Hypertext Transfer Protocol (HTTP)	value

■ REVIEW QUESTIONS

TRUE / FALSE

Circle T if the statement is true or F if the statement is false.

T   F   **1.**   Hexadecimal numbers operate on a base-10 number system.

T   F   **2.**   The <br /> tag creates a double space around the text.

T   F   **3.**   The letters href are a value to the <a></a> anchor tag.

T   F   **4.**   You can change the color of text on your Web pages with CSS styles.

T   F   **5.**   New HTML, XHTML, and CSS standards are agreed to and made public every few years.

T   F   **6.**   The <hr /> tag creates a single-space break.

T   F   **7.**   You must use the word-wrap feature in Notepad to ensure your paragraphs break at the end of each line when viewed later in a browser.

T   F   **8.**   The hexadecimal number FFFFFF is the value for white.

T   F   **9.**   The hexadecimal number FF0000 is the value for green.

T   F   **10.**   A pixel is approximately 1 centimeter by 1 centimeter.

FILL IN THE BLANK

Complete the following sentences by writing the correct word or words in the blanks provided.

1. The _____ tag creates a line across the page.

2. You can create a(n) _____ space in an HTML document with the <p> tag.

3. A(n) _____ is a communications system that is used to transfer data over networks.

4. A(n) _____ number lets you define a color with numbers and letters.

5. The _____ attribute changes a Web page's background color.

WRITTEN QUESTIONS

Write a short answer to each of the following questions:

1. Without looking back at the last step-by-step, write an example of how color styles can be defined using CSS for the h1, h2, and p tags. Make sure to include the location of these definitions on a Web page.

2. What hexadecimal value will create the color yellow?

3. Which tag(s) do you know of that don't use a separate closing tag but use a closing slash in the opening tag to close the tag?

4. What are three common errors that can be made when creating Web pages?

5. Why are there different versions of HTML, XHTML, or CSS?

■ PROJECTS

PROJECT 2–1: WHAT MAKES SOME PAGES SO HORRIBLE?

In the project activity from Lesson 1, you identified the greatest Web pages you could find. In this project, GreatApplications, Inc., wants you to identify the five worst pages you can find. These are to be used in a training seminar to help new employees learn how to create high-quality Web pages. Your managers suggested that you look for pages on the Web and find five examples of hard-to-read, unorganized, or boring Web pages to show new interns exactly what not to do.

Start your browser and use a search engine if necessary to search the Web for awful Web page examples. Record the title and URL of each page and list a few reasons why these pages make your list as poorly designed.

TABLE 2–3 Examples of unorganized Web pages

TITLE THAT APPEARS IN THE TITLE BAR	WEB ADDRESS OR URL	REASONS WHY THIS PAGE IS POORLY DESIGNED
1.		
2.		
3.		
4.		
5.		

PROJECT 2–2: TEAMWORK PROJECT

GreatApplications, Inc., is holding a design contest to see who can build the most informative and organized Web pages. Specifically, they are looking for a team that can create Web pages to introduce new products to customers over the Web.

The contest gives teams of three to five people two hours to create an informative Web page about a product of their choice. Form your team and brainstorm a new product to introduce. It could be a new cell phone, iPod, or computer game. It could be a new fashion or a new car. For the purpose of this contest, it doesn't really matter what product you pick, so don't take up too much of your time deciding what product you will use.

Create your team's Web page contest entry. Divide the writing responsibilities. Have one person enter the basic tags and serve as Webmaster. Each team member must research and write a portion of the Web page. Collaborate by editing and revising each other's writing. Use the techniques you have learned in this lesson to organize the information you want to present.

PROJECT 2–3: WEB PROJECT

We all know that teamwork is important. However, are there times when teamwork is harder than working alone? Answer the following questions about teams creating Web pages together.

1. As you worked together on the Teamwork Project, what problems did you encounter?

2. How did you organize your team? How did you divide the work? Which team members were responsible for which activities?

3. Did teamwork create a better Web page than you could have on your own? If so, how?

4. What advice would you give to other teams that are trying to create Web pages?

PROJECT 2–4: UNDERSTANDING STANDARDS

Ever wondered about upcoming changes in the standards governing HTML, XHTML, and CSS? Need to know what the current standards are for your Web pages? It's easy to find out. Go to Google, Yahoo!, Bing, or another search tool and try these search words. Create a Web

Design folder and bookmark key sites that can teach you more about the following:

HTML standards

XHTML standards

CSS standards

■ CRITICAL THINKING

ACTIVITY 2–1: MOVING TO THE TOP

Can you figure out how to create an internal hyperlink that will allow you to move from the bottom of your document to the very top? Use the steps you learned in Step-by-Step 2.3 to create a link just before the </body> tag that will link you to the top of the page. (*Hint*: Reverse the process.) Your link should look like this: To Top of Page.

ACTIVITY 2–2: COLOR BY NUMBER

Change the colors using hexadecimal numerical color values for your h1, h2, and p tag colors. Don't forget to add the # sign. Resave your page and take another look.

ACTIVITY 2–3: UPDATE YOUR PORTFOLIO

Keep your portfolio list up to date. Before you finish, add a link to your twelve.html page from your thirteen.html page.

■ CAPSTONE SIMULATION

What are your top 10 most important technical reference Web sites? What makes them important to you? Create a new HTML page that lists your most important personal Web pages. Keep adding to your Web resources page as you work through this text.

- Your page should have the title "Favorite Sites".

- The h1 heading should be called "Hyperlinks to my Favorite Sites".

- Create a numbered list for your links. (You might need to search back to Lesson 1 for help on this skill.)

LESSON 3

Power Techniques

Estimated Time:
1.5 hours

■ OBJECTIVES

Upon completion of this lesson, you should be able to:

- Control the size, style, and color of fonts.
- Download pictures from the Web.
- Insert pictures into your Web page.
- Change the size of graphics.
- Use tables to organize information.
- Turn pictures into hyperlinks.
- Insert a variety of data input options.

Multimedia such as pictures, sounds, and movies add interest to Web pages. There are several kinds of pictures, alternatively called graphics or images. They include *.gif* files (*Graphics Interchange Format*), *.jpg* or *.jpeg* (*Joint Photographic Experts Group*) files, and *.png* (*Portable Network Graphics*) files. The extensions .gif, .png, and .jpg tell your browser that these files are graphics and require special handling. We discuss these file types in more detail later in the lesson.

■ VOCABULARY

.gif

.jpg or .jpeg

.png

Graphics Interchange Format

Joint Photographic Experts
Group

Portable Network Graphics

Tables are important tools for organizing award-winning pages. You will learn how to create tables as well, so stay tuned. Tables allow the parts of a Web page to be divided, creating special spaces or compartments for each new element or piece of information you might want to include.

In this lesson, you will also learn a few extraordinary input tags that allow visitors to interact with your Web page. These tags allow you to easily collect information from users. First, you will learn how to change text in interesting ways in the first step-by-step activity in this lesson.

Texting to Perfection

The more you learn about HTML, XHTML, CSS, and XML, the more excitement you can add to your Web pages. For example, as you learned in Lesson 2, you can change the look of text. You can manipulate text in an almost unlimited number of ways. To start with, you can choose the fonts you want to use. Fonts define the style for letters and numbers. Each font has a unique, well-defined style. Here are some samples of a few common fonts in their unaltered forms:

- This is Times.
- This is Verdana.
- This is Arial.
- This is Courier.
- This is Teletype.

Fonts can be altered further with HTML and CSS styles, attributes, and values. When you change text and font colors using CSS definitions, you change the color of each identified text element for the entire page. If you want to have more control, for example, if you want to change the size, color, or style of a single paragraph, a single sentence, or even a single word, you can use the <style> tag.

Use <style> tag attributes and values to control:

- The size of words with <style="font-size:">
- The style of the font with <style="font-family:">
- The color of words with <style="color:">

Step-by-Step 3.1

In this step-by-step, you change the font family, font size, and font color by manipulating styles. So, let's get started.

1. Open your **thirteen.html** or **thirteen.htm** file (from Lesson 2) and then save the file using the **Save As** command with the filename **fourteen.html** or **fourteen.htm**. This way, you won't mess up your old file as you make changes to the new one.

2. Refer to the code shown in bold here and in bold at the top of **Figure 3–1** to make the following adjustments to your CSS code. Change the *p* color value to black. Create a new h3 color definition for purple. Adjust the background color to a soft blue using a hexadecimal number

WARNING

If you did not do the Step-by-Step 2.6 activity, you can just add the CSS code now, as shown in Step 2 between the <head></head> tags.

like #E6E6FA so that you can clearly see your changes. (Note: If you've already changed this background color to a soft blue, great, you don't have to change it now!)

```
<html>
<head>
<title>HTML and JavaScript</title>
<style type="text/css">
h1 {color:red}
h2 {color:blue}
h3 {color:purple}
p {color:black}
</style>
</head>
body style="background-color:#E6E6FA">
```

3. Create a hypertext link from the text Fancy Fonts in the list of links near the top of the page as shown here and in **Figure 3–1**.

```
<a href="#fonts">Fancy Fonts</a><br />
```

4. Add a new level h2 heading called **Fancy Fonts** just after the <hr /> tag and just before the </body> tag. This will finish the internal hypertext link you started in Step 3 and then change colors, font styles, and font sizes one line at a time by entering the font tags, attributes, and values exactly as shown here and repeated in bold in **Figure 3–1**.

```
<h2><a name="fonts">Fancy Fonts</a></h2>
<h3>Font Style Samples</h3>
<p style="font-family:verdana">This is the Verdana
font.</p>
<p style="font-family:times">This is the Times font.
</p>
<p style="font-family:courier">This is the Courier
font.</p>

<h3>Font Size Samples</h3>
<p style="font-size:150%">This is 150% normal size.
</p>
<p style="font-size:100%">This is 100% normal size.
</p>
<p style="font-size:75%">This is 75% normal size.
</p>

<h3>Font Color Samples</h3>
<p style="color:red">This is Red.</p>
<p style="color:white">This is White.</p>
<p style="color:blue">This is Blue.</p>
```

```
<h3>Multiple Font Style Samples</h3>

<p style="font-family:verdana;font-size:110%;
color:green">This is a sample of Verdana at 110% and
colored green.</p>

<p style="font-family:courier;font-size:140%;
color:yellow">This is a sample of Courier at 140% and
colored yellow.</p>

<p style="font-family:arial;font-size:70%;
color:orange">This is a sample of Arial at 70% and
colored orange.</p>

<hr />
```

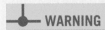 **WARNING**

Make sure you place a semi-colon (;) between separate font style elements.

5. Your tags should appear like those in **Figure 3–1**. Save your **fourteen.html** or **fourteen.htm** file to save your changes.

FIGURE 3–1 Applying font styles, sizes, and colors

```
<html>
<head>
<title>HTML and JavaScript</title>
<style type="text/css">
h1 {color:red}
h2 {color:blue}
h3 {color:purple}
p {color:black}
</style>
</head>

<body style="background-color:#E6E6FA">

<h1 style="text-align:center">Organizing Tags</h1>

<p>There are many ways to organize a Web page. This Web page will orga-
nize text, hypertext links, colors and fonts. You'll also demonstrate
single spacing, double spacing, and the use of line breaks. </p>
```

Continued on next page 》

FIGURE 3–1   Applying font styles, sizes, and colors

《 *Continued from previous page*

```
<p>This Web page will display how to organize Web pages in a number of
ways using: </p>

<a href="#powerful">Powerful Lines</a><br />
<a href="#hyperlinks">Hyperlinks to HTML, XHTML and JavaScript Sources
</a><br />
<a href="#previous">Hyperlinks to Previously Created Web Pages</a><br />
<a href="#fonts">Fancy Fonts</a><br />

Perfect Pictures <br />
Orderly Tables <br />
Extraordinary Extras <br />
<hr />

<h2><a name="powerful">Powerful Lines</a></h2>
A Horizontal Rule that is 10 pixels high.
<hr style="height:10px" />

A Horizontal Rule 30 pixels high.
<hr style="height:30px" />

A Horizontal Rule width set at 50%.
<hr style="width:50%" />

A Horizontal Rule width set at 25% and height set at 20 pixels.
<hr style="width:25%;height:20px" />

A Horizontal Rule without attributes and values.
<hr />

<h2><a name="hyperlinks">Hyperlinks to HTML, XHTML and JavaScript Sources
</a></h2>
<a href="http://www.microsoft.com">Microsoft</a><br />
<a href="http://sites.google.com">Google</a><br />
<a href="http://www.mozilla.org">Mozilla</a><br />
<a href="http://www.facebook.com">Facebook</a><br />
<a href="http://www.w3.org">W3</a><br />
<a href="http://www.wikipedia.org">Wikipedia</a><br />
<hr />
```

Continued on next page 》》

FIGURE 3–1   Applying font styles, sizes, and colors

《 *Continued from previous page*

```
<h2><a name="previous"> Hyperlinks to Previously Created Web Pages</a>
</h2>
<a href="one.html">One</a><br />
<a href="two.html">Two</a><br />
<a href="three.html">Three</a><br />
<a href="four.html">Four</a><br />
<a href="five.html">Five</a><br />
<a href="six.html">Six</a><br />
<a href="seven.html">Seven</a><br />
<a href="eight.html">Eight</a><br />
<a href="nine.html">Nine</a><br />
<a href="ten.html">Ten</a><br />
<a href="eleven.html">Eleven</a><br />
<hr />

<h2><a name="fonts"> Fancy Fonts</a></h2>
<h3>Font Style Samples</h3>
<p style="font-family:verdana">This is the Verdana font.</p>
<p style="font-family:times">This is the Times font.</p>
<p style="font-family:courier">This is the Courier font.</p>

<h3>Font Size Samples</h3>
<p style="font-size:150%">This is 150% normal size.</p>
<p style="font-size:100%">This is 100% normal size.</p>
<p style="font-size:75%">This is 75% normal size.</p>

<h3>Font Color Samples</h3>
<p style="color:red">This is Red.</p>
<p style="color:white">This is White.</p>
<p style="color:blue">This is Blue.</p>

<h3>Multiple Font Style Samples</h3>
<p style="font-family:verdana;font-size:110%;color:green">This is a
sample of Verdana at 110% and colored green.</p>
<p style="font-family:courier;font-size:140%;color:yellow">This is a
sample of Courier at 140% and colored yellow.</p>
<p style="font-family:arial;font-size:70%;color:orange">This is a sample
of Arial at 70% and colored orange.</p>
<hr />

</body>
</html>
```

6. Open the file **fourteen.html** in your browser to view your work as a Web page. Your changes should look like **Figure 3–2**, which shows the page in the Google Chrome browser. Make any corrections that appear necessary.

EXTRA FOR EXPERTS

Make sure you try your pages in several major browsers to make sure they work properly! Google created the Chrome browser to experiment with new ways of accessing the Web. See how a page can look in Chrome in **Figure 3–2**.

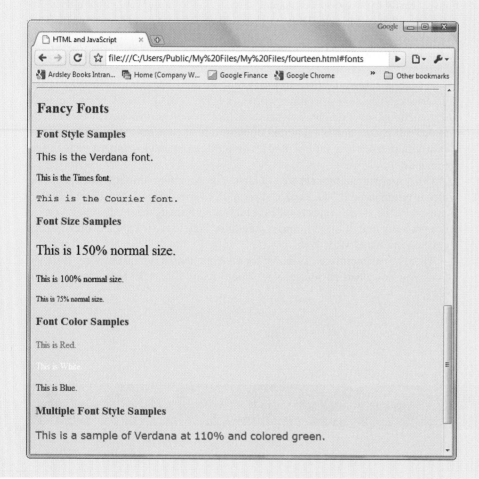

FIGURE 3–2
Various font styles, sizes, and colors in Google's Chrome browser

EXTRA FOR EXPERTS

There are other ways to change the look of text in a Web page. Can you guess what these tags do? Try these tags around certain words and see what effects they create when you view the page in a browser:

`<b></b>`

`<small></small>`

`<big></big>`

`<i></i>`

`<tt></tt>`

Downloading and Inserting Graphics

Pictures can be found in many places. You can find pictures in clip-art collections, import pictures from a digital camera, scan images into your computer with a scanner, draw your own pictures, or copy graphics from the Web. However, before you can easily use pictures in your Web pages, you need to convert them into one of the acceptable file formats. Three common file types for graphics used in Web pages are Graphics Interchange Format (GIF), Joint Photographic Experts Group (JPEG), and Portable Network Graphics Format (PNG), each indicated by their .gif, .jpg or .jpeg, and .png filename extensions, respectively.

The .gif graphics or image format was originally created by one of the first online companies, CompuServe, to provide a compressed graphics format that could transfer easily over low-speed modems. According to most Web gurus, GIF is pronounced with a soft g, as in JIFfy. GIF files have some unique characteristics: They can be used as regular images; they allow transparency in portions of the image so the background can bleed through; they can be animated and work like simple cartoons.

A second commonly used format is .jpg or .jpeg. It is pronounced J-Peg by Web artists in the know. It is often written as JPEG or JPG. This format adheres to an international set of graphics standards, is probably the format used by the camera on your cell phone, and is supported by most digital cameras today. JPEG images can be compressed to a variety of sizes so they can be made compact enough for Internet use.

Other graphic file formats are available. For example, a third file format is .png, which is pronounced PING, as in ping pong. PNG was designed to replace GIF files. Fortunately, the HTML rules handle each of these formats the same way. If you can work with any one of these formats, you know how to work with any other picture format on the World Wide Web.

There are many images available for noncommercial use on the Web. However, before you download an image, you should read "Ethics in Technology: Picture Piracy."

ETHICS IN TECHNOLOGY

Picture Piracy

One of the big ethical problems on the Web is picture piracy. Because it is so easy to pull pictures off the Web, many people do so without permission. Many pictures are copyrighted; that is, someone owns them. To legally use them, you need to obtain permission or pay the owner or the artist.

For instance, the Disney Corporation has many copyrighted images. A quick review of the legal page on the Disney Web site explains their terms of use for much of their property. To protect what is theirs, Disney legal teams have taken legal action against Web site creators who have used or altered Disney's copyrighted images without securing the appropriate permissions.

Consider which pictures you download and use from the Web. Are they free for you to use? Most sites have a link to "terms of use" for images and text on their page. There are sites that allow people to download images for noncommercial use. Stick to trustworthy sites, but even that is no guarantee an image isn't copyrighted. Use your best judgment and ask your instructor for advice if you have any question about an image.

Step-by-Step 3.2

In this step-by-step, you learn to download images and arrange them in a variety of ways in your document. The key thing you will need to remember is the name of your file and its appropriate filename extension: jpg or .jpeg, .png, or .gif. Keep your eye on those extensions!

1. Open your Web browser.

2. Use your favorite search engine, such as Google, to search the Web for a copyright-free image you can use in a Web page. Ask your instructor for help if necessary. In **Figure 3–3**, an image being saved is from the Cengage Learning Web site. For these steps, the image has been provided by your instructor.

> ⚠️ **WARNING**
>
> If you are not connected to the Internet, you will not be able to complete Steps 1–5. Your instructor will have given you a copy of the Data file for this lesson, levy.gif. You must save this file in the folder where you have been saving your HTML files. Begin this step-by-step with Step 6.

FIGURE 3–3
Image to use in a Web page

3. To download a picture from an online source, if you're on a Windows computer, right-click the image, as shown in the example in **Figure 3–4** and as shown in **Figures 3–5**. If you're using a Macintosh, click and hold your mouse button on the image.

4. Click the **Save Image As** or **Save Picture As** command on the short-cut menu. (Note: The command on your browser might be worded differently.)

5. Save your file in the exact same folder where you have been saving your Web pages.

> 📷 **EXTRA FOR EXPERTS**
>
> Use a variety of browsers. It will help you learn new and exciting features and stay on the cut-ting edge. Apple's Safari browser introduced a feature called cover flow, which lets you flip through your bookmarks like you would in iTunes. Created first as a Mac alternative to Internet Explorer, a PC version now exists, too.

FIGURE 3–4
With Firefox, choose **Save Image As**…

 WARNING

Just make sure you save your Data file levy.gif provided by your instructor in the exact same folder in which your HTML files are saved. Make a note of the graphics filename so you can find it later.

FIGURE 3–5
With Internet Explorer, select **Save Picture As**…

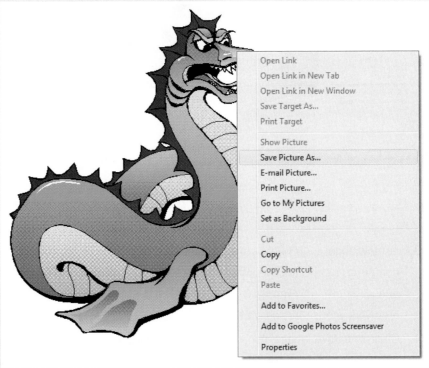

6. Open the **fourteen.html** or **fourteen.htm** file in your text editor.

7. Create a hypertext link from the words Perfect Pictures at the top of your page that hyperlinks to the new section you create at the end of your file. The text to be entered is shown in bold here and in **Figure 3–6**.

```
<a href="#pictures"> Perfect Pictures </a><br />
```

8. Add a new level 2 heading called **Perfect Pictures** just below the last <hr /> tag and just before the </body> tag. Include the <a name> tag to finish the internal hypertext link you started in the previous step and then enter an Image Source <img src="levy.gif"/> tag. Between the quotes, you enter the name of your image file. In our example, we are using an image file levy.gif. In another Web page, you could replace levy.gif with the name of your image file. Study the example shown here and in bold in **Figure 3–6** to help you execute this step properly. Remember, the image filename must be spelled correctly, must have the correct file extension, and must be saved in the same folder where you store your HTML files.

> **⊥— WARNING**
>
> A common error is created by transposing the R and the C in the <img src> tag. Think of this as the IMaGe SouRCe tag and you won't forget to place the letters in the right order.

```
<h2><a name="pictures"> Perfect Pictures </a></h2>
<img src="levy.gif" />
<hr />
```

9. Your tags should now appear like those in **Figure 3–6**. If everything looks correct, save your work as **fifteen.html** or **fifteen.htm**.

FIGURE 3–6   Inserting a graphic or image file

```
<html>
<head>
<title>HTML and JavaScript</title>
<style type="text/css">
h1 {color:red}
h2 {color:blue}
h3 {color:purple}
p {color:black}
</style>
</head>

<body style="background-color:#E6E6FA">

<h1 style="text-align:center">Organizing Tags</h1>

<p>There are many ways to organize a Web page. This Web page will
organize text, hypertext links, colors and fonts. You'll also demonstrate
single spacing, double spacing, and the use of line breaks. </p>

<p>This Web page will display how to organize Web pages in a number of
ways using: </p>

<a href="#powerful">Powerful Lines</a><br />
<a href="#hyperlinks">Hyperlinks to HTML, XHTML and JavaScript Sources
</a><br />
<a href="#previous">Hyperlinks to Previously Created Web Pages</a><br />
<a href="#fonts">Fancy Fonts</a><br />
<a href="#pictures"> Perfect Pictures </a><br />

Orderly Tables <br />
Extraordinary Extras <br />
<hr />
```

By now, you know the drill. Because nothing has changed in the code from this point on, we skip the Powerful Lines, Hyperlink sections, and Fancy Fonts sections of the code and jump down to the new code that needs to be added to the bottom of your updated HTML file. If you need to review the code for these earlier sections, see it in Figure 3–1. Add this code below your last <hr /> tag and before the </body> tag.

```
<h2><a name="pictures"> Perfect Pictures </a></h2>
<img src="levy.gif" />
<hr />

</body>
</html>
```

10. View your work in your Web browser. The image file levy.gif should look like **Figure 3–7** in your browser.

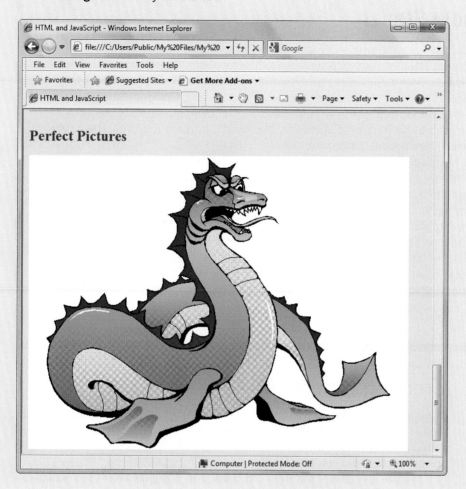

FIGURE 3–7
A GIF image as seen in the Internet Explorer browser

NET BUSINESS

Mozilla the Monopoly Slayer

For our sample, in Step-by-Step 3.2, we used a simple GIF graphic file of a dragon called levy.gif. Why a dragon named Levy? Back in ancient Internet history, Netscape Communications Corporation set out to defeat the first powerful graphical browser called Mosaic by creating a better browser. *Mozilla* was the code name for the Netscape browser. The original Mozilla image was that of a funky-looking dragon known as "Mozilla the Mosaic Slayer." Netscape won its battle with Mosaic, but the competition escalated as Netscape's Navigator found a new competitor for Web dominance, Microsoft's Internet Explorer. The battle between the two browsing titans was literally called a browser war.

The competition between the Netscape and Internet Explorer browsers was a positive thing. It inspired creativity and innovation, which improved the Web experience. In periods in which a near monopoly in browser dominance replaced competition, creativity and innovation slowed.

We use a dragon in this activity to symbolize the need to keep the browser competition going! For example, in the spirit of the first Mozilla, the Mozilla Organization created Firefox to compete against Internet Explorer. They succeeded in providing new alternatives and exciting solutions to the Web community. Other companies, such as Google and Apple, have also tried to compete against Microsoft's dominance with the Google Chrome and Apple Safari browsers. With luck, other new browsers will also break through and make their mark.

Our dragon is called Levy the Leviathan. Use your favorite search tool, such as Google or Bing, to look up Thomas Hobbes and his book *The Leviathan* from 1660 if you want more information about why we chose the name.

EXTRA FOR EXPERTS

An easy way to allow your Web page visitors to e-mail you with one click is to create the following tag: **<a href="mailto:youremail@ address.com">Your Name</a>.** When a visitor clicks the tag, if an e-mail program is on his or her computer, a new e-mail message window will open.

Creating Pictures of All Sizes

Pictures can be altered in a variety of ways by changing a tag's values. Images can be used as wallpaper to cover the entire background of a Web page. They can be aligned in the center, to the left side, or to the right side of a page. They can be made bigger or smaller, depending on your needs.

You can also change the size of the picture by using the height and width attributes. Controlling the exact size of a picture can be very helpful in conveying additional information. Proper use of pictures can make a page look sharp and interesting.

In the first part of Step-by-Step 3.3, you align your picture to the right of the page and make it small. In the second section, you align three dragons of varying sizes across the page, and then you place three dragons vertically on the Web page by manipulating the appropriate values.

Step-by-Step 3.3

Seven; count them. At the end of this step-by-step, you'll have seven images. And one size doesn't fit all. Learn to control the size and location of images in this step-by-step.

1. Open your **fifteen.html** or **fifteen.htm** file for text editing.

2. To add a second but smaller image to your page, near the end of your document, between your first <img src> tag and the last <hr /> tag, add the following tag, as shown in bold here and in **Figure 3–8**:

```
<p><img src="levy.gif" align="right" height="50"
width="50" /></p>
```

3. Save your changes as **sixteen.html** or **sixteen.htm**.

4. Open the file **sixteen.html** in your Web browser to view your changes. Click the **Perfect Pictures** link. The second image should appear smaller and right-aligned.

5. Next, create three more images that will appear across the screen, with each graphic appearing as a different size. To do so, enter the following tags below the second img src tag you entered in Step 2. (Peek ahead to **Figure 3-8** if you need to see all of the code in context.)

```
<img src="levy.gif" height="100" width="100" />
<img src="levy.gif" height="150" width="150" />
<img src="levy.gif" height="200" width="200" />
```

6. Save your changes using the same **sixteen.html** or **sixteen.htm** filename and view your new images in your Web browser. How do they look?

7. Just below the three tags you entered in the previous step, add two more img src tags, using <p> tags to cause several graphics to appear vertically. Enter these tags exactly as shown here. (Peek ahead to **Figure 3-8** if you need to see all of the code in context.)

```
<p><img src="levy.gif" height="150" width="150" /></p>
<p><img src="levy.gif" height="200" width="200" /></p>
<hr />
```

FIGURE 3-8 Dragons everywhere

```
<html>
<head>
<title>HTML and JavaScript</title>
<style type="text/css">
h1 {color:red}
h2 {color:blue}
h3 {color:purple}
p {color:black}
</style>
</head>

<body style="background-color:#E6E6FA">

<h1 style="text-align:center">Organizing Tags</h1>
```

Continued on next page »

FIGURE 3–8   Dragons everywhere

《 *Continued from previous page*

```
<p>There are many ways to organize a Web page. This Web page will
organize text, hypertext links, colors and fonts. You'll also demonstrate
single spacing, double spacing, and the use of line breaks. </p>

<p>This Web page will display how to organize Web pages in a number of ways
using: </p>

<a href="#powerful">Powerful Lines</a><br />
<a href="#hyperlinks">Hyperlinks to HTML, XHTML and JavaScript Sources</
a><br />
<a href="#previous">Hyperlinks to Previously Created Web Pages</a><br />
<a href="#fonts">Fancy Fonts</a><br />
<a href="#pictures"> Perfect Pictures </a><br />

Orderly Tables <br />
Extraordinary Extras <br />
<hr />
```

*We've skipped the Powerful Lines, Hyperlinks, and Fancy Fonts sections of the code and jumped down
to the new code that needs to be added to the bottom of your updated HTML file. If you need to review the
code for these earlier sections, see them in Figure 3–1. Add this code below your last entry made in the
previous step-by-step exercise.*

```
<h2><a name="pictures"> Perfect Pictures </a></h2>
<img src="levy.gif" />
<p><img src="levy.gif" align="right" height="50" width="50" /></p>
<img src="levy.gif" height="100" width="100" />
<img src="levy.gif" height="150" width="150" />
<img src="levy.gif" height="200" width="200" />
<p><img src="levy.gif" height="150" width="150" /></p>
<p><img src="levy.gif" height="200" width="200" /></p>
<hr />

</body>
</html>
```

8. Save your changes again as **sixteen.html** or **sixteen.htm**, and view
    the result in your Web browser. Your images will now look similar to
    Figure 3–9. Make corrections where necessary and review any changes
    in your browser.

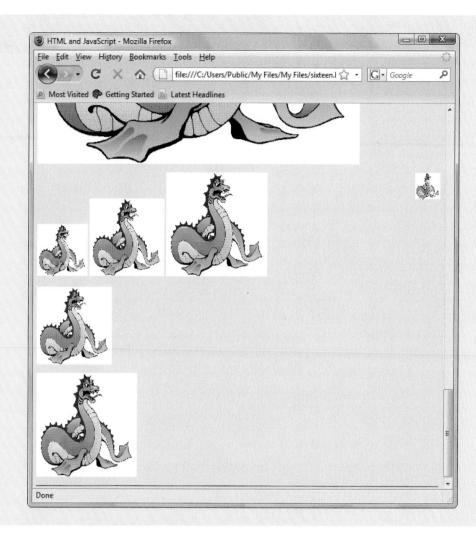

FIGURE 3–9
GIF images with changing attributes and values in a Firefox browser

EXTRA FOR EXPERTS

If you want a picture to work as a hyperlink, try this series of tags, attributes, and values:

<a href="http://website.domainad-dress.com/"><img src="levy.gif" height="50" width="50" /></a>

To use a picture as the background for your Web page, insert the background attribute in the <body> tag like this: <body background="levy.gif">

Creating Orderly Tables

Electronic tables are great organization tools. Tables are a grid of columns and rows that create boxes in which you can place text and images to keep them organized. Each intersection of a column and a row creates a box or cell. In Step-by-Step 3.4, you use tags to create a table with many cells. To create a table, you need to add the following three important tags: the row tag, the header tag, and the cell tag.

<tr> defines a table row
<th> defines a table header
<td> defines a table cell

Inside cells, you can insert many of the tags you have already learned so that text and graphics appear inside the table's cells. Tables can have borders by adding a border attribute with a number value. You can also make cells appear larger around pictures and text with the cell padding attribute. Within cells, you can align pictures and text to the center, left, or right.

Step-by-Step 3.4

Tables are a powerful tool to organize separate elements on a single Web page. In this step-by-step, you create and fill a table with images and text.

1. Open your **sixteen.html** or **sixteen.htm** file in your text editor, if it is not already open.

2. Create a hypertext link in your Web page at the top of the page that will hyperlink to the new section you are creating. The text to be entered is shown in bold here and in **Figure 3–10**.

   ```
   <a href="#tables"> Orderly Tables </a><br />
   ```

3. Refer to **Figure 3–10** and add a new level 2 heading called **Orderly Tables** just below the last <hr /> tag you created in a previous step-by-step and just before the </body> tag. Include the <a name> tag so you can complete the internal hyperlink you started in Step 2.

   ```
   <h2><a name="tables">Orderly Tables</a></h2>
   ```

4. Below the new heading, near the end of your document, enter the <table> tags, attributes, and values, exactly as shown here and in bold in **Figure 3–10**.

   ```
   <table border="5" cellpadding="10" align="center">
   <tr>
           <th>Images</th>
           <th>Colors</th>
           <th>Fonts</th>
   </tr>
   <tr>
           <td><img src="levy.gif" height="50"
           width="50"></td>
           <td bgcolor="red" align="center">Red</td>
           <td align="center"><font face="times"
           size="7" color="red">Times</td>
   </tr>
   <tr>
           <td><img src="levy.gif" height="75"
           width="50"></td>
           <td bgcolor="green"
           align="center">Green</td>
           <td align="center"><font face="courier"
           size="10" color="green">Courier</td>
   </tr>
   </table>
   <hr />
   ```

5. Your tags should now match those in **Figure 3–10**. Save your work as
    seventeen.html or **seventeen.htm**.

FIGURE 3–10   Creating a table in HTML

```
<html>
<head>
<title>HTML and JavaScript</title>
<style type="text/css">
h1 {color:red}
h2 {color:blue}
h3 {color:purple}
p {color:black}
</style>
</head>

<body style="background-color:#E6E6FA">

<h1 style="text-align:center">Organizing Tags</h1>

<p>There are many ways to organize a Web page. This Web page will
organize text, hypertext links, colors and fonts. You'll also demonstrate
single spacing, double spacing, and the use of line breaks. </p>

<p>This Web page will display how to organize Web pages in a number of
ways using: </p>

<a href="#powerful">Powerful Lines</a><br />
<a href="#hyperlinks">Hyperlinks to HTML, XHTML and JavaScript Sources</
a><br />
<a href="#previous">Hyperlinks to Previously Created Web Pages</a><br />
<a href="#fonts">Fancy Fonts</a><br />
<a href="#pictures"> Perfect Pictures </a><br />
<a href="#tables"> Orderly Tables </a><br />

Extraordinary Extras <br />
<hr />
```

*We've skipped the Powerful Lines, Hyperlink sections, Fancy Fonts and Perfect Pictures sections of the code
and jumped down to the new code that needs to be added to the bottom of your updated HTML file. Add
this code below your last entry made in the previous step-by-step exercise.*

```
<h2><a name="tables">Orderly Tables</a></h2>
<table border="5" cellpadding="10" align="center">
```

Continued on next page >>

FIGURE 3–10 Creating a table in HTML

《 *Continued from previous page*

```
<tr>
        <th>Images</th>
        <th>Colors</th>
        <th>Fonts</th>
</tr>
<tr>
        <td><img src="levy.gif" height="50" width="50"></td>
        <td bgcolor="red" align="center">Red</td>
        <td align="center"><font face="times" size="7" color="red">Times
        </td>
</tr>
<tr>
        <td><img src="levy.gif" height="75" width="50"></td>
        <td bgcolor="green" align="center">Green</td>
        <td align="center"><font face="courier" size="10"
        color="green">Courier</td>
</tr>
</table>
<hr />

</body>
</html>
```

6. Open the **seventeen.html** file using your favorite Web browser to view your work as a Web page. Click the link for **Orderly Tables**. Your new page displays the table with text and images and should look like **Figure 3–11**. Make any corrections that are necessary.

FIGURE 3–11
An HTML table as seen in a Chrome browser

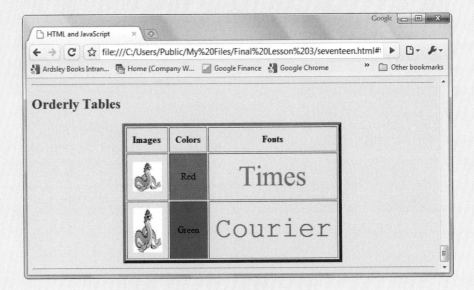

NET BUSINESS

Business on the Web

For many years, the Web was a tough place to make a living. The truth is that it took many years before the commercial potential of the Web began to be realized. Some of the Web companies that have made considerable money online include America Online, Yahoo!, Amazon, eBay, Apple iTunes, and Google.

Some succeeded online by daring to go where no one else dared to go. Many said that the Web would never replace bookstores. The people of Amazon took exception to that theory and began selling books on the Web. They sold so many books that other bookstores quickly realized that they had to go online or give away a big portion of their business to Amazon. Barnes & Noble was one of the first major booksellers to join Amazon on the Net.

Sony discovered that the Web was a great place to sell music CDs, but then Apple set up iTunes and people started downloading music instead of buying CDs and CD sales dropped rapidly. eBay expanded online auctions. Google sells advertising online. Expedia and Orbitz sell travel packages. And these are just a few examples.

Think about this for a few minutes: What other kinds of products and services can you think of that could become big sellers online? Can you set up an online business and make lots of money from the Web?

Adding Extraordinary Extras

In Step-by-Step 3.5, you learn to use a few extra tags that add extraordinary power to your Web pages. These tags allow those who visit your Web page to interact with the page. Many data input or <form> tag options will give you ways to ask questions of visitors to your Web page. These tags give extra functionality to your Web page and can make your Web page extraordinary.

You use the following four basic input tags throughout these next step-by-steps:

- **Text box**: A box in which Web site visitors can enter responses such as name and address information

- **Drop-down list**: A list that appears when a Web site visitor clicks an arrow to display a list of possible options to view and select responses

- **Radio button**: Sometimes referred to as an option button, a circular button that allows a Web site visitor to choose one option from a group of options

- **Check box**: A box that allows a user to click to place a check mark in its center so a Web site visitor can select more than one option from a group of options

Step-by-Step 3.5

In the final steps in this lesson, you create four different types of input options using HTML tags.

1. Open your **seventeen.html** or **seventeen.htm** file in your text editor if it is not already open.

2. Create an internal hypertext link from the top of your Web page that links to the new section you are creating for your input options. Call this link **Extraordinary Extras**, as shown here in bold and in bold in **Figure 3–12**.

```
<a href="#extras">Extraordinary Extras</a><br />
```

3. Add a new level 2 heading called **Extraordinary Extras** near the end of the page just below the last <hr /> tag you created and just before the </body> tag. Then enter the attributes and values exactly as shown here and in bold in **Figure 3–12**.

```
<h2><a name="extras">Extraordinary Extras</a></h2>
<h3> Text Input Box </h3>
<form>
Enter your first name: <input type="text" size="25"
/><br />
Enter your last name: <input type="text" size="30"
/><br />
<input type="submit" />
</form>

<h3> Selection List Input </h3>
The favorite team is:<br />
<form>
<select>
<option>Chicago Bulls</option>
<option>Utah Jazz</option>
<option>Los Angeles Lakers</option>
<option>Cleveland Cavaliers</option>
<option>New Jersey Nets</option>
<option>Phoenix Suns</option>
</select><br />
input type="submit"  />
</form>
```

```
<h3> Radio Button Input </h3>
The best place to eat is:<br />
<form>
<input type="radio" name="best">Wendy's<br />
<input type="radio" name="best">Five Guys<br />
<input type="radio" name="best">Taco Bell<br />
<input type="radio" name="best">Burger King<br />
<input type="radio" name="best">Kentucky Fried
Chicken<br />
<input type="submit"  />
</form>

<h3> Checkbox Input </h3>
I  like to eat:<br>
<form>
<input type="checkbox" />Hamburgers<br />
<input type="checkbox" />Tacos<br />
<input type="checkbox" />Chicken Strips<br />
<input type="checkbox" />Fries<br />
<input type="checkbox" />Hot Dogs<br />
<input type="submit"  />
</form>
<hr />
```

4. Save your work as **eighteen.html** or **eighteen.htm**.

FIGURE 3–12   A variety of data input tags

```
<html>
<head>
<title>HTML and JavaScript</title>
<style type="text/css">
h1 {color:red}
h2 {color:blue}
h3 {color:purple}
p {color:black}
</style>
</head>

<body style="background-color:#E6E6FA">

<h1 style="text-align:center">Organizing Tags</h1>
```

Continued on next page ⟫

FIGURE 3–12   A variety of data input tags

《 *Continued from previous page*

```
<p>There are many ways to organize a Web page. This Web page will
organize text, hypertext links, colors and fonts. You'll also demonstrate
single spacing, double spacing, and the use of line breaks. </p>

<p>This Web page will display how to organize Web pages in a number of
ways using: </p>

<a href="#powerful">Powerful Lines</a><br />
<a href="#hyperlinks">Hyperlinks to HTML, XHTML and JavaScript Sources
</a><br />
<a href="#previous">Hyperlinks to Previously Created Web Pages</a><br />
<a href="#fonts">Fancy Fonts</a><br />
<a href="#pictures"> Perfect Pictures </a><br />
<a href="#tables"> Orderly Tables </a><br />
<a href="#extras">Extraordinary Extras</a><br />
<hr />
```

We've skipped the Powerful Lines, Hyperlinks, Fancy Fonts, and Perfect Pictures sections of the code and
jumped down to the new code that needs to be added to the bottom of your updated HTML file. Add this
code below the last <hr /> tag you entered in the previous step-by-step exercise.

```
<h2><a name="extras">Extraordinary Extras</a></h2>
<h3> Text Input Box </h3>
<form>
Enter your first name: <input type="text" size="25" /><br />
Enter your last name: <input type="text" size="30" /><br />
<input type="submit" />
</form>

<h3> Selection List Input </h3>
The favorite team is:<br />
<form>
<select>
<option>Chicago Bulls</option>
<option>Utah Jazz</option>
<option>Los Angeles Lakers</option>
<option>Cleveland Cavaliers</option>
<option>New Jersey Nets</option>
<option>Phoenix Suns</option>
</select><br />
<input type="submit"   />
</form>
```

Continued on next page 》

FIGURE 3–12   A variety of data input tags

《 Continued from previous page

```
<h3> Radio Button Input </h3>
The best place to eat is:<br />
<form>
<input type="radio" name="best">Wendy's<br />
<input type="radio" name="best">Five Guys<br />
<input type="radio" name="best">Taco Bell<br />
<input type="radio" name="best">Burger King<br />
<input type="radio" name="best">Kentucky Fried Chicken<br />
<input type="submit"  />
</form>

<h3> Checkbox Input </h3>
I  like to eat:<br>
<form>
<input type="checkbox" />Hamburgers<br />
<input type="checkbox" />Tacos<br />
<input type="checkbox" />Chicken Strips<br />
<input type="checkbox" />Fries<br />
<input type="checkbox" />Hot Dogs<br />
<input type="submit"  />
</form>
<hr />

</body>
</html>
```

5. Open the **eighteen.html** file in your favorite Web browser. Click the **Extraordinary Extras** link and try all the input options. They should appear like those shown in **Figure 3–13**. Try them all. Do they all work as you would have expected? Correct any errors you find, resave, and try them again.

WARNING

It is considered impolite to download pictures to your school network that you don't intend to use. Graphics take up a great deal of space on a computer. Downloading hundreds and hundreds of pictures and not using them is a waste of network server drive space. Consider deleting any pictures you aren't actually using.

FIGURE 3–13
Input tags in a Safari browser

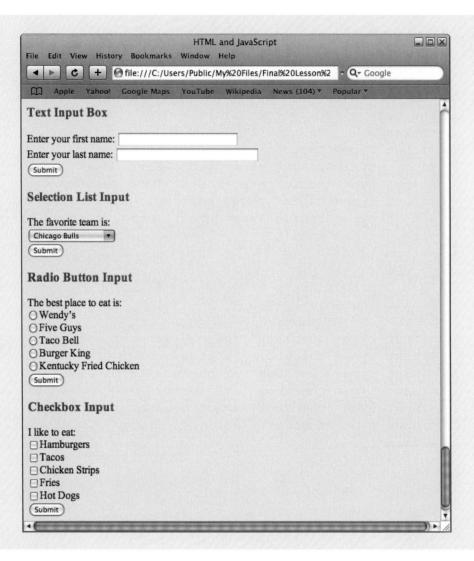

TECHNOLOGY CAREERS

Artists on the Web

There was a time when a Web page would be made entirely of words or text. Today, pictures and graphics dominate Web pages, attracting a greater number of visitors than ever before. For this reason, artists are in great demand among Web site development companies.

If you are considering an artistic career, consider the Web. You might find that much of your artwork will end up on the Web. Big corporations with Web sites and Web site developers are always on the lookout for great artistic talent.

You can create your art using any medium or method you like. Scanners can convert your pictures into digital images. Digital files can be converted into formats that will work on the Web such as GIF, PNG, or JPG. You can also use a variety of graphics software to create your works of art or to improve any art you have scanned into Web images.

The best training for a Web artist is to take as many art classes as you can. The graphics tools you need to use to convert your artwork are easily learned, whereas the skills of an artist take much more time to develop.

SUMMARY

In this lesson, you learned:

- How to control the size, style, and color of fonts.
- How to download and insert graphics in your Web pages.
- How to change the size and placement of graphics.
- How to create tables to organize information.
- How to insert a variety of data input options into a Web page.

◼ VOCABULARY REVIEW

Define the following terms:

.gif

.jpg or .jpeg

.png

Graphics Interchange Format

Joint Photographic Experts Group

Portable Network Graphics

◼ REVIEW QUESTIONS

TRUE / FALSE

Circle T if the statement is true or F if the statement is false.

T   F   **1.**   You can only change the color of a font with attributes and values placed in the \<body> tag.

T   F   **2.**   You can make an image either bigger or smaller.

T   F   **3.**   GIF stands for Greater Image Format.

T   F   **4.**   All images are available for you to use free over the Internet.

T   F   **5.**   The border can be made thicker or thinner around a table and its cells.

T   F   **6.**   The .png format was designed to replace .gif files, but so far, both still work just fine online.

T   F   **7.**   The .jpg file format allows for greater or lesser compression of file size.

T   F   **8.**   GIF images can be animated.

T   F   **9.**   Fonts all look the same in HTML until you change their size and look with HTML values.

T   F   **10.**   You can only change the color of a font with attributes and values by using CSS tags.

FILL IN THE BLANK

Complete the following sentences by writing the correct word or words in the blanks provided.

1. You can use \<img_____> to place pictures and text in an orderly fashion on a Web page.

2. \<_____> tags allow you to collect information about people who visit your site.

3. The _____ image format allows for transparency or transparent images.

4. The \<select>\<_____> tag creates an item in a drop-down list in a form.

5. The _____ image format is an international standard established by photographic experts that can be compressed.

WRITTEN QUESTIONS

Write a short answer to each of the following questions:

1. In 150–200 words, why are artists in such demand on the Web?

2. In less than 10 words, when is it illegal to take pictures off the Web without permission?

3. In 20 words or less, why is it important not to download pictures to your school or workplace network if you do not plan to use them?

4. Without looking back at the lesson, write two sample lines of code that create a link within a page.

5. Without looking back at the lesson, write a sample line of code that creates a link to an online Web page.

■ PROJECTS

PROJECT 3–1: GOT GAME?

GreatApplications, Inc., wants to enter the online video game business. However, before it starts programming the next great online video game, it wants to survey potential customers to see what kinds of online games they want to play and buy.

Brainstorm 10 questions that help GreatApplications, Inc., learn what its customers want in a video game program. Using your new skills, create an online survey to gather information from potential customers, such as the respondents' names and e-mail addresses. Ask questions that utilize drop-down lists, radio buttons, selection items, and check boxes. Include a submit button for each question.

PROJECT 3–2: TEAMWORK PROJECT

GreatApplications, Inc., is asking your team to plan a world tour to demonstrate its new software video games to people in five major cities. Your team has been asked to create a calendar of events for the tour using <table> tags. The tour must be conducted during a single month and should involve five major cities.

When you create your calendar, create links to tourist information about the cities that you will be visiting on the tour. Use cell padding and cell borders to make the table interesting. You can even put pictures (be sure you have permission to use the images) in the cells to illustrate the five cities you have selected for the software rollout.

PROJECT 3–3: WEB PROJECT

How fast can you substitute the levy.gif graphic for another graphic? Think about another graphic you like. How could you manipulate the attributes and values to display your new graphic in a variety of sizes? Go for it! Make the changes!

CRITICAL THINKING

ACTIVITY 3–1: THE WEB'S PLACE IN HISTORY

Prepare a 100- to 250-word answer to each of the following questions.

1. How important is the Web and HTML to the world's economy?

2. How can the Web benefit small businesses, such as a family-owned flower shop, a local antique store, or a fancy hair salon?

3. Over 500 years ago, Johannes Gutenberg invented movable type, which led to an explosion in the amount of printed material available to common people. He changed the history of the world. Imagine a world 500 years from now; how do you think people will look back on the invention of the Web and HTML?

ACTIVITY 3–3: THE TOPIC IN QUESTION

Each of these extraordinary input boxes asks the user to supply a different kind of information. What kinds of responses would you expect from the following <form> attributes?

Text:
Option button:
Radio button:
Check box:

ACTIVITY 3–2: THINKING ABOUT HTML AND CSS

Using sample code or short lists, answer each of the following questions.

1. Using both CSS and <style=> code samples, how can you change fonts to make the text on your Web pages more interesting?

2. How can table tags enhance a Web page?

3. What extra features or tags would you like to see added to HTML? What tags do you think should be added to give more power to HTML?

■ CAPSTONE SIMULATION

The local city zoo has hired you to create a Web page that describes some of the animals they currently have on display. They want your Web page to be well organized. They also want you to include images of the animals along with a short, descriptive paragraph about each animal. Use the information you learned in this lesson about tables, fonts, and images to complete this assignment.

Project Requirements:

■ Your Web page should have an appropriate title at the top.

■ Your animal images should be kept to an appropriate size within the Web page.

Be sure you have permission to use the images in your Web page.

■ The descriptive paragraph for each animal should be displayed in a variety of font faces and colors.

■ Your table should have a visible border that separates each cell.

Probably the best way for you to find animal images to use in your page is to surf the Web. Once you have found an animal picture that you want to use, check the terms of use to be sure you can use the image for noncommercial purposes. Right-click the image, and then use the Save Picture As command or Save Image As command to download the image to your computer. Keep in mind, however, that it is inappropriate for you to download copyrighted images from the Web. Please avoid using any image that displays a copyright message on it or on the Web page where it is located.

LESSON 4

HTML Structural Design Techniques

■ OBJECTIVES

Upon completion of this lesson, you should be able to:

- Create a frameset.
- Add a navigation bar.
- Make a welcome page.
- Create a nested frameset.
- Include a title bar frame and page.
- Utilize frame and frameset options.

HTML provides many features that help Web page developers organize information. You are now familiar with HTML tables, but in this lesson you will learn about HTML frames. Frames are similar to tables in that they help Web designers divide up the browser screen space into two or more rectangular areas. However, frames provide additional functionality; they allow the designer to change the ways in which Web pages normally behave. Frames allow Web developers to combine two or more Web pages on the same screen, and these pages can interact with each other in various ways. Frames also support several attributes that may allow, or in some cases disallow, the user to adjust the appearance of the resulting Web page.

■ VOCABULARY

border attribute

cols attribute

frames

frame separator

frameset tag

left-hand navigation

name attribute

navigation bar

nested frameset

noresize attribute

pixel

rows attribute

src attribute

target attribute

title bar

Creating an HTML Frameset

In Lesson 2, you learned how to make your Web browser link from one Web page to another page through the use of hyperlinks. Now it is time to learn how to make your Web browser display two or more Web pages on the screen at the same time. The HTML tags that will help you accomplish this are the <frameset> tag and the <frame> tag.

▶ **VOCABULARY**

frameset tag

frames

As its name implies, the *frameset tag* allows you to define a set of rectangular areas on your browser screen called *frames* (see **Figure 4–1**). Each frame is capable of displaying a different Web page. In a way, you can make your Web browser behave as though you had multiple Web browsers running on your computer at the same time. However, a frameset allows a Web page in one frame to communicate with a page in a different frame. For example, a hyperlink in one frame can cause a Web page to be loaded into a different frame. You learn more about this concept later in this lesson.

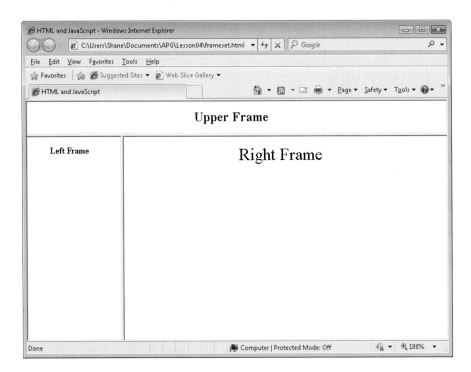

FIGURE 4–1   Three frames on a Web page

When you create your first HTML frameset file, you will notice that it has many things in common with the other HTML pages you created in the previous lessons. However, you should also recognize an important difference. Specifically, a frameset page does not contain the familiar <body> and </body> tags that are such an important part of standard Web pages. Instead, the frameset page contains <frameset> and </frameset> tags that mark the beginning and the end of frame definitions.

In addition, the frameset tag can contain a rows attribute or a cols attribute. The purpose of the *rows attribute* is to give you the means to define horizontal frames and to specify the height of each frame. Similarly, the cols attribute allows you to create vertical frames and to designate the width of each frame. Because you can define only horizontal or vertical frames within any given frameset, the <frameset> tag may contain a rows attribute or a *cols attribute*, but not both.

As you will see in the following step-by-step, the frameset tags encapsulate two or more <frame> tags. In turn, the <frame> tags contain at least two important attributes called name and src that allow you to give each frame a name and to specify the source Web page that you want to display in each frame. The purpose of the *src attribute* (source) is quite clear, but the function of the *name attribute* is not immediately apparent. Don't worry: You will learn more about this attribute in Step-by-Step 4.2.

▶ **VOCABULARY**
rows attribute
cols attribute
src attribute
name attribute

Step-by-Step 4.1

In this step-by-step, you create your first frameset file. As you will see, it's a simple task. You work in your text editor to enter basic HTML codes.

1. Open Notepad, SimpleText, or your favorite text editor.

2. Create a new blank document, if necessary.

3. Enter the HTML text shown in **Figure 4–2** in the exact order as shown in the figure. Don't leave out a single angle bracket (<) or slash (/). Every character and letter is important.

— **WARNING**

As you have already learned, you can save files with either an .htm or .html extension. Be careful! If you used the .htm extension, you must change all the filenames in **Figure 4–2** accordingly. For example, change navbar.html to navbar.htm in the frameset file.

FIGURE 4–2   Your first frameset file

```
<html>

<head>
<title>HTML and JavaScript</title>
</head>

<frameset cols="180,*">
<frame name="LeftFrame" src="navbar.html">
<frame name="RightFrame" src="welcome.html">
</frameset>

</html>
```

4. Save your newly created HTML text file as **frameset-1.html** or **frameset-1.htm** in the same folder you saved the files from the previous lessons.

 NOTE

The asterisk (*) means "whatever is left."

Adding a Navigation Bar

One design that is commonly used by professional Web designers is to place a Web page in a narrow left-hand frame that contains many hyperlinks. When the user clicks on any of these links, the appropriate Web page is displayed in the larger right-hand frame. This design technique is often referred to as ***left-hand navigation***, and the Web page containing the hyperlinks is called a navigation bar. A ***navigation bar*** is a series of hyperlinks, usually organized horizontally or vertically on a Web page or in a frame. It is used to navigate a Web site. **Figure 4–3** shows an example of a Web page with a navigation bar.

> **VOCABULARY**
>
> **left-hand navigation**
>
> **navigation bar**
>
> **target attribute**
>
> **pixel**

Navigation bar

FIGURE 4–3   Two-frame Web page

The Target Attribute

You do not have to learn any new HTML tags to create your navigation bar. The navigation bar is created by using tags you have already used in previous lessons. However, you will use a new attribute in the <a> tag that will associate the links in the left-hand frame to the Web pages in the right-hand frame. The ***target attribute*** tells the browser which frame it should use to display the target Web page. It is important to note that the target attribute uses the frame name that you defined with the name attribute in the <frame> tag in Step-by-Step 4.1.

> **EXTRA FOR EXPERTS**
>
> The numbers that accompany the rows and cols attributes can be absolute *pixel* values or percentage values. A ***pixel*** is an individual "dot" of light on a computer screen. In the file you just created, you made the frameset column 180 pixels wide. There are thousands of pixels on a typical computer screen, far too many to count. Therefore, it is sometimes easier to specify percentage values of a screen instead of counting pixels. A percentage value will automatically determine the proper number of pixels to dedicate to a frame. For example, you can enter the tag <frameset cols="20%, *">.

Step-by-Step 4.2

In this step-by-step, you learn how to create a navigation bar to link to the previous 18 Web pages you created in Lessons 1, 2, and 3. Your navigation bar will contain an unordered list of 18 hyperlinks, and these links will refer to the Web pages you saved as one.html, two.html, three.html, through eighteen.html. Open Notepad, SimpleText, or your favorite text editor, if it is not already open.

1. Click **File** on the menu bar, and then click **New** to create a new blank document.

2. Enter the HTML text exactly as shown in **Figure 4–4**.

   Hint: You can take advantage of the copy and paste commands to help you enter the 18 <li tags>, which are very similar. To enter the <li> tags, type the first **<li><a href="one.html" target="RightFrame">one.html </a></li>** tag, copy the tag, and paste it to the next line. Now that the tag is copied, simply select **one**, and then type **two** in both places in the tag. Repeat this for all 18 tags, entering each subsequent number for the appropriate filenames.

FIGURE 4–4 Navigation tags in a frames page

```html
<html>

<head>
<title>HTML and JavaScript</title>
</head>

<body>
<div align="center"><b>Web Pages</b></div>
<ul>
<li><a href="one.html" target="RightFrame">one.html</a></li>
<li><a href="two.html" target="RightFrame">two.html</a></li>
<li><a href="three.html" target="RightFrame">three.html</a></li>
<li><a href="four.html" target="RightFrame">four.html</a></li>
<li><a href="five.html" target="RightFrame">five.html</a></li>
<li><a href="six.html" target="RightFrame">six.html</a></li>
<li><a href="seven.html" target="RightFrame">seven.html</a></li>
<li><a href="eight.html" target="RightFrame">eight.html</a></li>
<li><a href="nine.html" target="RightFrame">nine.html</a></li>
<li><a href="ten.html" target="RightFrame">ten.html</a></li>
<li><a href="eleven.html" target="RightFrame">eleven.html</a></li>
```

Continued on next page »

FIGURE 4–4   Navigation tags in a frames page

《 *Continued from previous page*

```
<li><a href="twelve.html" target="RightFrame">twelve.html</a></li>
<li><a href="thirteen.html" target="RightFrame">thirteen.html</a></li>
<li><a href="fourteen.html" target="RightFrame">fourteen.html</a></li>
<li><a href="fifteen.html" target="RightFrame">fifteen.html</a></li>
<li><a href="sixteen.html" target="RightFrame">sixteen.html</a></li>
<li><a href="seventeen.html" target="RightFrame">seventeen.html</a></li>
<li><a href="eighteen.html" target="RightFrame">eighteen.html</a></li>
</ul>
</body>

</html>
```

INTERNET

Normally when a user clicks on a hyperlink, the target Web page will be loaded into the same frame as the link. The target attribute overrides this behavior and sends the proper Web page to the "target" frame.

3. Save your newly created HTML file as **navbar.html** or **navbar.htm** in the same folder as the other files you have created in these lessons.

Creating a Web Site Welcome Page

Typically, a professional Web site developer will create a welcome page that users see when they first access the site. As you learned in Lesson 1, the primary purpose of the welcome page is simply to give users a good first impression of the Web site and to ensure that they recognize the purpose of the Web site. For example, a company that wants to sell books, music, or other products over the Web wants to create a welcome page that will catch the user's eye, display exciting examples of their media products, emphasize the company name, and allow easy access to the various parts of the Web site.

Step-by-Step 4.3

In this step-by-step, you create a simple welcome page. In fact, you do not have to enter any HTML tags for this page that you have not already used in earlier lessons. As you enter the tags, keep in mind that this page has a particular purpose—it is your welcome page. As you learn more about creating Web pages, you could continue to enhance this page to liven up your Web site and give the user a memorable experience. One of the primary goals of commercial Web sites is to give users a reason to return to the site again and again.

1. Open Notepad, SimpleText, or your favorite text editor, if it is not already open.

2. Click **File** on the menu bar, and then click **New** to create a new blank document.

3. Enter the HTML text exactly as shown in **Figure 4–5**.

FIGURE 4–5   Creating a simple welcome page

```
<html>

<head>
<title>HTML and JavaScript</title>
</head>

<body>
<div align="center"><font size="6">Welcome</font></div>
<br>
<div align="center"><font size="5">to</font></div>
<br>
<div align="center"><font size="6">HTML and JavaScript</font></div>
</body>

</html>
```

4. Save your newly created file as **welcome.html** or **welcome.htm** in the same folder where you have been saving the HTML files for the lessons in this book.

5. Open the file **frameset-1.html** in your Web browser and view the **frameset-1.html** document you created in Step-by-Step 4.1. Your screen should look similar to **Figure 4–6**. The left frame displays the HTML file navbar.html, while the right frame displays the HTML file welcome. html. These HTML files are the files specified with the src attribute in the frameset file frameset-1.html.

NOTE

Remember that the files you created in previous lessons (one.html, two.html, three.html, and so on) must be located in the same folder as the files you create in this lesson. If they are not in the same folder, your hyperlinks will not function correctly.

FIGURE 4–6
A welcome page with a navigation bar

welcome.html

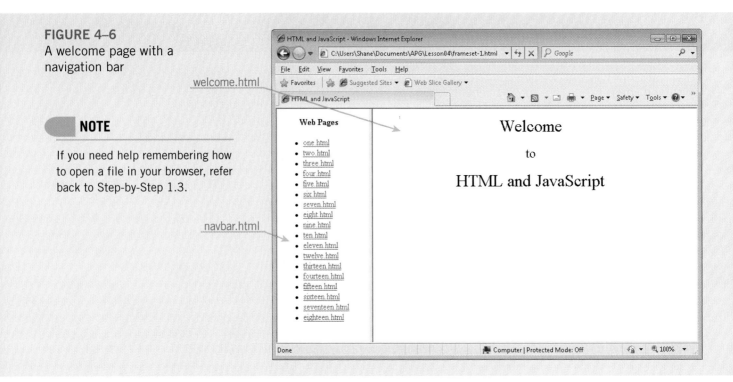

navbar.html

NOTE

If you need help remembering how to open a file in your browser, refer back to Step-by-Step 1.3.

Creating a Nested Frameset

There are times when it is desirable to place a third frame into your frameset to display a horizontal frame across the top of your browser window. You can then place a new Web page into this new frame that functions as a consistent title for your Web page.

If you recall the discussion about horizontal and vertical frames in the first part of this lesson, you should be asking yourself an important question. To be specific, we stated early on that it is only possible for a frameset to contain either horizontal frames or vertical frames, but not both. So, you might be curious: How are you supposed to create a horizontal frame in which to display your title page if you already have vertical frames defined in your existing frameset?

A ***nested frameset*** solves this problem. The term *nested* is a word that programmers and Web developers use to describe a structure, keyword, or tag that contains one or more additional instances of the same item. In this case, you will use a <frameset> tag inside another <frameset> tag to create both vertical and horizontal frames.

▶ **VOCABULARY**
nested frameset

Step-by-Step 4.4

In this step-by-step, you create a nested frameset by adding additional <frameset> tags to your existing document. These tags define the new frame. You then save the HTML file with a new filename, preserving your original HTML file.

1. Open Notepad, SimpleText, or your favorite text editor, if it is not already open.

2. Click **File** on the menu bar, and then click **Open** to open the Open dialog box.

3. Click the **File type** arrow, click **All Files**, and then navigate to the folder where you stored your HTML files for this book.

4. Open the **frameset-1.html** or **frameset-1.htm** file you created in Step-by-Step 4.1 for editing.

5. Modify the HTML document by adding the tags shown in bold here and in **Figure 4–7**.

```
<frameset rows="60,*">
<frame name="UpperFrame" src="title.html">
<frameset cols="180,*">
<frame name="LeftFrame" src="navbar.html">
<frame name="RightFrame" src="welcome.html">
</frameset>
</frameset>
```

FIGURE 4–7   Creating a nested frameset

```
<html>

<head>
<title>HTML and JavaScript</title>
</head>

<frameset rows="60,*">
<frame name="UpperFrame" src="title.html">
<frameset cols="180,*">
<frame name="LeftFrame" src="navbar.html">
<frame name="RightFrame" src="welcome.html">
</frameset>
</frameset>

</html>
```

6. Use the **Save As** command to save the changes in a new file as **frameset-2.html** or **frameset-2.htm** in the folder where you have been saving the files for the lessons in this book.

Creating a Title Bar

Just as the Web page you created in Step-by-Step 4.2 is referred to as a navigation bar, a page that has the specific purpose of displaying a constant title for a Web site is commonly called a *title bar*. In this step-by-step, you create a title bar to be displayed in the new frame you defined in Step-by-Step 4.4 in the file frameset-2.html. **Figure 4–8** shows an example of a Web page with a title bar.

▶ **VOCABULARY**
title bar

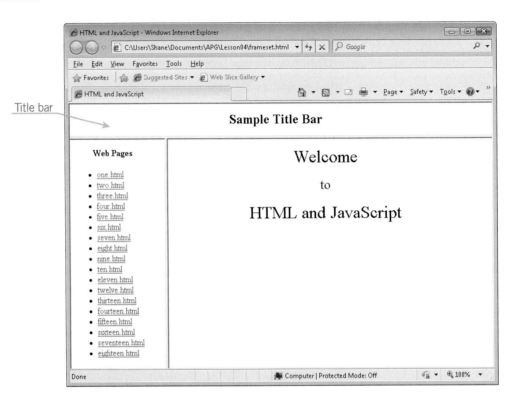

Title bar

FIGURE 4–8   Three frames with a navigation bar, title bar, and welcome page

Like the welcome.html or welcome.htm page HTML file you created in Step-by-Step 4.3, you do not have to use any new HTML tags to create this title bar Web page. But, as with welcome pages, professional Web developers will typically go to great lengths to create a title bar that will be eye-catching and memorable. Yours, however, will be very simple so that you can more easily grasp this new concept.

There is another aspect of frame-based Web pages that is worth mentioning here. By default, the browser will display semithick lines between each frame, and these lines are called *frame separators*. When the user moves the mouse over a frame separator, the pointer changes shape to indicate that the frame separator can be moved. The user can simply click and drag the separator to a new location. As you will learn in the next section, depending on your Web page design, this might or might not be a desirable characteristic of frames.

▶ **VOCABULARY**
frame separators

Step-by-Step 4.5

Frames help organize Web pages. In this step-by-step, you create a title frame that helps to organize your Web page. You also see how frames can be resized by dragging the frame separator.

1. Open Notepad, SimpleText, or your favorite text editor, if it is not already open.

2. Create a new blank document.

3. Enter the HTML text exactly as shown in bold in **Figure 4–9**.

FIGURE 4–9   HTML text for a title page

```
<html>

<head>
<title>HTML and JavaScript</title>
</head>

<body>
<div align="center"><font size="5"><b>HTML and JavaScript</b></font></div>
</body>

</html>
```

4. Save your newly created HTML file as **title.html** or **title.htm**.

5. Open your Web browser and open the **frameset-2.html** or **frameset-2.htm** file to view the frameset-2.html document you created in Step-by-Step 4.4 as a Web page. You should see a Web page that looks like the one shown in **Figure 4–10**.

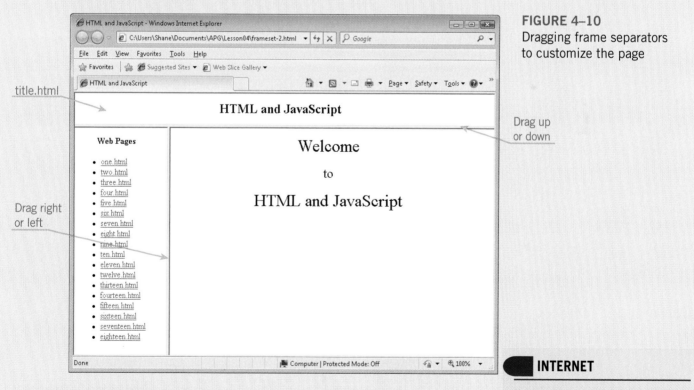

FIGURE 4–10
Dragging frame separators to customize the page

title.html

Drag up or down

Drag right or left

6. Frame pages can be customized by the user. Slowly roll your mouse over the bars (called frame separators) between the frames, as shown in **Figure 4–10**. When the mouse pointer changes to a double arrow, click and drag the bar to the left or right (for vertical frames), or up or down (for horizontal frames).

INTERNET

Frames are a great way to learn how Web pages can be organized into sections or parts. Tables provide another way to split a page into sections for artistic and organizational purposes.

Using Advanced HTML Options

Let's take a minute to make a couple of observations about the frames and framesets you have created so far. First, your Web browser is displaying frame separators that make it abundantly obvious where one frame ends and where another frame begins. Second, if you position your mouse cursor directly over any of these frame separators, you will see your mouse pointer change shape to indicate that the frame separator can be moved. This means the user can change the appearance of your Web pages simply by clicking and dragging a frame separator to a different position, as you experienced in the previous step-by-step.

The frame and frameset characteristics we have just described might be desirable in some situations. However, there are occasions when professional Web developers do not want the browser to display frame separators, nor would they want the user to change the layout of the screen at will. This is especially true when the developer includes custom-made graphic images in their Web pages. Such images are frequently designed to be a specific size and to fit within a frame. If the browser displays frame separators, or if the user were to change the size of the frames, the entire layout of the page could be disrupted, and the resulting clutter of images would be very unappealing.

Fortunately, two important HTML attributes can be used within the <frameset> and <frame> tags to address these issues, as shown in **Figure 4–11**. First, you can use the ***border attribute*** within the <frameset> tag to adjust the appearance of the frame separators. In addition, you can also use the ***noresize attribute*** within the <frame> tag to instruct the browser that the user should not be able to change the size of the frames. These two attributes can be used separately or together to get the appearance and behavior you want.

▶ **VOCABULARY**

border attribute

noresize attribute

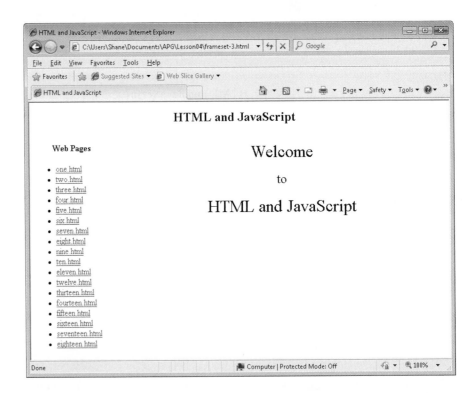

FIGURE 4–11   Eliminating frame separators on a Web page

Step-by-Step 4.6

In this step-by-step, you enter the tags that will make it impossible for a user to change the size of the frames in your Web page.

1. Open Notepad, SimpleText, or your favorite text editor, if it is not already open.

2. Open the HTML file **frameset-2.html** or **frameset-2.htm** you created in Step-by-Step 4.4 for text editing.

3. Modify the HTML document by adding the HTML text shown in bold here and in **Figure 4–12.**

```
<frameset border="0" rows="60,*">
<frame name="UpperFrame" noresize src="title.html">
<frameset border="0" cols="180,*">
<frame name="LeftFrame" noresize src="navbar.html">
<frame name="RightFrame" noresize src="welcome.html">
</frameset>
</frameset>
```

FIGURE 4–12   Using <frameset> and <frame> attributes

```
<html>

<head>
<title>HTML and JavaScript</title>
</head>

<frameset border="0" rows="60,*">
<frame name="UpperFrame" noresize src="title.html">
<frameset border="0" cols="180,*">
<frame name="LeftFrame" noresize src="navbar.html">
<frame name="RightFrame" noresize src="welcome.html">
</frameset>
</frameset>

</html>
```

4. Save your changes in a new HTML file as **frameset-3.html** or **frameset-3.htm** in the folder where you have been saving the other files you created in these lessons.

5. Open your Web browser and view the **frameset-3.html** document you just saved as a Web page. The Web page in your browser should not have frame separators. Refer back to **Figure 4–11**.

TECHNOLOGY TIMELINE

HTML Creation Tools

HTML is powerful, but it can take a long time to enter all the tags by hand. Someone finally asked, "Is there any way to make HTML files simpler to create?" A few years after HTML became the standard way of communicating online, enterprising programmers created software tools that take the pain out of typing in all those angle brackets and tags. Some of the most popular Web page development tools include Adobe Dreamweaver, Adobe GoLive, and Microsoft Expression. Each of these tools helps you create Web pages in much the same way professionals create documents in word-processing or desktop publishing software. In a program like Dreamweaver, most of the tags are created for you automatically as you design your page. However, don't believe for a minute that you do not need to know HTML tags to use these powerful and exciting Web page creation tools. There will be times when you will need to edit or make corrections to the tags created by these products. A tag view is always available.

SUMMARY

In this lesson, you learned:

- How to create a frameset.
- How to interpret frameset attributes and values.
- How to create a navigation bar in a frame.
- How to make a simple welcome page in a frame.

- How to insert nested tags and attributes.
- How to add a title bar frame to a frameset.
- How to remove the borders in a frameset.

 **VOCABULARY REVIEW**

Define the following terms:

border attribute	left-hand navigation	pixel
cols attribute	name attribute	rows attribute
frame	navigation bar	src attribute
frame separator	nested frameset	target attribute
frameset tag	noresize attribute	title bar

REVIEW QUESTIONS

TRUE / FALSE

Circle T if the statement is true or F if the statement is false.

T   F   **1.**   A frameset can display either rows or columns, but not both.

T   F   **2.**   The rows attribute is used to define vertical frames.

T   F   **3.**   The <body> and </body> tags are required in a frameset page.

T   F   **4.**   The <head> and </head> tags are allowed in frameset pages.

T   F   **5.**   You must type in all HTML tags when you use programs like Dreamweaver, Expression, or GoLive.

T   F   **6.**   There is no value in knowing and understanding HTML tags if you create Web pages with Web design software.

T   F   **7.**   The only way to calculate the width of a frame is to count pixels.

T   F   **8.**   By default, a user can move the frame separators displayed by the Web browser.

T   F   **9.**   The border attribute makes frame separators disappear.

T   F   **10.**   The noresize attribute makes frame separators disappear.

FILL IN THE BLANK

Complete the following sentences by writing the correct word or words in the blanks provided.

1. The _____ attribute creates horizontal frames.

2. The _____ attribute creates vertical frames.

3. The _____ attribute specifies the filename of a Web page to display in a frame.

4. The _____ attribute identifies a specific frame.

5. The _____ attribute is used within anchor <a> tags.

6. The _____ attribute can be used to make frame separators disappear.

7. The _____ attribute prevents viewers of a Web page from changing the size of frames.

8. A single "dot" of light on a computer screen is called a(n) _____.

9. A frameset that is defined within another frameset is called a(n) _____ frameset.

10. A(n) _____ is a semithick line displayed by Web browsers between frames.

WRITTEN QUESTIONS

Write a short answer to each of the following questions:

1. What is the purpose of a navigation bar as described in this lesson?

2. What is a welcome page? What is the primary goal of this page?

3. What is a nested frameset? Why would a Web page designer use one?

4. What are pixel values and percentage values, and how are they specified within a <frameset> tag?

5. Why is it not always a good idea to allow users to adjust the row and/or column separators on a frame-based Web page?

■ PROJECTS

PROJECT 4–1: ORGANIZE RESEARCH INFORMATION

In Project 1-1, you used your Web searching skills to locate information on HTML, XHTML, and CSS. Your manager has asked that you organize the information you collected in a new frame-based Web page using two columns only.

GreatApplications, Inc., has asked you to create a Web site with left-hand navigation that will organize the information you collected in Project 1-1 and Table 1-3. This way, these helpful Web pages can be made available to everyone in the company online. Create a navigation frame on the left-hand side of your frameset page, and have the information you are linking to appear on the right-hand side. You can do all of this with tags you have learned in this lesson.

PROJECT 4–3: TOP-SIDE NAVIGATION

In Project 4-1, you created a left-hand navigation system that will allow you to share with your colleagues at GreatApplications, Inc., information about HTML. In this Web project, challenge yourself. Change the Web page you created in Project 4-1 to a site that navigates from the top bar of the page. Create two rows in your frameset. In the top frame, create your navigation system using 20 percent of the screen. In the bottom frame, display the information. Save this project as **Project 4-3.html** or **Project 4-3.htm**.

PROJECT 4–2: CONDUCT A SURVEY AS A TEAM

In this teamwork project, you are to conduct a survey. To complete the survey, you and your team members must visit at least 100 different Web sites. With teamwork, this won't be as difficult as it might first appear. If your team consists of five members, for example, you each need to visit only 20 sites.

As a team, revisit both the best and the worst pages you have listed. Visit other sites if necessary. You must, as a team, survey exactly 100 sites, collecting data as you go. Divide the task with each member taking a certain percentage of the sites to view while recording the results of applying the following questions to each Web site.

SURVEY QUESTIONS

1. Viewing the source code of your 100 Web pages, how many use <frame> tags or some type of frame organization to organize their Web pages?

2. Viewing the source of your Web pages, how many of these sites use <table> tags to organize their Web pages?

3. What percentage of these sites uses left-hand navigation?

4. How many of these sites use navigation systems at the top of the Web page?

5. How many of these Web sites use an attractive graphic or logo in the title bar area at the top of the Web page?

6. What percentage of the Web sites visited, in the opinion of your team members, have effective welcome pages?

■ CRITICAL THINKING

ACTIVITY 4–1: WHAT DID YOU LEARN?

In your opinion, what are the top 10 most important things you have learned about HTML and creating Web pages while completing the previous four lessons? Prepare a 100–250 word report explaining why each of these top 10 items has been placed on your list. Save your answer (in a text file) as **Activity 4-1**.

ACTIVITY 4–2: CHANGING HTML

As you conclude your studies of HTML, think about the top three weaknesses that you see in HTML. What are the top three things you would change about HTML? What are the weaknesses or things that you feel can be improved? Explain thoroughly, in a 100–250 word report, how you would like to see HTML become better, easier to use, and more helpful to you as a Web developer. Save your answer as **Activity 4-2**.

■ CAPSTONE SIMULATION

Professional Web designers often need to understand and utilize the flexibility of HTML frames to give Web sites the desired appearance. For example, some commercial Web sites are designed with top, bottom, or right-hand navigation bars rather than the left-hand-oriented navigation bar presented in this lesson. Using what you learned about frames and framesets, reorganize the Web site shown in **Figure 4–10** so that it illustrates the use of right-hand navigation. Also change the structure of the Web site's frames so that the navigation bar spans the full height of the browser window and the title bar does *not* span the whole width. Your reorganized Web page should look similar to **Figure 4–13**.

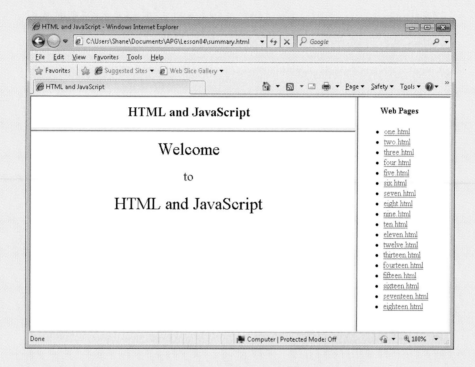

FIGURE 4–13   Sample Web site with right-hand navigation

Project Requirements:

■ You may use the **title.html**, **welcome.html**, and **navbar.html** files you created in this lesson to provide the content for your new frameset.

■ The upper (title) frame should be about 60 pixels high, and the right (navigation) frame should be about 180 pixels wide.

■ Each frame should be defined as not resizable.

■ You might want to use concepts from previous lessons (such as fonts and images) to improve the appearance of your title and welcome pages.

LESSON 5

Introduction to Cascading Style Sheets

■ OBJECTIVES

Upon completion of this lesson, you should be able to:

- Create a Cascading Style Sheet.
- Control hyperlink behavior with CSS.
- Create style classes.
- Share style classes among Web pages.
- Control HTML table appearance with CSS.

■ VOCABULARY

active

cascading style

Cascading Style Sheet

.css

CSS files

hover

look and feel

normal

style

style class

style sheets

visited

Virtually every HTML tag supports the inclusion of one or more optional attributes. Some attributes affect the way the tag operates or the way in which it is processed by the Web browser. Other attributes do not affect functionality, but rather the appearance of an element on a Web page. In older versions of the HTML standard, it was often a challenge for Web developers to learn and remember all of the various attributes that could affect the way the browser would render the visual components of a Web page. But with the latest HTML 4.01 standard, all of these attributes have been consolidated into a globally accessible attribute called style.

In Lesson 2 and Lesson 3, you received a brief introduction to the concept of HTML styles. A *style* is simply a collection of one or more attributes that are applied to the visual components of a Web page. Such components might include text, graphics, input buttons, and Web page elements. The simplest way to use styles is to include them with an individual HTML tag, and there are several instances of this in the pages you created in Lessons 2 and 3. Consider the following example:

```
<body style="background-color:#E6E6FA">
```

This style applies a background color to the entire body of a Web page. If you want to apply another attribute to this Web page (such as a particular font), you could create the tag such as this:

```
<body style="background-color:#E6E6FA;
font-family:New York">
```

This approach to using styles works great in some situations, but it is not always the best option. Consider, for example, an ordered or unordered list on a Web page that contains dozens, or perhaps hundreds, of line items. It quickly becomes overwhelming to apply a style to each <li> tag in the list. You can see that it would be very tedious to type, or even copy and paste, the same style attribute into dozens or hundreds of <li> tags. For this reason, HTML supports the concept of a cascading style. A *cascading style* is a collection of one or more attributes that can be specified once within the header of a Web page and then applied to many instances of a particular tag.

Consider the following example:

```
<style type="text/css">

li {font-family:Verdana;font-color:red}

</style>
```

Using this cascading style, the font-family and font-color attributes will be applied to *every* occurrence of the <li> tag within the current HTML document. As you learned in Lesson 3, multiple tags can be included within the cascading style definition. The tags shown in **Figure 5–1** create a cascading effect for many parts of a Web page. Cascading styles save Web designers an enormous amount of time!

▶ **VOCABULARY**

style

cascading style

FIGURE 5–1 A cascading style definition

```
<style type="text/css">
  h1 {color:red}
  h2 {color:blue}
  h3 {color:purple}
  p {color:black}
</style>
```

So now that you have a basic understanding of HTML styles and cascading styles, let's increase your knowledge even more by discussing the concept of Cascading Style Sheets, or CSS.

Creating Cascading Style Sheets

A *Cascading Style Sheet* is a collection of one or more cascading style codes that has been extracted from the header of a Web page and stored in a separate file in a specific (CSS) format. By convention, Cascading Style Sheet files are always given a *.css* extension so that Web developers can immediately recognize them as Cascading Style Sheets (often just called *CSS files or style sheets*). The two primary motivations for using style sheets are to simplify the header section of HTML documents and to keep all of the style definitions in one place where they can be easily found and modified.

Web development companies can create an entire Web site that can be sold to different customers. CSS makes it possible to customize the appearance and behavior (often called *look and feel*) of the Web site for each customer simply by changing the values in the style sheets. This is a good way for companies to maximize their profits by minimizing the effort required to support multiple customers.

▶ **VOCABULARY**
Cascading Style Sheet

.css

CSS files or style sheets

look and feel

▣ **EXTRA FOR EXPERTS**

Nearly every professionally developed Web page will contain two sections: the header and the body. Strictly speaking, the header section is optional, but it is required by many HTML companion technologies such as CSS (and JavaScript, as you will learn later in Unit 2). The header section includes everything defined between the <head> and </head> tags.

Step-by-Step 5.1

In this step-by-step, you create your first CSS file. So you can get started quickly and see the results of your efforts, you start by making a minor modification to the Web page you created in Lesson 3 in Step-by-Step 3.5. You modify the code that is between the <head> and </head> tags. You then create a CSS file using your text editor. When you save a CSS file, you have to be careful to add the .css file extension.

1. Open Notepad, SimpleText, or your favorite text editor.

2. Click **File** on the menu bar, and then click **Open** to open the **eighteen.html** or **eighteen.htm** file you created in Step-by-Step 3.5 in your text editor.

3. Click **File** on the menu bar, click **Save As**, and then save the HTML file as **nineteen.html** or **nineteen.htm** in the same folder you saved the files from the previous lessons to preserve the eighteen.html file.

4. Modify the header of this HTML file by deleting the lines marked in strikeout and adding the line shown in bold here. The resulting Web page header should appear as shown in **Figure 5–2**.

```
<head>
<title>HTML and JavaScript</title>
<style type="text/css">
h1 {color:red}
h2 {color:blue}
h3 {color:purple}
p {color:black}
</style>
<link href="nineteen.css" rel="stylesheet"
type="text/css"></link>
</head>
```

FIGURE 5–2   nineteen.html file header

```
<head>
<title>HTML and JavaScript</title>
<link href="nineteen.css" rel="stylesheet" type="text/css"></link>
</head>
```

EXTRA FOR EXPERTS

Make sure you don't forget to include the **rel** and **type** attributes within your <link> tags. The **stylesheet** and **text/css** values tell the Web browser that the file specified by the **href** attribute will be a Cascading Style Sheet in CSS format. The fact that the filename ends with a .css extension is not sufficient. In addition, do *not* forget to include the closing </link> tag. If you do, the results will not be good!

5. Save your changes in the HTML file **nineteen.html** or **nineteen.htm**.

6. Click **File** on the menu bar, and then click **New** to create a new blank document.

7. Enter the CSS text exactly as shown in **Figure 5-3**.

FIGURE 5–3   Your first Cascading Style Sheet (CSS file)

```
h1 {color:red}
h2 {color:blue}
h3 {color:purple}
p {color:black}
```

8. Click **File** on the menu bar, click **Save**, and then save your newly created CSS file as **nineteen.css** in the same folder where you have been saving your files for these lessons.

9. Start your favorite Web browser, and then open the **nineteen.html** or **nineteen.htm** file to view the file as a Web page. The Web page on your screen should look like the one shown in **Figure 5–4**.

WARNING

Be sure to type the .css file extension when you type the filename. Do not overwrite the nineteen.html file.

FIGURE 5–4
Web page using a Cascading Style Sheet

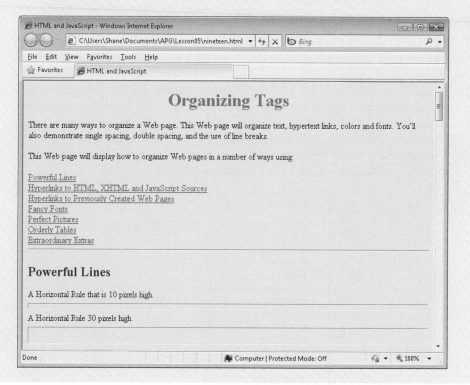

Exploring Hyperlink Styles

By now, you should be familiar with the purpose of hyperlinks in Web pages and the HTML tags that create them. However, you should also be aware that the appearance and behavior of hyperlinks can be modified with Cascading Style Sheets. By default, the Internet Explorer browser, as well as many popular browsers, displays text hyperlinks in an underlined, blue font. The navbar.html Web page file you created in Lesson 4 (and shown in **Figure 5–5**) is a good example of text links formatted with this default font and style.

FIGURE 5–5   Navigation bar with default style links

If you move the mouse pointer over any of these 18 hyperlinks, the pointer changes shape to the hand pointer, but the text link itself does not change. The link still appears as underlined, blue text. Also, if you point to a link (eighteen.html, for example) and then press and hold the left mouse button, the text link still appears as underlined, blue text; it does not change. However, once you release the mouse button, thereby clicking the link, you open the associated Web page in the browser. When you go back to the page with links, the link text will have changed from underlined, blue to a shade of purple (still underlined), as shown in **Figure 5–6**. This change in appearance indicates that the link has been visited.

FIGURE 5–6   Navigation bar with default visited link

The default hyperlink scenario just described illustrates the four possible states of a link: normal, hover, active, and visited. The *normal* state of a hyperlink is the way it appears when the mouse pointer is not over it and it has never been clicked. The *hover* state defines the link's appearance when the mouse pointer is over it but has not yet been clicked. A link's *active* state is when it has the focus on a Web page and pressing the mouse button gives it focus. And, finally, as you might expect, the *visited* state specifies a link's appearance after it has been clicked at least once.

▶ VOCABULARY

normal

hover

active

visited

Step-by-Step 5.2

In this step-by-step, you create a style sheet that defines text attributes for all four hyperlink states. You also apply this style sheet to the navbar.html file you created in Lesson 4. The resulting Web page is frame based, so you need to retrieve and modify several files. In Web development, once you know you have files that work, it is best to make changes to these files rather than recreate new similar files and risk introducing errors. The changes you make to each file are minor and should require very little time.

1. Open Notepad, SimpleText, or your favorite text editor if it is not already open.

2. Open the **frameset-1.html** or **frameset-1.htm** file in the text editor. This is the file you created in Step-by-Step 4.1.

3. Click **File** on the menu bar, click **Save As**, and then save the HTML file as **frameset-4.html** or **frameset-4.htm** in the same folder you saved the files from the previous lessons to preserve the frameset-1.html file.

4. Modify the **frameset-4.html** or **frameset-4.htm** file to change the name of the source file for the left frame, as shown in this step and in bold in **Figure 5–7**.

   ```
   <frame name="LeftFrame" src="navbar-2.html">
   ```

FIGURE 5–7   frameset-4.html file

```
<html>

<head>
<title>HTML and JavaScript</title>
</head>

<frameset cols="180,*">
<frame name="LeftFrame" src="navbar-2.html">
<frame name="RightFrame" src="welcome.html">
</frameset>

</html>
```

5. Save the changes to the file **frameset-4.html** or **frameset-4.htm**.

6. Open the **navbar.html** or **navbar.htm** file in your text editor. This is the file you created in Step-by-Step 4.2.

7. Click **File** on the menu bar, click **Save As**, and then save the HTML file as **navbar-2.html** or **navbar-2.htm** in the same folder you saved the files from the previous lessons to preserve the navbar.html file.

8. Modify the header of this HTML file by adding the tag line, as shown in this step and in bold in **Figure 5–8**.

```
<link href="navbar-2.css" rel="stylesheet"
type="text/css"></link>
```

FIGURE 5–8   Cascading Style Sheet navbar-2.html file header

```
<head>
<title>HTML and JavaScript</title>
<link href="navbar-2.css" rel="stylesheet" type="text/css"></link>
</head>
```

9. Add a new hyperlink in the navbar-2.html file for the new **nineteen.html** or **nineteen.htm** file you created in Step-by-Step 5.1. The link to the nineteen.html file appears just below the link to the eighteen.html file. You create the link by adding the code shown in this step and in bold in **Figure 5–9**.

```
<li><a href="nineteen.html"
target="RightFrame">nineteen.html</a></li>
```

FIGURE 5–9   Cascading Style Sheet navbar-2.html file

```
<html>

<head>
<title>HTML and JavaScript</title>
<link href="navbar-2.css" rel="stylesheet" type="text/css"></link>
</head>

<body>
<div align="center"><b>Web Pages</b></div>
<ul>
```

Continued on next page »

FIGURE 5–9   Cascading Style Sheet navbar-2.html file

《 *Continued from previous page*

```
<li><a href="one.html" target="RightFrame">one.html</a></li>
<li><a href="two.html" target="RightFrame">two.html</a></li>
<li><a href="three.html" target="RightFrame">three.html</a></li>
<li><a href="four.html" target="RightFrame">four.html</a></li>
<li><a href="five.html" target="RightFrame">five.html</a></li>
<li><a href="six.html" target="RightFrame">six.html</a></li>
<li><a href="seven.html" target="RightFrame">seven.html</a></li>
<li><a href="eight.html" target="RightFrame">eight.html</a></li>
<li><a href="nine.html" target="RightFrame">nine.html</a></li>
<li><a href="ten.html" target="RightFrame">ten.html</a></li>
<li><a href="eleven.html" target="RightFrame">eleven.html</a></li>
<li><a href="twelve.html" target="RightFrame">twelve.html</a></li>
<li><a href="thirteen.html" target="RightFrame">thirteen.html</a></li>
<li><a href="fourteen.html" target="RightFrame">fourteen.html</a></li>
<li><a href="fifteen.html" target="RightFrame">fifteen.html</a></li>
<li><a href="sixteen.html" target="RightFrame">sixteen.html</a></li>
<li><a href="seventeen.html" target="RightFrame">seventeen.html</a></li>
<li><a href="eighteen.html" target="RightFrame">eighteen.html</a></li>
<li><a href="nineteen.html" target="RightFrame">nineteen.html</a></li>
</ul>
</body>

</html>
```

10. Save your changes in the **navbar-2.html** or **navbar-2.htm** file in the same folder as your frameset-4.html file.

11. Click **File** on the menu bar, and then click **New** to create a new blank document.

12. Enter the CSS text exactly as shown in bold in Figure 5-10.

FIGURE 5–10   Define four hyperlink styles

```
a:link {color:blue;text-decoration:none}
a:visited {color:purple;text-decoration:none}
a:hover {color:green;text-decoration:underline}
a:active {color:red;text-decoration:underline}
```

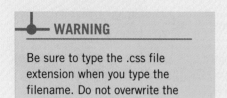

WARNING

Be sure to type the .css file extension when you type the filename. Do not overwrite the navbar-2.html file.

FIGURE 5–11
Two-frame Web page with CSS navbar

13. Save your newly created CSS file as **navbar-2.css** in the same folder as the other files you created in this lesson.

14. Start your favorite Web browser and open your **frameset-4.html** or **frameset-4.htm** file in the browser. The resulting Web page should look like **Figure 5–11**.

    Note: The nineteen.html link might be purple or visited in your Web page if you clicked it in the last step-by-step.

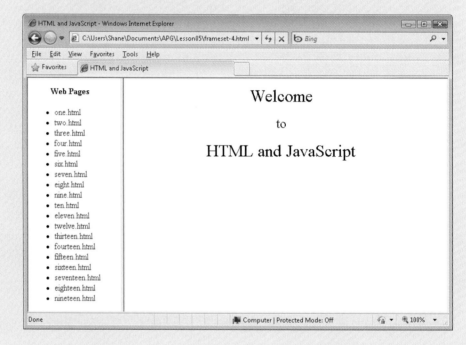

15. Move your mouse over the hyperlinks in the navigation bar. Each link should become underlined and change color as the mouse pointer passes over it.

16. Point to a hyperlink and then press and hold the left mouse button. The color of the link text should change to another color.

17. Click the link. The Web page for the link you click opens in the right frame. After a link is clicked, it should appear as active until it loses focus. Then, the color should change to purple, indicating that it has been visited, as shown in **Figure 5–12**.

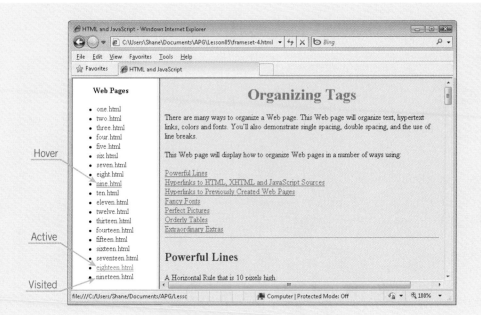

FIGURE 5–12
Navigation bar with hover, active, and visited links

Working with Style Classes

Cascading styles are very useful for applying multiple attributes to many different display elements without having to key those attributes numerous times. However, this approach is not always the solution you are looking for as you design your Web pages. Suppose, for example, that you have various sections (or divisions) of text on a Web page and you would like to apply a different set of attributes to each division. Obviously, applying a single style globally to the entire page will not yield the results you want. Fortunately, CSS technology allows you to define style classes that can be applied to certain tags within your Web page without affecting other tags of the same type. A *style class* is a named group of attributes that are defined in a Cascading Style Sheet and that can be applied to specified tags within an HTML document.

▶ **VOCABULARY**
style class

Step-by-Step 5.3

In this step-by-step, you create three different style classes that will be applied to three different divisions of text on a Web page. The class names prevent one class from being applied to all three lines of text.

1. Open Notepad, SimpleText, or your favorite text editor if it is not already open.

2. Open the **frameset-4.html** or **frameset-4.htm** file in your text editor. This is the file you created in the previous step-by-step.

3. Click **File** on the menu bar, click **Save As**, and then save the HTML file as **frameset-5.html** or **frameset-5.htm** in the same folder you saved the files from the previous lessons to preserve the frameset-4.html file.

4. Change the name of the source file for the right frame, as shown in this step and in bold in **Figure 5–13**.

```
<frame name="RightFrame" src="welcome-2.html">
```

FIGURE 5–13   frameset-5.html file

```
<html>

<head>
<title>HTML and JavaScript</title>
</head>

<frameset cols="180,*">
<frame name="LeftFrame" src="navbar-2.html">
<frame name="RightFrame" src="welcome-2.html">
</frameset>


</html>
```

5. Save your changes to the **frameset-5.html** or **frameset-5.htm** file.

6. Open the file **welcome.html** or **welcome.htm** file in your text editor. This is the file you created in Step-by-Step 4.3.

7. Click **File** on the menu bar, click **Save As**, and then save the HTML file as **welcome-2.html** or **welcome-2.htm** in the same folder you saved the files from the previous lessons to preserve the welcome.html file.

8. Modify the header of this file by adding a style sheet link. Also modify the body of the file by changing the <div> tags and removing the <font> tags, as shown in bold in this step and in bold in **Figure 5–14**.

```
<html>

<head>
<title>HTML and JavaScript</title>
<link href="welcome-2.css" rel="stylesheet"
type="text/css"></link>
</head>
<body>
<div class="text1">Welcome</div>
<br>
<div class="text2">to</div>
<br>
<div class="text3">HTML and JavaScript</div>
</body>
```

FIGURE 5–14   welcome-2.html file

```
<html>

<head>
<title>HTML and JavaScript</title>
<link href="welcome-2.css" rel="stylesheet" type="text/css"></link>
</head>

<body>
<div class="text1">Welcome</div>
<br>
<div class="text2">to</div>
<br>
<div class="text3">HTML and JavaScript</div>
</body>

</html>
```

9. Save your changes to the **welcome-2.html** or **welcome-2.htm** file in the same folder as the frameset-5.html file.

10. Click **File** on the menu bar, and then click **New** to create a new blank document.

11. Enter the CSS text exactly as shown in **Figure 5–15**.

FIGURE 5–15   Your first style classes

```
.text1 {color:red;font-size:32;text-align:center}

.text2 {color:green;font-size:24;text-align:center}
.text3 {color:blue;font-size:32;text-align:center}
```

12. Save your newly created CSS file as **welcome-2.css** in the same folder as the other files you created in this lesson.

13. Start your favorite Web browser and open your **frameset-5.html** or **frameset-5.htm** file in the browser. The resulting Web page should look like the one shown in **Figure 5–16**.

> **WARNING**
>
> Be sure to type the .css file extension when you type the filename. Do not overwrite the welcome-2.html file.

FIGURE 5–16
Welcome page using CSS classes

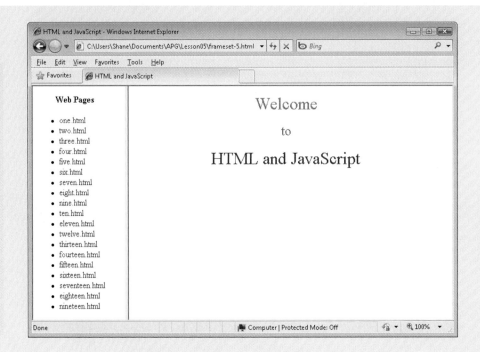

INTERNET

How does your Web browser know the difference between a cascading style and a style class? Cascading styles are given names that correspond with a defined HTML tag such as **body**, **h2**, or **li**. Style classes can be given any arbitrary name, but the name must always be preceded by the dot (.) character. When you invoke the style class within an HTML tag by means of the **class** attribute, you specify the class name *without* the dot.

Sharing Style Classes

As was demonstrated in the previous section, a single Web page can make use of multiple style classes. However, it is also true that a single style class can be used by multiple Web pages. All that is required for two or more Web pages to share a style class is for these Web pages to link in the style sheet in which the style class is defined. This is often done when the Web pages sharing the class are all displayed in a common frameset. However, this is not a requirement. Two or more Web pages that are completely unrelated to each other can still share a style class definition as long as they have access to the appropriate CSS file.

Step-by-Step 5.4

In this step-by-step, you create a common style sheet that is linked by two different Web pages within a common frameset. This CSS file contains a style class that gives the Web pages a common pale yellow background color.

1. Open Notepad, SimpleText, or your favorite text editor if it is not already open.

2. Open the **frameset-5.html** or **frameset-5.htm** file in your text editor. This is the file you created in the previous step-by-step.

3. Click **File** on the menu bar, click **Save As**, and then save the HTML file as **frameset-6.html** or **frameset-6.htm** in the same folder you saved the files from the previous lessons to preserve the frameset-5.html file.

4. Change the name of the source files for the left and right frames, as shown in this step and in bold in **Figure 5–17**.

```
<frame name="LeftFrame" src="navbar-3.html">
<frame name="RightFrame" src="welcome-3.html">
```

FIGURE 5–17   frameset-6.html file

```
<html>

<head>
<title>HTML and JavaScript</title>
</head>

<frameset cols="180,*">
<frame name="LeftFrame" src="navbar-3.html">
<frame name="RightFrame" src="welcome-3.html">
</frameset>

</html>
```

5. Save your changes to the file **frameset-6.html** or **frameset-6.htm** in the same folder as the other files for this lesson.

6. Open the **navbar-2.html** or **navbar-2.htm** file in your text editor. This is the file you created in Step-by-Step 5.2.

7. Click **File** on the menu bar, click **Save As**, and then save the HTML file as **navbar-3.html** or **navbar-3.htm** in the same folder you saved the files from the previous lessons to preserve the navbar-2.html file.

8. Modify the header of this file by adding a second style sheet link. Also add a class attribute to the <body> tag, as shown in this step and in bold in **Figure 5–18**.

```
<link href="common.css" rel="stylesheet"
type="text/css"></link>
<body class="bgcolor1">
```

FIGURE 5–18   navbar-3.html file

```
<html>

<head>
<title>HTML and JavaScript</title>
<link href="navbar-2.css" rel="stylesheet" type="text/css"></link>
<link href="common.css" rel="stylesheet" type="text/css"></link>
</head>

<body class="bgcolor1">
<div align="center"><b>Web Pages</b></div>
<ul>
<li><a href="one.html" target="RightFrame">one.html</a></li>
<li><a href="two.html" target="RightFrame">two.html</a></li>
<li><a href="three.html" target="RightFrame">three.html</a></li>
<li><a href="four.html" target="RightFrame">four.html</a></li>
<li><a href="five.html" target="RightFrame">five.html</a></li>
<li><a href="six.html" target="RightFrame">six.html</a></li>
<li><a href="seven.html" target="RightFrame">seven.html</a></li>
<li><a href="eight.html" target="RightFrame">eight.html</a></li>
<li><a href="nine.html" target="RightFrame">nine.html</a></li>
<li><a href="ten.html" target="RightFrame">ten.html</a></li>
<li><a href="eleven.html" target="RightFrame">eleven.html</a></li>
<li><a href="twelve.html" target="RightFrame">twelve.html</a></li>
<li><a href="thirteen.html" target="RightFrame">thirteen.html</a></li>
<li><a href="fourteen.html" target="RightFrame">fourteen.html</a></li>
<li><a href="fifteen.html" target="RightFrame">fifteen.html</a></li>
<li><a href="sixteen.html" target="RightFrame">sixteen.html</a></li>
<li><a href="seventeen.html" target="RightFrame">seventeen.html</a></li>
<li><a href="eighteen.html" target="RightFrame">eighteen.html</a></li>
<li><a href="nineteen.html" target="RightFrame">nineteen.html</a></li>
</ul>
</body>

</html>
```

9. Save your changes to the file **navbar-3.html** or **navbar-3.htm** in the same folder as the frameset-6.html file.

10. Open the **welcome-2.html** or **welcome-2.htm** file in your text editor. This is the file you created in Step-by-Step 5.3.

11. Click **File** on the menu bar, click **Save As**, and then save the HTML file as **welcome-3.html** or **welcome-3.htm** in the same folder you saved the files from the previous lessons to preserve the welcome-2.html file.

12. Modify the header of this file by adding a second style sheet link. Also add a class attribute to the <body> tag, as shown in this step and in bold in **Figure 5–19**.

```
<link href="common.css" rel="stylesheet"
type="text/css"></link>

<body class="bgcolor1">
```

FIGURE 5–19   welcome-3.html file

```
<html>

<head>
<title>HTML and JavaScript</title>
<link href="welcome-2.css" rel="stylesheet" type="text/css"></link>
<link href="common.css" rel="stylesheet" type="text/css"></link>
</head>

<body class="bgcolor1">
<div class="text1">Welcome</div>
<br>
<div class="text2">to</div>
<br>
<div class="text3">HTML and JavaScript</div>
</body>

</html>
```

13. Save your changes to the **welcome-3.html** or **welcome-3.htm** file in the same folder as the frameset-6.html file.

14. Click **File** on the menu bar, and then click **New** to create a new blank document.

15. Enter the CSS text exactly as shown in **Figure 5–20**.

FIGURE 5–20   common.css file

```
.bgcolor1 {background-color:#EFEFCF}
```

16. Save your newly created file as **common.css** in the same folder as navbar-3.html and welcome-3.html.

17. Start your favorite Web browser and open your **frameset-6.html** or **frameset-6.htm** file in the browser. The Web page on your screen should look similar to the Web page shown in **Figure 5–21**.

FIGURE 5–21
Two Web pages
sharing a common
style class

Background color
might look different
on your screen

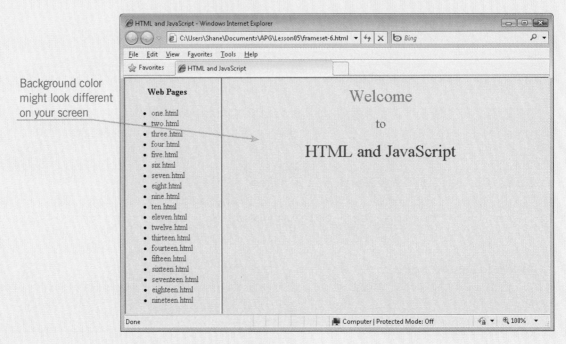

Exploring Table Styles

So far, all of the experience you have gained with HTML styles has related to formatting text in some way. All of the styles, cascading styles, and style classes you created in this and preceding lessons have related to such elements as font color, background color, text alignment, and so on. But rest assured that styles can be used to manage all kinds of HTML tag attributes, not just those related to text. Consider HTML tables, for example. Tables support a variety of attributes that are used to define column widths, border thickness and style, and cell padding, as well as other table features. Because it is common for Web designers to want different tables on their Web pages to have different attributes, this is a perfect opportunity to make use of style classes.

Step-by-Step 5.5

In this step-by-step, you modify the "Orderly Tables" section of the nineteen.html file you created in the first section of this lesson. You learn how to set table attributes as well as individual table cell attributes.

1. Open Notepad, SimpleText, or your favorite text editor if it is not already open.

2. Open the **frameset-6.html** or **frameset-6.htm** file in your text editor if it is not already open. This is the file you created in the previous step-by-step.

3. Click **File** on the menu bar, click **Save As**, and then save the HTML file as **frameset-7.html** or **frameset-7.htm** in the same folder you saved the files from the previous lessons to preserve the frameset-6.html file.

4. Change the name of the source files for the left frame, as shown in this step and in bold in **Figure 5–22**.

```
<frame name="LeftFrame" src="navbar-4.html">
```

FIGURE 5–22   frameset-7.html file

```
<html>

<head>
<title>HTML and JavaScript</title>
</head>

<frameset cols="180,*">
<frame name="LeftFrame" src="navbar-4.html">
<frame name="RightFrame" src="welcome-3.html">
</frameset>

</html>
```

5. Save the changes to the file **frameset-7.html** or **frameset-7.htm**.

6. Open the **navbar-3.html** or **navbar-3.htm** file in your text editor. This is the file you created in the previous step-by-step.

7. Click **File** on the menu bar, click **Save As**, and then save the HTML file as **navbar-4.html** or **navbar-4.htm** in the same folder you saved the files from the previous lessons to preserve the navbar-3.html file.

8. Modify the body of this navbar-4.html file by adding a new link to the **twenty.html** file below the link to the nineteen.html file, as shown in this step and in bold in **Figure 5–23**.

```
<li><a href="twenty.html"
target="RightFrame">twenty.html</a></li>
```

FIGURE 5–23   navbar-4.html file body tags

```
<body class="bgcolor1">
<div align="center"><b>Web Pages</b></div>
<ul>
<li><a href="one.html" target="RightFrame">one.html</a></li>
<li><a href="two.html" target="RightFrame">two.html</a></li>
<li><a href="three.html" target="RightFrame">three.html</a></li>
<li><a href="four.html" target="RightFrame">four.html</a></li>
<li><a href="five.html" target="RightFrame">five.html</a></li>
<li><a href="six.html" target="RightFrame">six.html</a></li>
<li><a href="seven.html" target="RightFrame">seven.html</a></li>
<li><a href="eight.html" target="RightFrame">eight.html</a></li>
<li><a href="nine.html" target="RightFrame">nine.html</a></li>
<li><a href="ten.html" target="RightFrame">ten.html</a></li>
<li><a href="eleven.html" target="RightFrame">eleven.html</a></li>
<li><a href="twelve.html" target="RightFrame">twelve.html</a></li>
<li><a href="thirteen.html" target="RightFrame">thirteen.html</a></li>
<li><a href="fourteen.html" target="RightFrame">fourteen.html</a></li>
<li><a href="fifteen.html" target="RightFrame">fifteen.html</a></li>
<li><a href="sixteen.html" target="RightFrame">sixteen.html</a></li>
<li><a href="seventeen.html" target="RightFrame">seventeen.html</a></li>
<li><a href="eighteen.html" target="RightFrame">eighteen.html</a></li>
<li><a href="nineteen.html" target="RightFrame">nineteen.html</a></li>
<li><a href="twenty.html" target="RightFrame">twenty.html</a></li>
</ul>
</body>
```

9. Save your changes to the file **navbar-4.html** or **navbar-4.htm** in the same folder as the frameset-7.html file.

10. Open the **nineteen.html** or **nineteen.htm** file in your text editor. This is the file you created in Step-by-Step 5.1.

11. Click **File** on the menu bar, click **Save As**, and then save the HTML file as **twenty.html** or **twenty.htm** in the same folder you saved the files from the previous lessons to preserve the nineteen.html file.

12. Modify the header of this file by updating the CSS file specified in the <link> tag, as shown here and in bold in **Figure 5–24**.

```
<link href="twenty.css" rel="stylesheet"
type="text/css"></link>
```

13. Modify the "Orderly Tables" section in the body of this file, as shown here and in bold in **Figure 5–24**.

```
<h2><a name="tables">Orderly Tables</a></h2>
<table class="table1">
<tr>
  <th>Images</th>
  <th>Colors</th>
  <th>Fonts</th>
</tr>
<tr>
  <td class="row1"><img src="levy.gif"
  height="50" width="50"></td>
  <td class="row1">Red</td>
  <td class="row1"><font face="times"
  size="7" color="red">Times</td>
</tr>
<tr>
  <td class="row2"><img src="levy.gif"
  height="75" width="50"></td>
  <td class="row2">Green</td>
  <td class="row2"><font face="courier"
  size="10" color="green">Courier</td>
</tr>
</table>
<hr />
```

FIGURE 5–24   twenty.html file

```
<html>

<head>
<title>HTML and JavaScript</title>
<link href="twenty.css" rel="stylesheet" type="text/css"></link>
</head>

<body style="background-color:#E6E6FA">
```

Because the only changes to the code from this point on are in the Orderly Tables section, skip the Powerful Lines, Hyperlink, Fancy Fonts, and Perfect Pictures sections of the code and jump down to the Orderly Tables section of your HTML file. Make the changes as shown below in bold to the Orderly Tables section. Do not make any changes to the Extraordinary Extras section.

```
<h2><a name="tables">Orderly Tables</a></h2>
<table class="table1">
```

Continued on next page ≫

FIGURE 5–24   twenty.html file

《 *Continued from previous page*

```
<tr>
  <th>Images</th>
  <th>Colors</th>
  <th>Fonts</th>
</tr>
<tr>
  <td class="row1"><img src="levy.gif" height="50" width="50"></td>
  <td class="row1">Red</td>
  <td class="row1"><font face="times" size="7" color="red">Times</td>
</tr>
<tr>
  <td class="row2"><img src="levy.gif" height="75" width="50"></td>
  <td class="row2">Green</td>
  <td class="row2"><font face="courier" size="10"
color="green">Courier</td>
</tr>
</table>
<hr />
```

14. Save your changes to the file **twenty.html** or **twenty.htm** in the same folder as the frameset-7.html file.

15. Open the file **nineteen.css** in your text editor. This is the file you created in Step-by-Step 5.1.

16. Click **File** on the menu bar, click **Save As**, and then save the HTML file as **twenty.css** in the same folder you saved the files from the previous lessons to preserve the nineteen.css file.

17. Enter the CSS text exactly as shown in this step and in bold in **Figure 5–25**.

```
.table1 {border-color:black;border-style:solid;
border-width:5}
.row1 {background-color:#EFCFCF;padding:10;
text-align:center}
.row2 {background-color:#CFEFCF;padding:10;
text-align:center}
```

FIGURE 5–25   twenty.css file

```
h1 {color:red}
h2 {color:blue}
h3 {color:purple}
p {color:black}

.table1 {border-color:black;border-style:solid;border-width:5}

.row1 {background-color:#EFCFCF;padding:10;text-align:center}
.row2 {background-color:#CFEFCF;padding:10;text-align:center}
```

18. Save your changes to the file **twenty.css** in the same folder as the twenty.html file.

19. Start your favorite Web browser, and open your **frameset-7.html** or **frameset-7.htm** file in the browser. Click the **twenty.html** link in the left frame, and then click the **Orderly Tables** link in the right frame. Your Web page should look similar to **Figure 5–26**.

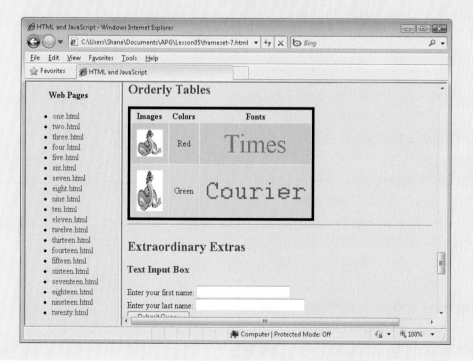

FIGURE 5–26
HTML table using style classes

INTERNET

Whenever you create a Cascading Style Sheet that is indented for use with a single Web page, it is a good idea to give the HTML file and the CSS file the same name (for example, **twenty.html** and **twenty.css**). However, this is just a programming convention; it is not required by HTML or by CSS.

SUMMARY

In this lesson, you learned:

- How to create a Cascading Style Sheet.
- How to control hyperlink behavior with CSS.
- How to create style classes.
- How to share a style class among Web pages.
- How to control HTML table appearance with CSS.

■ VOCABULARY REVIEW

Define the following terms:

active	CSS files	style
cascading style	hover	style class
Cascading Style Sheet	look and feel	style sheets
.css	normal	visited

■ REVIEW QUESTIONS

TRUE / FALSE

Circle T if the statement is true or F if the statement is false.

T F   **1.** Styles, cascading styles, and Cascading Style Sheets are all created in exactly the same way.

T F   **2.** The terms Cascading Style Sheet, style sheet, and CSS file are synonymous.

T F   **3.** Cascading Style Sheets are linked to Web pages by means of the <style> tag.

T F   **4.** CSS files use the style keyword to define cascading styles.

T F   **5.** The appearance and behavior of Web page hyperlinks can be modified with CSS.

T F   **6.** HTML hyperlinks maintain exactly two states: normal and visited.

T F   **7.** You may define any number of style classes within a CSS file.

T F   **8.** A style class definition may be shared by two or more Web pages.

T F   **9.** A style class definition may be shared by two or more Web pages, but only if those pages reside in a common frameset.

T F **10.** CSS files can contain cascading styles or style classes, but not both.

FILL IN THE BLANK

Complete the following sentences by writing the correct word or words in the blanks provided.

1. A(n) _____ is defined as an attribute within an individual HTML tag.

2. Cascading styles are defined by using the _____ tag.

3. The _____ attribute is used within the <link> tag to specify the filename of a Cascading Style Sheet.

4. The _____ attribute identifies the file format of a linked style sheet.

5. The _____ state of a hyperlink is applied when the mouse pointer passes over it.

6. The _____ state of a hyperlink is invoked when the mouse button is clicked.

7. The _____ state of a hyperlink is invoked when the link has been clicked at least once.

8. A(n) _____ may be defined within the header of an HTML file or within a CSS file.

9. The _____ attribute may be used in any HTML tag to invoke a style class.

10. A style class name is always preceded by a(n) _____ character.

WRITTEN QUESTIONS

Write a short answer to each of the following questions:

1. Explain the difference between a style, a cascading style, and a Cascading Style Sheet.

2. Name and briefly describe the four states of hyperlinks.

3. What is a style class? How does it differ from a cascading style?

4. Explain how style classes can be shared among Web pages.

5. Describe how CSS can affect the appearance of HTML tables.

■ PROJECTS

PROJECT 5–1: REVIEWING YOUR WORK

Review the HTML files you created in previous lessons (one.html through eighteen.html). Identify which ones include cascading styles. Rework these Web pages so that they use a Cascading Style Sheet instead. If you want to preserve the original HTML files, give your modified files new names (for example, eighteen-2.html). The basic steps for replacing a cascading style with a style sheet are as follows:

- Delete the cascading style code (<style> tags) from the HTML file.
- Add a <link> tag with the appropriate href, rel, and type attributes.
- Create a CSS file that contains the deleted style codes.
- Make sure the CSS filename and the value of the href attribute in the HTML file's <link> tag match (for example, eighteen.css).

Please note that not all of your original 18 HTML files use cascading styles.

PROJECT 5–2: MORE EXPERIENCE WITH HYPERLINK STYLES

Review the navbar-2.html file you created in Step-by-Step 5.2. Modify the appropriate style sheet so that your navigation hyperlinks behave differently. For example, use a bold font when a link is in its hover state or use an italic font for visited links. You can also change the font colors used to enhance the appearance of the Web page and improve the user experience. See how creative you can be!

To preserve your original navbar-2.css file, give your new style sheet a new name and update the <link> tag in the HTML file appropriately.

PROJECT 5–3: CREATING A COMMON BACKGROUND

Return to the one.html through twenty.html files you created in Lessons 2, 3, and 5. Insert the appropriate HTML tags so that all of these files use the common.css file you created for Step-by-Step 5.4. Make all of these pages display with the pale yellow background color so that they better match the background color of the leftmost navigation frame (like the welcome-3.html file does). *Hint*: This only involves adding a class attribute to the <body> tag of your files.

CRITICAL THINKING

ACTIVITY 5–1: WHAT'S THE BENEFIT?

Your supervisor at GreatApplications, Inc., has been asked to modify the company Web site so that it uses Cascading Style Sheets. He asks you to explain what possible benefits the company could realize from this change. Identify and briefly describe at least three ways in which GreatApplications can benefit by using CSS.

ACTIVITY 5–2: IS THERE A DOWNSIDE?

Whenever new technologies are introduced to software and Web developers, they are intended to provide certain benefits. However, there is almost always a downside to a new technology. What potential problems might be introduced by CSS technology?

CAPSTONE SIMULATION

All of the frame-based Web pages in this lesson display exactly two frames—left and right. Review the work you did in Lesson 4 to create a three-frame Web page. Modify the appropriate HTML and/or CSS files to turn your final project in this lesson into a three-frame Web page. Make sure that the page in the upper frame makes use of its own new CSS file and also the common .css file you created in Step-by-Step 5.4. Also ensure that the colors of the displayed text and background match the other files in the frameset.

To preserve your original HTML and CSS files, give your new style sheet a new name and update the <link> tag in the HTML files appropriately.

UNIT I REVIEW

HTML Basics

HTML TAG AND ATTRIBUTE SUMMARY

TAGS OR ATTRIBUTES	PURPOSE	LESSON
\<a> \</a>	Anchor tag used to define hyperlinks	2
align	Attribute used to specify the horizontal alignment of a table	3
bgcolor	Attribute used to specify table cell background color	3
\<body> \</body>	Tag used to define the beginning and ending of the main body of an HTML document	1
border	Attribute used to specify table or frame border width	3, 4
\ 	Tag used to denote a single-spaced line break	2
cellpadding	Attribute used to add padding to table cells	3
\<center> \</center>	Tag used to center text horizontally on a Web page	1
class	Attribute used to specify a particular style class	5
color	Attribute used to specify text font color	3
cols	Attribute used to define columns in a frameset	4
\<div>	Tag used to delimit the beginning and ending of a text division	5
face	Attribute used to specify a text font face	3
\<font> \</font>	Tag used to delimit the beginning and ending of text font settings	3
\<form> \</form>	Tag used to define the beginning and ending of a user input form	3
\<frame> \</frame>	Tag used to mark the beginning and ending of a frame definition	4
\<frameset> \</frameset>	Tag used to mark the beginning and ending of a frameset definition	4

continued

TAGS OR ATTRIBUTES	PURPOSE	LESSON
<h1> </h1>	Tag used to mark the beginning and ending of a level 1 heading	1
<h2> </h2>	Tag used to mark the beginning and ending of a level 2 heading	1
<h3> </h3>	Tag used to mark the beginning and ending of a level 3 heading	1
<h4> </h4>	Tag used to mark the beginning and ending of a level 4 heading	1
<h5> </h5>	Tag used to mark the beginning and ending of a level 5 heading	1
<h6> </h6>	Tag used to mark the beginning and ending of a level 6 heading	1
<head> </head>	Tag used to define the beginning and ending of the HTML document header	2
height	Attribute used to specify image height	3
<hr />	Tag used to mark a horizontal rule (line)	2
href	Attribute used to specify a target Web page or CSS file	2, 5
<html> </html>	Tag used to define the beginning and ending of an HTML file	1
<img />	Tag used to indicate the placement of a graphic image	3
<input />	Tag used to define a user input control	3
<li> </li>	Tag used to designate a line item within an ordered or unordered list	1
<link> </link>	Tag used to link a CSS file to a Web page	5
name	Attribute used to name anchors and frames	2, 4
noresize	Attribute used to prevent user resizing of frames	4
<ol> </ol>	Tag used to designate an ordered (sequentially numbered) list	1
<option> </option>	Tag used to define an option within a drop-down selection box	3
<p> </p>	Tag used to define the beginning and ending of a paragraph	1
rel	Attribute used within <link> tags to specify the relationship between documents	5
rows	Attribute used to define rows in a frameset	4
<select> </select>	Tag used to define the beginning and ending of a drop-down selection box	3
size	Attribute used to specify a text font size	3
src	Attribute used to specify the source of an image or frame	3, 4
style	Style attribute used to modify various tags	2, 5
<style> </style>	Tag used to define a cascading style	2, 5
<table> </table>	Tag used to define the beginning and ending of a table	3
target	Attribute used within anchor tags to specify a target frame	4

continued

TAGS OR ATTRIBUTES	PURPOSE	LESSON
<td> </td>	Tag used to delimit a table cell within a row	3
<th> </th>	Tag used to delimit a table header cell within a row	3
<title> </title>	Tag used to define the title of a Web page	1
<tr> </tr>	Tag used to delimit a table row	3
type	Attribute used to define style type or an input control type	2, 3
<ul> </ul>	Tag used to designate an unordered (bulleted) list	1
width	Attribute used to specify image width	3

■ REVIEW QUESTIONS

MATCHING

Match the correct term in the right column to its description in the left column.

1. The specialized Web language used to instruct Web browsers on how Web elements should appear

2. A popular scripting language used to create miniapplications and multimedia effects

3. A collection of two or more frames on a Web page

4. Usually appear in pairs enclosed in angle brackets

5. Operating in base-16, a system that uses letters as well as numbers to express values

6. Common name given to a vertical or horizontal list of hyperlinks on a Web site home page

7. The definition of attribute

8. A protocol used to transfer data from Web servers to Web browsers

9. HTML tag used to attach a Cascading Style Sheet to a Web page

10. Graphical format that adheres to international standards; compact enough for Internet use

11. Image file format designed to be small enough to transfer over low-speed modems

12. HTML tag used to define one or more cascading styles

13. Term used by programmers that describes a structure, keyword, or tag that contains one or more additional instances of the same item

14. Software program that makes it possible to avoid having to manually enter every single tag

15. Attribute used to apply a particular CSS style to various kinds of HTML tags

A. Dreamweaver

B. frameset

C. GIF

D. HTML

E. navigation bar

F. HTTP

G. hexadecimal

H. <link>

I. tags

J. nested

K. <style>

L. value

M. JPEG

N. class

O. JavaScript

WRITTEN QUESTIONS

Compose a brief answer to each of the following questions. Save the answers in a single document file named HTML Unit Summary.

1. List and explain the functions of five HTML tags that you believe can be found on most Web pages.

2. List and explain the origin of each of the following file formats. In your explanation, indicate which formats are used for Web pages.
   A. .txt
   B. .docx
   C. .htm
   D. .html
   E. .css

3. Explain how the anchor tag is used and written to create hyperlinks to sites on the Web and to individual Web pages on your personal computer. In your explanation, indicate how graphics can be turned into hyperlinks.

4. Explain how framesets work and how Web pages can be targeted to appear in different frames.

5. Explain the difference between a style, a cascading style, and a Cascading Style Sheet.

■ CROSS-CURRICULAR PROJECTS

In this exercise, you will demonstrate a practical use for HTML. You're going to design a frames page that will help you organize excellent sources of information in at least five academic subject areas. The four required areas are Language Arts, Science, Social Studies, and Math. Pick another subject area that interests you, such as Foreign Language, Music, Art, Physical Education, or Technology. Use Web search tools such as *www.yahoo.com* or *www.google.com* to find legitimate academic resources in these subject areas. Choose sites that you will want to return to again and again for information.

This will take some careful thinking and planning on your part. Here's the trick—create a left-hand navigation bar that will access these resource pages for each of these subject areas. Invent your own filenames for your frameset and navigation bar pages. The title bar page is optional. Include at least one Cascading Style Sheet with your project. Test all of the links to make sure each one works.

LANGUAGE ARTS 1

Find five Web sites related to the study of Language Arts, and place them on a target page that will appear in the right frame of your cross-curricular frames page. Name this file **la-1.html** or **la-1.htm**.

SCIENCE 1

Find five Web sites related to the study of Science, and place them on a target page that will appear in the right frame of your cross-curricular frames page. Name this file **sci-1.html** or **sci-1.htm**.

SOCIAL STUDIES 1

Find five Web sites related to the study of Social Studies, and place them on a target page that will appear in the right frame of your cross-curricular frames page. Name this file **ss-1.html** or **ss-1.htm**.

MATH 1

Find five Web sites related to the study of Math, and place them on a target page that will appear in the right frame of your cross-curricular frames page. Name this file **m-1.html** or **m-1.htm**.

YOUR CHOICE OF SUBJECT 1

Find five Web sites related to the study of a subject of your choice, and place them on a target page that will appear in the right frame of your cross-curricular frames page. Name this file **mychoice-1.html** or **mychoice-1.htm**.

REVIEW PROJECTS

PROJECT 1–1: CREATING A WEB SITE

You've probably been thinking, "I have created dozens of Web pages, but when can I branch out and create a Web site entirely of my own?" Well, now is your chance to harness all of your Web design creativity.

Pick an appropriate topic or theme for your Web site. Using all of the skills you learned in this unit, create an awesome Web site. Invent your own HTML filenames, and use a CSS file for your styles.

PROJECT 1–2: EVALUATING WEB SITES

By now, you probably think your Web pages compose the most awesome site on the Web. And it's probably true! However, it's time to find out. Team up in groups of three or four. Share your Web pages from both the Cross-Curricular Projects and Project 1-1 with your teammates. If any team member is having problems making elements of his or her pages work, solve these problems as a group. Give each other suggestions on how pages can be improved.

SIMULATION

JOB 1–1: HTML REFERENCE RESOURCES

Imagine you have just become the lead Web page designer and Web development Team Manager responsible for the GreatApplications, Inc., Web site. To sharpen your team's skills in cutting-edge technology, you have decided to create a Web page cataloging sites that will help your team members learn more about HTML, JavaScript, Flash, and other Web page creation tools such as Dreamweaver or Expression Web 2. Look at pages you worked on in this unit involving cataloging the HTML learning sites. Add these to your new Web site. Then, reference some of the dominant Web site development companies online, including Adobe, creator of Dreamweaver; Microsoft, creator of Expression Web 2; and other online multimedia development tools. Use search engines such as *www.yahoo.com* or *www.google.com* to find the resources you need. Invent your own filenames.

JOB 1–2: WEB PAGE DEVELOPMENT JOBS

Do you want a career in the high-tech online industry? If you do, you'd first better find out what types of jobs are available and whether they are to your liking.

Go online and visit some of the major career Web sites such as *www.flipdog.com* or *www.monster.com* and search for 10 jobs related to Web page development. If you have trouble finding these types of jobs on these sites, try using the keyword **Online Job Search** in your search engine.

Create a short report that lists 10 of the jobs you have found and explains a little bit about the qualifications you would need to accept these jobs in the high-tech Web design industry. Save your work as **Job 1-2**.

■ SUMMARY PROJECT

This is your opportunity to demonstrate that you have mastered all of the major concepts in this unit. Consider the information in Table U1–1. This table summarizes the various HTML topics that were presented in the first three lessons.

Your job is to organize this information into a Web page that is laid out as shown in Figure U1–1. Frame A will contain a list of hyperlinks that represent the first three lessons in the book. Frame B will contain its own list of hyperlinks that correspond to the topics covered in one of the lessons. Frame B will be updated each time the user clicks a hyperlink in Frame A. Frame C will contain a Web page that illustrates one of the topics listed in Frame B, and the Web page will change when a user clicks a different link in Frame B. Figure U1–2 shows an example of how the completed Web page might look if the user clicks on Lesson 1 in Frame A and Headings in Frame B.

TABLE U1–1

LESSON NUMBER	TOPICS COVERED
1	headings ordered lists unordered lists
2	horizontal lines background colors hyperlinks text colors
3	fonts images tables input controls

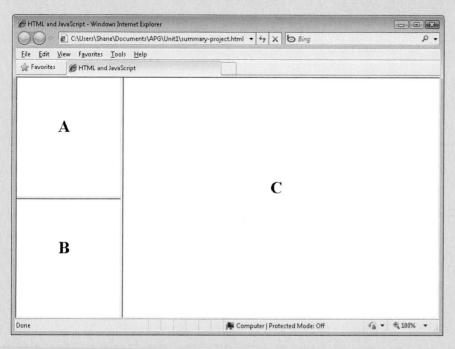

FIGURE U1–1   Three-frame page layout

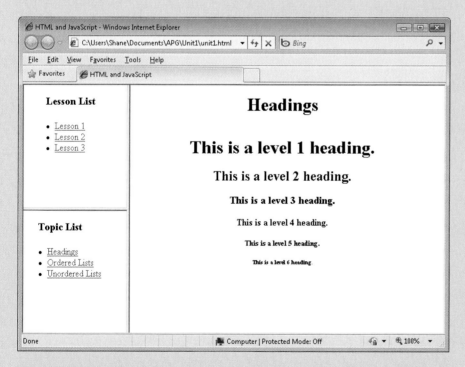

FIGURE U1–2   Sample Web page for Unit 1 Summary Project

PROJECT REQUIREMENTS

- You must use a nested frameset to create the proper Web page layout.

- Make the two left frames about 25% of the screen width.

- The two frames on the left side should each use about 50% of the screen height.

- Create a CSS file to contain all of the various style elements you want to incorporate on your Web pages.

- Name your main frameset page **unit1.html**.

- You will need to create three Web pages for your topic lists. Name your three files **topics1.html**, **topics2.html**, and **topics3.html**.

- You will need to create 11 Web pages for your example pages. Name your files **example1.html**, **example2.html**, **example3.html**, and so on.

■ PORTFOLIO CHECKLIST

Include the following files from this unit in your student portfolio:

_____   HTML Unit Summary Questions

_____   Language Arts 1

_____   Science 1

_____   Social Studies 1

_____   Math 1

_____   Your Choice of Subject 1

_____   Project 1-1

_____   Project 1-2

_____   Job 1-1

_____   Job 1-2

_____   Summary Project

UNIT II

JAVASCRIPT BASICS

LESSON 6

Introducing JavaScript

■ OBJECTIVES

Upon completion of this lesson, you should be able to:

- Display Web page text with JavaScript.
- Use HTML formatting tags both in and around JavaScript code.
- Create conditional statements with JavaScript.
- Use the JavaScript alert() method.
- Access the browser status line with JavaScript.

HTML is undoubtedly the most widely used technology on the World Wide Web. It is the backbone on which all Web pages are based. However, HTML has limitations, so over time, developers have created a wide variety of other technologies to enhance and extend the basic capabilities of standard HTML. One of these widely used companion technologies is JavaScript. JavaScript provides Web developers with tools to add functionality and a little flair to static Web pages.

■ VOCABULARY

binary code

compiler

condition

conditional statement

interpretation

keywords

methods

objects

operators

parameter list

programming language

properties

<script> </script> tags

scripting language

status line

syntax

token

variable

Hello World Wide Web

JavaScript is sometimes referred to as a ***programming language***, but it is more accurate to call it a ***scripting language***. The difference between a programming language and a scripting language is subtle but important to understand. Both types of languages must be converted from a human-readable form to a machine-readable form.

For programming languages, the process is performed before the program runs by a specialized piece of software called a ***compiler***. The programmer controls this conversion process.

With a scripting language, however, there is no need for the programmer to explicitly initiate the code-conversion process. It happens automatically when the source code is processed by the target program. To be more specific, an HTML document must be written by a person and then processed by a Web browser. When that document contains embedded JavaScript code, that code is interpreted by the browser and converted into its machine-readable form when the page is loaded. ***Interpretation*** is the term programmers use to describe the line-by-line conversion process that occurs automatically at run time.

In many cases, the output of a JavaScript function will be nothing more than one, or perhaps several, lines of text that are inserted into the host Web page. The resulting HTML page is then processed by the browser just as it would be if it had been keyed into the source document by a person.

The real power of embedding JavaScript code into Web pages comes from the fact that the resulting text can change from one day to the next or even from one minute to the next. It is entirely possible for one person to enter a particular URL into his Web browser and see a Web page that is completely different from the page that is seen by another person who enters the exact same URL. These different-looking Web pages can be the result of differences in time, differences in location, or even differences in Web browsers. JavaScript is capable of detecting various conditions in the current operating environment and reacting accordingly. This concept is explored in greater detail in Step-by-Step 6.3.

It is easy for a Web browser to detect whether a particular Web page contains embedded JavaScript code. All that is required is for the person who creates the document to use the <script> tag to mark the beginning of a JavaScript section and the </script> tag to indicate the end of that section. The Web browser will interpret everything between these two tags as JavaScript source code rather than standard HTML text. The browser will then convert the script (via the interpretation process) into its equivalent machine-readable form called ***binary code***. This binary code will then be executed, and its output (if any) will be inserted into the HTML text stream and displayed as if it had been typed into the original HTML document by a person.

It is important for you to understand that the scripts you embed between the <script> and </script> tags cannot be just any text you care to put in there. On the contrary, the text must conform to certain rules, or the Web browser will display an unpleasant error message on the screen when you try to view your page. This is precisely why JavaScript is called a scripting language—because it must adhere to specific rules of grammar known as program ***syntax***. In this lesson, you learn about JavaScript objects and methods, as well as JavaScript keywords and operators. Once you have mastered these basic language elements, you will be able to start building useful, sophisticated scripts in no time.

The primary purpose of JavaScript is to generate text that will be inserted into the standard HTML text stream. JavaScript is essentially made up of a number of invisible entities called ***objects*** that contain a well-defined set of capabilities. For JavaScript programmers to make use of these capabilities, they must call upon the services of one or more specialized functions known as ***methods*** within those objects. The programmer invokes the services of these methods by entering the name of the object, followed by a period (the . character), followed by the method name.

Method names are always followed by a parameter list, even though the list is sometimes empty. Perhaps the best way to understand method parameters is to visualize a list of ingredients for a recipe. The ***parameter list*** simply provides the method with the information it needs to perform its function correctly. The syntax of the parameter list consists of an opening parenthesis, zero or more parameter items, and a closing parenthesis. For example, if you want to invoke the write method of the JavaScript object called "document," you enter the following line of code:

```
document.write("A string of text.");
```

Now that you have seen a simple example of JavaScript coding, you can incorporate this concept in an actual HTML document with embedded JavaScript.

▶ VOCABULARY
parameter list

— **WARNING**

Your particular Web browser might display various warning messages as you try to work through the following JavaScript activities. If you see such a warning, simply click the option to enable JavaScript. None of the activities in this book are capable of damaging your computer system in any way.

Step-by-Step 6.1

In this step-by-step, you create a very simple HTML file with embedded JavaScript. Pay particular attention to the <script> </script> tags and the JavaScript code that appears between them.

1. Open Notepad, SimpleText, or your favorite text editor.

2. Create a new blank document, if necessary.

3. Enter the HTML and JavaScript text exactly as shown in **Figure 6–1**.

FIGURE 6–1   js-one.html file

```
<html>

<head>
<title>HTML and JavaScript</title>
</head>

<body>
<script>
   document.write("Hello World Wide Web!");
</script>
</body>


</html>
```

4. Save your newly created HTML text file as **js-one.html** or **js-one.htm** in the same folder you saved the files from the previous lessons.

5. Start your favorite Web browser, and then open the **js-one.html** or **js-one.htm** file to view the file as a Web page. The Web page on your screen should look like the one shown in **Figure 6–2**.

FIGURE 6–2
Your first Web page with embedded JavaScript

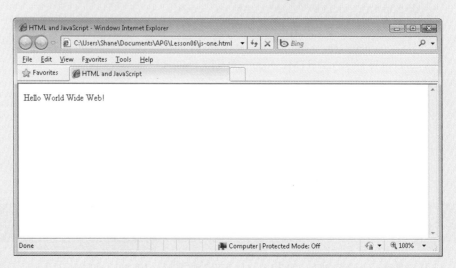

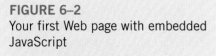

WARNING

If your browser displays the message, "To help protect your security, Internet Explorer has restricted this webpage from running scripts or ActiveX controls that could access your computer. Click here for options." click the message bar, click Allow Blocked Content, and then click Yes in the Security Warning dialog box.

At this point, you might be thinking that this Web page does not look all that impressive. But don't give up on JavaScript yet because you are just getting started. By the time you have worked through a few more step-by-steps, you will begin to see that JavaScript is capable of much more than this simple Web page demonstrates.

Enhancing Your Web Page

As was mentioned earlier in this lesson, the JavaScript method **document.write()** simply inserts a string of characters into the standard HTML text stream. Another way to think of it is that after the browser has finished processing the HTML document, the end result is that the <script> tag, the </script> tag, and everything in between the two will be stripped out of the page and replaced by the output of the write() method. This is the parameter of the write() method. Any HTML formatting tags you put before or after the <script> </script> tags will be processed just as they would be in a page without any embedded JavaScript code. To illustrate this point, modify the Web page you just created in Step-by-Step 6.1. HTML formatting tags can enhance the "Hello World Wide Web!" message so that it looks a little more appealing on the screen.

Step-by-Step 6.2

In this step-by-step, you add HTML formatting tags and a second embedded script. The formatting tags will make the resulting Web page look a little nicer. A second message on the page helps you to understand the interaction between HTML and JavaScript.

1. Open Notepad, SimpleText, or your favorite text editor if it is not already open.

2. If the **js-one.html** or **js-one.htm** file is not already open in the text editor, click File on the menu bar, and then click **Open** to open the **js-one.html** or **js-one.htm** file you created in the previous step-by-step.

3. Click **File** on the menu bar, click **Save As**, and then save the HTML file as **js-two.html** or **js-two.htm** in the same folder to preserve the js-one.html file.

4. Add the two sections of HTML and JavaScript code after the <body> tag and then after the </script> tag exactly as shown in bold in this step and in bold in **Figure 6–3**.

```
<div align="center">
<h1>


</h1>
<h3>
<script>
  document.write("Welcome to the exciting
  world of JavaScript");
</script>
</h3>
</div>
```

FIGURE 6–3   js-two.html file

```
<html>

<head>
<title>HTML and JavaScript</title>
</head>

<body>
<div align="center">
<h1>
<script>
  document.write("Hello World Wide Web!");
</script>
</h1>
<h3>
<script>
  document.write("Welcome to the exciting world of JavaScript");
</script>
</h3>
</div>
</body>

</html>
```

5. Save the changes to the file **js-two.html** or **js-two.htm**.

6. Start your favorite Web browser and then open the **js-two.html** or **js-two.htm** file to view the file as a Web page in the browser. The Web page on your screen should look like the one shown in **Figure 6–4**.

FIGURE 6–4
Formatted JavaScript Web page

If you understand the HTML material presented in Unit 1, you should be able to clearly see the purpose of the <div> and header tags that were added to this document. You should also understand that the output string generated by the first occurrence of the document.write() method is inserted into the HTML text stream between the <div> </div> tags as well as between the <h1> </h1> tags. Likewise, the output string produced by the second occurrence of document.write() appears between the <div> </div> tags and the <h3> </h3> tags.

In other words, the <h1> </h1> tags only affect the appearance of the first output string, and the <h3> </h3> tags only affect the appearance of the second output string. The <div> </div> tag pair will affect the display position of both output strings.

Creating Conditional Statements in JavaScript

The astute student might look at the previous two step-by-steps and ask "Why use JavaScript to display text messages on the screen? Wouldn't it be much easier to enter the text into the HTML document and not bother with the script tags and the use of the document.write() method?"

Well, yes, it would be easier to enter the code that can display simple static text messages in a browser using HTML. In fact, the Web browser would display the resulting Web page slightly faster because it would not need to call on the services of the JavaScript interpreter. However, JavaScript is capable of performing a lot more functions than simply writing text to the screen. So, you learn with a simple example, and then expand your knowledge and abilities by creating more exciting Web pages that have to use JavaScript.

In the next step-by-step, you use one of the most powerful features of the JavaScript language, the *conditional statement*. Every programming language possesses the ability to make decisions. Or, to put it in more technical terms, every language gives programmers the ability to evaluate a specific condition and then perform different actions depending on the results of that evaluation.

The syntax of the conditional statement in JavaScript is very important. The statement begins with the keyword *if*, and then a condition is specified within a pair of parentheses. A *keyword* is recognized as part of the language definition. It is reserved by the language and cannot be used as a *variable*—a user-defined name for a memory location whose value can change over time. Some examples of keywords are **if**, **else**, and **return**.

The condition is followed by a statement block that consists of an opening brace ({), one or more JavaScript statements, and then a closing brace (}). The shell of a JavaScript conditional statement is as follows:

```
if (<condition>)
{
    statement 1;
    statement 2;
    statement 3;
        .
        .
        .
    statement N;
}
```

VOCABULARY
conditional statement
keyword
variable

The JavaScript **if** statement also supports an optional **else** clause, which defines the action to take if the specified condition is not true. The **else** keyword appears immediately after the statement block of the if clause and is accompanied by a statement block of its own. An example of a JavaScript conditional statement that includes the optional **else** clause follows:

```
if (<condition>)
{
    statement i1;
    statement i2;
    statement i3;

        .

        .

        .

    statement iN;
}
else
{
    statement e1;
    statement e2;
    statement e3;

        .

        .

        .

    statement eN;
}
```

Now that you know the basic structure of JavaScript **if** and **if-else** statements, you can learn a little about the condition part of the syntax (shown as <condition> in the preceding JavaScript examples). A JavaScript condition will always consist of two *tokens* separated by a relational *operator*. A token can either be a variable name (such as x or count) or a literal constant (such as *10* or "*hello*"). The relational operator may be any one of the symbols shown in **Table 6–1**.

▶ **VOCABULARY**

tokens

operator

TABLE 6–1   Relational Operators

OPERATOR	MEANING
==	Is equal to
!=	Is not equal to
<	Is less than
>	Is greater than
<=	Is less than or equal to
>=	Is greater than or equal to

Now that you have learned how to create conditional statements in JavaScript, you can put that knowledge to work in an actual program.

Step-by-Step 6.3

In this step-by-step, you include a simple conditional statement in your Web document and learn a useful programming technique in the process. It is fairly common for Web content developers to want the Web page to perform a different task depending on the type of browser a particular user is using to view the Web page. You enter a JavaScript program that determines whether the active browser is Internet Explorer, and based on that determination, the page reacts accordingly.

1. Open Notepad, SimpleText, or your favorite text editor if it is not already open.

2. If it is not already open in the text editor, click **File** on the menu bar, and then click **Open** to open the file **js-two.html** or **js-two.htm** you created in the previous step-by-step.

3. Click **File** on the menu bar, click **Save As**, and then save the file as **js-three.html** or **js-three.htm** in the same folder you saved the files from the previous step-by-steps to preserve the js-two.html file.

4. Enter the JavaScript code exactly as shown here and in bold in **Figure 6–5**.

```
<script>
  if (navigator.appName == "Microsoft
  Internet Explorer")
{
  document.write("You are using Internet
  Explorer.");
}
else
{
  document.write("You are not using Internet
  Explorer.<br>");
  document.write("Perhaps you are using
  Firefox or Safari.");
}
</script>
```

FIGURE 6–5   js-three.html file

```html
<html>

<head>
<title>HTML and JavaScript</title>
</head>

<body>
<div align="center">
<h1>
<script>
  document.write("Hello World Wide Web!");
</script>
</h1>
<h3>
<script>
  document.write("Welcome to the exciting world of JavaScript");
</script>
</h3>
<script>
  if (navigator.appName == "Microsoft Internet Explorer")
  {
    document.write("You are using Internet Explorer.");
  }
  else
  {
    document.write("You are not using Internet Explorer.<br>");
    document.write("Perhaps you are using Firefox or Safari.");
  }
</script>
</div>
</body>

</html>
```

5. Save your changes to the **js-three.html** or **js-three.htm** file.

6. Start your favorite Web browser and then open your **js-three.html** or **js-three.htm** file to view the file as a Web page in the browser. The Web page on your screen should look like the one shown in **Figure 6–6** or **Figure 6–7** depending on the browser you are using.

FIGURE 6–6
Web page viewed with Internet Explorer 8

FIGURE 6–7
Web page viewed with Firefox 3.5

Even though you didn't add a lot of code to the JavaScript program, you did apply several important concepts. Take a minute to review those concepts to make sure you have a solid understanding of what is happening.

First of all, the condition being evaluated in this JavaScript code fragment is:

```
(navigator.appName == "Microsoft Internet Explorer")
```

Earlier in this lesson, you learned that JavaScript objects contain special functions called methods that perform various tasks. It is also true that JavaScript objects contain *properties* that programmers can access to obtain information about the object. In this case, you are utilizing the **appName** property of the **navigator** object to determine the application name of the current Web browser. In this context, the term *navigator* can be used interchangeably with the term *browser*. If this name is Microsoft Internet Explorer, the program knows that the user is running some version of Internet Explorer. Otherwise, it knows that the user is not running Internet Explorer but is using a different kind of browser.

The second important concept to learn here is that once the condition has been evaluated, either the **if** statement block or the **else** statement block will be executed—never both. If the result of the condition is true, the **if** block will run. If the condition is false, the **else** statement block will run. It's as simple as that.

There is one final point in this example you need to recognize. So far, you learned the concept of embedding JavaScript code into HTML documents. But it turns out that it is also possible, as well as useful, to embed HTML tags in JavaScript text strings. Look carefully at the first call to document.write() inside the **else** statement block. Notice that the **
** tag is embedded within the output text string. The purpose of this tag is to tell the browser to execute a break command so that the second string of text will appear on a separate line, rather than on the same line as the first text string. When your Web page displayed in the browser, the message appeared on two lines.

TECHNOLOGY TIMELINE

What's with Those Semicolons?

If you were to study the source code for many JavaScript-enabled Web pages, you would discover that most of them contain semicolons (;) at the end of each statement, but not all of them. Strictly speaking, the rules of JavaScript syntax do not require a semicolon at the end of each line. However, all of the examples in this book, and in most other JavaScript references, include the terminating semicolons. This is because many other programming languages (such as C, Pascal, Java, and so on) require the presence of semicolons and will report syntax errors if they are not found. Using semicolons in your JavaScript code will help you get used to this coding standard and will ease the transition to other languages should you ever need to do so. After all, it is easier to learn a good habit than to unlearn a bad one, right?

Using the JavaScript alert() Method

In the first three step-by-steps in this lesson, you used the document.write() method, a common way for JavaScript programs to convey a message to a user viewing a Web page. However, scripts can get a Web page visitor's attention in other ways as well. One such way is by means of the JavaScript **alert()** method.

The purpose of the alert() method is to allow a JavaScript program to display a special dialog box that will notify the user that an unexpected event has occurred or that some kind of user input is required. Just as the write() method is part of the document object and the appName property is part of the navigator object, the alert() method is also part of an object called **window**. The window object is just like every other JavaScript object in most respects, but it does have one unique characteristic. Specifically, window is considered to be the JavaScript default object, which means it is not necessary to use its name explicitly. In other words, any method or property that appears in a script without an explicit reference to an object is automatically assumed to be part of the window object. Therefore, JavaScript programmers can alert users by invoking either window.alert(), or, simply, alert(). Most developers use the latter, shorter form.

Step-by-Step 6.4

In this step-by-step, you add code to your JavaScript file, which alerts the user as to the Web browser that he or she is using to view the Web page. This alert dialog box appears on the screen in addition to the Web browser text message you created in Step-by-Step 6.3.

1. Open Notepad, SimpleText, or your favorite text editor if it is not already open.

2. If the **js-three.html** or **js-three.htm** file is not already open in the text editor, click **File** on the menu bar and then click **Open** to open the **js-three.html** or **js-three.htm** file you created in the previous step-by-step.

3. Click **File** on the menu bar, click **Save As**, and then save the file as **js-four.html** or **js-four.htm** to preserve the js-three.html file.

4. Enter the JavaScript code to create the alerts just below each document.write() method, as shown in this step and exactly as shown in bold in **Figure 6–8**.

```
alert("Internet Explorer detected.");

alert("Internet Explorer not found.");
```

FIGURE 6–8   js-four.html file

```html
<html>

<head>
<title>HTML and JavaScript</title>
</head>

<body>
<div align="center">
<h1>
<script>
  document.write("Hello World Wide Web!");
</script>
</h1>
<h3>
<script>
  document.write("Welcome to the exciting world of JavaScript");
</script>
</h3>
<script>
  if (navigator.appName == "Microsoft Internet Explorer")
```

Continued on next page ≫

FIGURE 6–8   js-four.html file

《 *Continued from previous page*

```
    {
       document.write("You are using Internet Explorer.");
       alert("Internet Explorer detected.");
    }
    else
    {
       document.write("You are not using Internet Explorer.<br>");
       document.write("Perhaps you are using Firefox or Safari.");
       alert("Internet Explorer not found.");
    }
    </script>
    </div>
    </body>

    </html>
```

5. Save your changes to the **js-four.html** or **js-four.htm** file.

6. Start your favorite Web browser and then open the **js-four.html** or **js-four.htm** file to view the file as a Web page in the browser. The Web page on your screen should look like the one shown in **Figure 6–9** or **Figure 6–10** depending on the browser you are using to view the Web page.

FIGURE 6–9
Web page viewed with
Internet Explorer 8

FIGURE 6–10
Web page viewed with Firefox 3.5

7. Click **OK** in the warning box to close it.

Hopefully, this step-by-step has helped you see how the alert() method can be useful in various Web page development situations. It is normally used in JavaScript programs when the user needs to be made aware that some unexpected error condition has occurred. It can also be used when the program needs some kind of user acknowledgement before proceeding. For example, you might use an alert box that says "The following process might take several minutes to complete. Click OK to proceed." In either case, the alert() method is an effective way to convey a message to the user.

TECHNOLOGY TIMELINE

Which Came First—Java or JavaScript?

Many people who only have a casual knowledge of Internet technologies tend to think that the Java programming language and the JavaScript scripting language are the same thing. Even those who know they are not the same thing might not know how they relate to each other or which one was developed first. The history of these languages is interesting. Java was created first by Sun Microsystems, Inc. Sun released its cross-platform programming language to the general public in 1995, and it has grown in popularity at an unprecedented rate ever since.

But Sun was not the only company looking for ways to enhance the capabilities of standard HTML. Netscape Communications Corporation was also busy working on technologies to give Web developers a way to embed user-programmable scripts into static HTML documents. They knew that they needed to incorporate a well-defined syntax into their design. Netscape employees observed how popular the Java language was becoming, so they licensed the Java name from Sun and used the Java syntax in their own scripting language. The result of Netscape's efforts became known as JavaScript, and it has also enjoyed a great deal of success in the Internet software development sector.

Accessing the Browser Status Line

You probably have noticed that when your Web browser loads an HTML document that contains many objects such as text and graphics, it displays various messages in a bar at the bottom of the browser window. This area is called the *status line*, and it can be accessed from within a JavaScript program. In addition to the document.write() method and the alert() method, the status line is another way in which a JavaScript Web page can communicate information to the user.

Accessing the status line of the browser is a very simple task. The message (if any) that the browser displays in the status line is stored as a simple text string in a window object property called **status**. When a JavaScript program assigns a new string value to the status property, the browser responds by displaying this value as a message on the status line.

▶ **VOCABULARY**
status line

┷━ **WARNING**

Some versions of Firefox have JavaScript access to the status line disabled by default. To allow status line access, open the Options dialog box by clicking **Tools** on the menu bar and then clicking **Options**. In the Options dialog box, click the **Content** tab and make sure the "Enable JavaScript" option is checked. Next, open the Advanced JavaScript Settings dialog by clicking the **Advanced** button. Make sure the "Change status bar text" option is checked and then save your JavaScript settings.

Step-by-Step 6.5

In this step-by-step, you add two new JavaScript statements that assign text strings to the window object's status property. **Window** is the default JavaScript object. These statements simply reinforce the messages that are already being displayed by the alert() method.

1. Open Notepad, SimpleText, or your favorite text editor if it is not already open.

2. If the **js-four.html** or **js-four.htm** file is not already open in the text editor, click **File** on the menu bar, and then click **Open** to open the **js-four.html** or **js-four.htm** file you created in the previous step-by-step.

3. Click **File** on the menu bar, click **Save As**, and then save the file as **js-five.html** or **js-five.htm** to preserve the js-four.html file.

4. Enter the status JavaScript code just below the document.write() method code and above the alert() method code exactly as shown in this step and in bold in **Figure 6–11**.

```
window.status = "Internet Explorer detected.";

window.status = "Internet Explorer not found.";
```

FIGURE 6-11   js-five.html file

```
<html>

<head>
<title>HTML and JavaScript</title>
</head>

<body>
<div align="center">
<h1>
<script>
  document.write("Hello World Wide Web!");
</script>
</h1>
<h3>
<script>
  document.write("Welcome to the exciting world of JavaScript");
</script>
</h3>
<script>
  if (navigator.appName == "Microsoft Internet Explorer")
  {
    document.write("You are using Internet Explorer.");
    window.status = "Internet Explorer detected.";
    alert("Internet Explorer detected.");
  }
  else
  {
    document.write("You are not using Internet Explorer.<br>");
    document.write("Perhaps you are using Firefox or Safari.");
    window.status = "Internet Explorer not found.";
    alert("Internet Explorer not found.");
  }
</script>
</div>
</body>

</html>
```

5. Save your changes to the **js-five.html** or **js-five.htm** file.

6. Start your favorite Web browser and then open the **js-five.html** or **js-five.htm** file to view the file as a Web page in the browser. The Web page on your screen should look like the one shown in **Figure 6-12** or **Figure 6-13** depending on the browser you are using.

FIGURE 6–12
Web page viewed with
Internet Explorer 8

Status line

FIGURE 6–13
Web page viewed with Firefox 3.5

Status line

7. Click **OK** in the warning box to close it.

In this step-by-step, you used the browser's status line to merely echo the same message that is displayed in an alert dialog box. This was done for the sake of simplicity, but it is not typical for professional Web developers to do this. Normally, the status line is used to let the user know what the browser is doing. This is especially helpful whenever the browser is about to perform an operation that could take an unusually long time to complete. For example, it is common to see a "Loading…" message or something similar whenever the browser initiates the download of a large graphic image, large program, or large data file. Displaying this type of message helps the user know that the browser is really doing something and that the system hasn't crashed.

TECHNOLOGY TIMELINE

Hello World!

The next time you are in a local bookstore, take a few minutes to skim through the first chapter of several different programming books. In many cases, you will see that the first programming example in these books will demonstrate how to display the phrase "Hello, World!" in that particular computer language. Why do you suppose it is so common for authors to begin their books this way? Well, the answer is simple.

In 1978, two employees of Bell Laboratories, Brian Kernighan and Dennis Ritchie, published a book titled *The C Programming Language*. This book has proven itself to be one of the most enduring programming tutorials in the history of computer software. Over the past 30 years, this book has undergone only one revision, and the second edition is still in print today! The very first programming exercise in this book explains how to use the C function **printf()** to display the phrase "Hello, World!" Though it is unlikely that Kernighan and Ritchie intended to start an informal tradition among authors of programming books, that is exactly what they did! We took the liberty of modifying the phrase slightly to "Hello World Wide Web!", but the first JavaScript program in this book is still based on their simple example from over 30 years ago.

SUMMARY

In this lesson, you learned:

- The purpose of JavaScript.
- How to display Web page text with JavaScript.
- How to use JavaScript objects.
- How to use JavaScript methods.
- How to use HTML formatting tags both in and around JavaScript code.

- How to create conditional statements with JavaScript.
- How to use the JavaScript alert() method.
- How to access the browser status line with JavaScript.

■ VOCABULARY REVIEW

Define the following terms:

binary code	methods	<script> </script> tags
compiler	objects	scripting language
condition	operators	status line
conditional statement	parameter list	syntax
interpretation	programming language	token
keywords	properties	variable

■ REVIEW QUESTIONS

TRUE / FALSE

Circle T if the statement is true or F if the statement is false.

T   F   **1.**   Strictly speaking, JavaScript is a programming language, not a scripting language.

T   F   **2.**   Compilers convert human-readable source code into machine-readable binary code.

T   F   **3.**   JavaScript requires a compiler.

T   F   **4.**   JavaScript code is embedded in HTML documents between <script> and </script> tags.

T   F   **5.**   Web browsers can process HTML tags that are placed between the <script> and </script> tags.

T   F   **6.**   Embedding HTML tags in JavaScript output strings will cause a syntax error.

T   F   **7.**   JavaScript objects include both properties and methods.

T   F   **8.**   JavaScript method names are always followed by a list of zero or more parameters.

T   F   **9.**   The default JavaScript object is called document.

T   F   **10.**   JavaScript requires a semicolon at the end of each statement.

FILL IN THE BLANK

Complete the following sentences by writing the correct word or words in the blanks provided.

1. The symbols { and } are called _____.

2. The JavaScript _____ object contains a method called write().

3. The JavaScript if statement supports an optional _____ clause.

4. JavaScript conditions are composed of two _____ separated by a relational operator.

5. The _____ relational operator means "is not equal to."

6. The JavaScript scripting language incorporates the syntax of the _____ programming language.

7. The appName property belongs to the JavaScript _____ object.

8. The status property and the alert() method belong to the JavaScript _____ object.

9. The JavaScript window object is considered to be the _____ object.

10. appName and status are both examples of JavaScript object _____.

WRITTEN QUESTIONS

Write a short answer to each of the following questions:

1. How does JavaScript enhance the capabilities of HTML?

2. What is a JavaScript object? What are methods and properties?

3. Describe the syntax of a JavaScript conditional statement.

4. What is the unique characteristic of the JavaScript window object?

5. Briefly describe three ways in which a JavaScript program can convey information to the user.

■ PROJECTS

PROJECT 6–1: BASIC JAVASCRIPT KNOWLEDGE

Review the JavaScript-enabled Web page you created for Step-by-Step 6.1. GreatApplications, Inc., would like you to modify this page so the phrase "Hello World Wide Web!" is replaced with "Welcome to GreatApplications!" Save your new Web page as **Project 6-1.html** or **Project 6-1.htm**, and make sure it functions correctly by viewing it in a Web browser.

PROJECT 6–3: BROWSER TYPES

Review the JavaScript-enabled Web page you created for Step-by-Step 6-5. This page is "Internet Explorer oriented," meaning that it is looking to see whether Internet Explorer is the current browser. Internet Explorer browsers are processed by the **if** statement block, whereas any other type of browser is processed within the **else** statement block. Change this Web page so that it is no longer Internet Explorer oriented, but rather oriented toward a different browser, such as Firefox, Safari, or Chrome. In your new Web page, your browser of choice will be processed within the **if** clause, whereas Internet Explorer and all other browsers are processed by the **else** clause. Make sure that you change the output text appropriately in addition to the **if** statement condition. Save your results as **Project 6-3.html** or **Project 6-3.htm**, and view the file in at least two different browsers to ensure that it functions correctly.

PROJECT 6–2: HTML FORMATTING TAGS

Review the JavaScript-enabled Web page you created for Step-by-Step 6-3. This document contains HTML formatting tags that are located outside the <script> and </script> tags, as well as embedded within the output text strings (the <br> tag). Demonstrate your ability to work with HTML formatting tags in both ways by enhancing the appearance of this Web page. Give the page an appropriate background color, and also make the output text appear in a new color (other than black) by means of external HTML tags. Then cause the output text to appear in a different font by embedding <font> tags within the JavaScript code. Save your resulting Web page as **Project 6-2.html** or **Project 6-2.htm**, and view it in your favorite browser.

■ CRITICAL THINKING

ACTIVITY 6–1: MAKING DECISIONS

In the introduction of Step-by-Step 6-3, we mentioned that the conditional statement is one of JavaScript's most powerful features. This claim is merely an echo of a statement made more than 30 years ago by the great computer scientist Joseph Weizenbaum. In 1976, Weizenbaum wrote a book titled *Computer Power and Human Reason* in which he presented the idea that the real power of computer systems is their ability to make decisions (although they can never fully replace human compassion and wisdom). Think about this idea for few minutes and then answer the following questions:

1. How useful would computers be if they could not make decisions?

2. Describe the general structure of the JavaScript decision-making construct.

3. What does it mean to "evaluate a condition"?

4. Why do you suppose the **else** clause of the **if-else** statement is optional?

ACTIVITY 6–2: THE JAVASCRIPT APPNAME PROPERTY

Revisit for a moment the Web page you created for Step-by-Step 6-3. In this exercise, we check the appName property of the navigator object to see if the active browser is "Microsoft Internet Explorer." If the appName property does not contain this value, what does it contain? Can you think of a way to find out? Try rewriting this Web page so that instead of checking the value of the appName property, it simply displays the value. Then view your new Web page in different browsers to see what it displays. Name your new Web page **Activity 6-2.html** or **Activity 6-2.htm**.

■ CAPSTONE SIMULATION

Put your newly acquired knowledge of JavaScript to work by revisiting the Web page you created in Lesson 1 (in Step-by-Step 1.2) and named **one.html** or **one.htm**. Modify this Web page so that all of the output text is generated with the document.write() method. The resulting Web page should look exactly like the one produced by the one.html page, as shown in **Figure 6–14**.

Project Requirements:

■ Start with the HTML code you created in Lesson 1 Step-by-Step 1.2.

■ Replace the HTML text strings with JavaScript document.write() statements.

■ Name your new Web page **capstone-6.html** or **capstone-6.htm**.

■ View your new Web page in a browser and confirm the results.

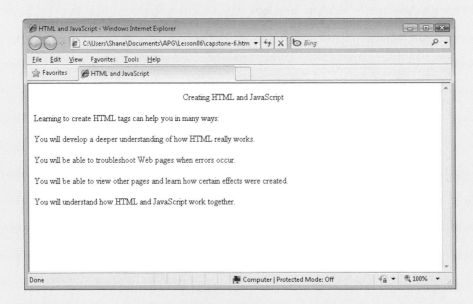

FIGURE 6–14   Results of capstone-6.html

LESSON 7

Using Images with JavaScript

■ OBJECTIVES

Upon completion of this lesson, you should be able to:

- Name and describe JavaScript events.
- Create an image rollover.
- Make a hyperlink rollover.
- Construct a cycling banner.
- Display random images.
- Create a JavaScript slide show.

The effective use of graphic images can be essential to the overall success of a Web page. That principle holds true whether the Web page is based on HTML or JavaScript technology. Standard HTML gives you the ability to incorporate interesting visual effects with images, but JavaScript gives you some additional capabilities to enhance the visual appeal of a Web page.

■ VOCABULARY

ad banner

array

cycling banner

decrement

entity code

event

floating-point number

function

hyperlink rollover

image rollover

increment

index

real number

slide show

variable

Making Graphic Images Come Alive

This lesson focuses on the JavaScript features that are commonly used to make graphic images "come alive" on Web pages. Once you learn these new techniques, you will be able to quickly identify these JavaScript features used on pages throughout the World Wide Web. You no longer need to wonder how the designers of these interesting pages are able to create such eye-catching effects.

Before you can accomplish anything spectacular with images, you need to acquire an understanding of JavaScript events. For the purpose of this book, you can think of an *event* as a system-level response to the occurrence of some specific condition. Some of these conditions are generated by the Web browser software, but most of them are caused by the user performing some action. Such actions might include moving the mouse, clicking on a button, or even selecting a block of text on the screen. But regardless of how a particular event is generated, JavaScript gives you the ability to create Web pages that react to it. Furthermore, when these reactions are implemented skillfully, the user is able to use and interact with your Web page successfully.

Another important concept you need to master when working with images is how to use JavaScript functions. A *function* is nothing more than a segment of JavaScript code that can be invoked or called just like the document.write() and window.alert() methods that you used in Lesson 6. In fact, there is really no difference between a method and a function, except that methods have already been defined as part of the objects that make up the JavaScript programming environment. Functions, on the other hand, are written by the programmer and may contain any number of JavaScript statements, including calls to JavaScript methods and other functions.

It might not be obvious to you at this point how JavaScript events and functions relate to the use of graphic images in Web pages. As you work though this lesson, you will begin to see the connection. In fact, that is the very purpose of the activities in this lesson. You will use events and functions with images to create some interesting effects that improve the quality of your Web pages immensely.

VOCABULARY

event

function

image rollover

WARNING

To complete the step-by-step exercises in this lesson, you need to get a copy of the Data files for this lesson from your instructor. These files include **lions.gif**, **tigers.gif**, **bears.gif**, **ohmy.gif**, **blueArrow.gif**, and **redArrow.gif**. You must save these files in the folder where you have been saving your HTML files for this book. Ask your teacher for assistance if necessary.

Teaching an Image to Roll Over

In Lesson 3, you learned how to include a graphic image on your Web page, and you also learned how to turn an image into a hyperlink. In this lesson, you learn how to use the power of JavaScript to make a graphical hyperlink respond to mouse movements.

To be more specific, you learn to use the JavaScript programming technique called an *image rollover* to change the appearance of an image whenever a visitor to the Web site moves the mouse pointer over the image. The first thing you need to know to implement a rollover is how to make use of the JavaScript events called *onMouseOver* and *onMouseOut*. The *onMouseOver* event is generated whenever the user moves the mouse pointer over a particular object. Likewise, the *onMouseOut* event is generated when the user moves the mouse pointer off of the object. All you need to learn is how to use JavaScript to detect when these events occur and then take some appropriate action. In Step-by-Step 7.1, you display a blue arrow on the screen and then change the arrow to red when the mouse pointer rolls over it. You then change the arrow color back to blue when the mouse pointer rolls off of the image. Sounds simple, right?

Step-by-Step 7.1

In this step-by-step, you create a very simple image rollover with JavaScript. This involves writing some JavaScript functions that respond to the *onLoad*, *onMouseOver*, and *onMouseOut* events.

1. Make sure that the image files **blueArrow.gif** and **redArrow.gif** are properly saved in the same folder where you have been saving your Web pages.

2. Open Notepad, SimpleText, or your favorite text editor and then create a new blank document, if necessary.

3. Enter the HTML and JavaScript text exactly as shown in **Figure 7–1**.

FIGURE 7–1   js-six.html file

> **WARNING**
>
> To complete this next step-by-step, you need access to the following Data files that your instructor will have given you: **blueArrow.gif** and **redArrow.gif**. These files must be stored in the folder where you have been saving your HTML files for this book. Ask your teacher for assistance if necessary.

```
<html>

<head>
<title>HTML and JavaScript</title>
<script>
var blueArrow = new Image;
var redArrow = new Image;

function startup()
{
  blueArrow.src = "blueArrow.gif";
  redArrow.src = "redArrow.gif";
  return;
}

function turnBlue()
{
  document.arrow.src = blueArrow.src;
  return;
}

function turnRed()
{
  document.arrow.src = redArrow.src;
  return;
}
</script>
</head>
```

Continued on next page 》

FIGURE 7–1   js-six.html file

« *Continued from previous page*

```html
<body onLoad="startup()">
  <div align="center">
    <a href="webpage.html"
       onMouseOut="turnBlue()" onMouseOver="turnRed()">
      <img name="arrow" src="blueArrow.gif">
    </a>
  </div>
</body>

</html>
```

4. Save your newly created file as **js-six.html** or **js-six.htm** in the same folder that you saved the files from the previous lessons.

5. Start your favorite Web browser, and then open the **js-six.html** or **js-six.htm** file to view the file as a Web page. The Web page on your screen should initially look like the one shown in **Figure 7–2**.

6. Move the mouse pointer over the **arrow image**. The Web page on your screen should now look like the one shown in **Figure 7–3**.

FIGURE 7–2
Web page in "mouse-out" state

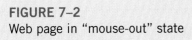

WARNING

If your browser displays the message, "To help protect your security, Internet Explorer has restricted this webpage from running scripts or ActiveX controls that could access your computer. Click here for options." click the message bar, click Allow Blocked Content, and then click Yes in the Security Warning dialog box.

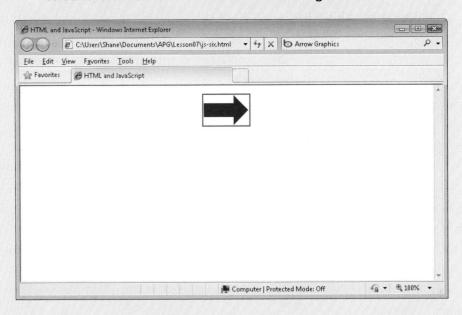

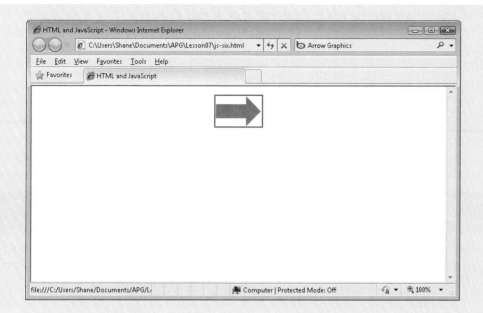

FIGURE 7–3
Web page in "mouse-over" state

The HTML/JavaScript source code you just entered to create the file js-six.html in Figure 7–1 introduces several new features that you have not seen before. It is important that you understand these new concepts because you use them throughout this lesson.

First, you might have noticed that the <script> and </script> tags are in the header section of the HTML document rather than in the body section. This placement ensures that the Web browser processes the JavaScript code before it begins to display the contents of the document on the screen. This is an important point for this particular document because you want the browser to create image objects for the blueArrow and redArrow variables before it loads the body of the Web page. Then, when the Web page has finished loading, the *onLoad* event is processed and the startup() function is called. The **startup()** function assigns the appropriate image filenames to the **src** property of the image objects.

After the Web page is displayed on the screen, the browser continuously monitors the position of the mouse pointer. If the pointer passes over the location of the arrow image, the *onMouseOver* event will fire, and the **turnRed()** function will be called. This function changes the **src** (source) property of the image to that of the redArrow object, and the image turns red on the screen. Similarly, if the mouse pointer moves away from the arrow image, the *onMouseOut* event will fire, and the **turnBlue()** function is called. This function changes the src (source) property of the image to that of the blueArrow object, and the image returns to blue on the screen.

How does the browser know which image to modify in response to the onMouseOver and onMouseOut events? In this Web page, the turnRed() and turnBlue() functions set the **src** (source) property of a document object called **arrow**. This name comes from the <img> tag within the HTML code. Notice that it contains an attribute called **name**. This is the name of the Web page image object as far as JavaScript is concerned. Suppose that this Web page contained several images rather than a single image. Most Web pages have several images. For a Web page with multiple images, you need to give each one a unique name. Then, you can reference any image on the page from within your JavaScript functions.

▶ **VOCABULARY**
variable

EXTRA FOR EXPERTS

A JavaScript *variable* is nothing more than a name that is assigned to a literal value or to an object.

EXTRA FOR EXPERTS

Image borders. When a graphic is defined as a hyperlink, the browser displays the image with a rectangular border around it. If this default border detracts from the appearance of the page, you can adjust its size with an image attribute called **border**. Including the statement **border="0"** in the <img> tag removes the border completely.

Teaching a Hyperlink to Roll Over

▶ VOCABULARY
hyperlink rollover

Now that you know how to make an image rollover, you can learn how to create a *hyperlink rollover*. As you might expect, a hyperlink rollover is very similar to an image rollover. The only difference is that a hyperlink rollover is triggered when the user moves the mouse pointer over a hyperlink, rather than when the mouse pointer rolls over an image. If you are expecting the JavaScript code required to make a hyperlink rollover to be similar to the code for an image rollover, you won't be disappointed. The changes you make in Step-by-Step 7.2 are quite subtle. Are you ready to give it a try?

Step-by-Step 7.2

In this step-by-step, you change your Web page so that JavaScript events are fired when the mouse pointer passes over a hyperlink rather than an image. However, the arrow image still changes color as it did in the previous step-by-step.

1. Open Notepad, SimpleText, or your favorite text editor, if it is not already open.

2. If the **js-six.html** or **js-six.htm** file is not already open in the text editor, click **File** on the menu bar and then click **Open** to open the **js-six.html** or **js-six.htm** file you created in Step-by-Step 7.1.

3. Click **File** on the menu bar, click **Save As**, and then save the HTML file as **js-seven.html** or **js-seven.htm** in the same folder to preserve the js-six.html file.

4. Change the HTML code shown in this step in bold and in **Figure 7–4** in bold so that the resulting HTML file looks exactly as shown in **Figure 7–4**.

```
<a href="webpage.html"
   onMouseOut="turnBlue()"
     onMouseOver="turnRed()">
  Next Page
</a>
<p>
 <img name="arrow" src="blueArrow.gif">
</p>
```

FIGURE 7–4   js-seven.html file

```html
<html>

<head>
<title>HTML and JavaScript</title>
<script>
var blueArrow = new Image;
var redArrow = new Image;

function startup()
{
  blueArrow.src = "blueArrow.gif";
  redArrow.src = "redArrow.gif";
  return;
}

function turnBlue()
{
  document.arrow.src = blueArrow.src;
  return;
}

function turnRed()
{
  document.arrow.src = redArrow.src;
  return;
}
</script>
</head>

<body onLoad="startup()">
  <div align="center">
    <a href="webpage.html" onMouseOut="turnBlue()" onMouseOver="turnRed()">
      Next Page
    </a>
    <p>
     <img name="arrow" src="blueArrow.gif">
    </p>
  </div>
</body>

</html>
```

5. Save the changes to the file **js-seven.html** or **js-seven.htm**.

6. Start your favorite Web browser and then open the **js-seven.html** or **js-seven.htm** file to view the file as a Web page. The Web page on your screen should look like the one shown in **Figure 7–5**. Do not move the mouse, yet.

FIGURE 7–5
Web page in "mouse-out" state

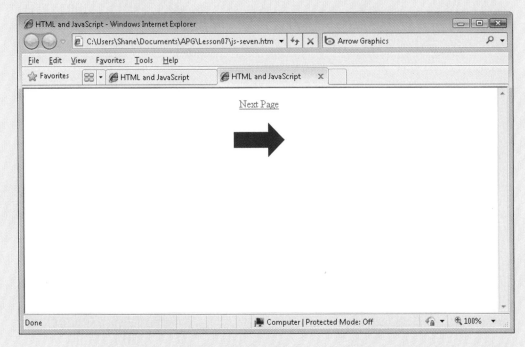

7. Now, move the mouse pointer over the **Next Page** link; the arrow changes color to red, and the Web page on your screen should look like **Figure 7–6**.

FIGURE 7–6
Web page in "mouse-over" state

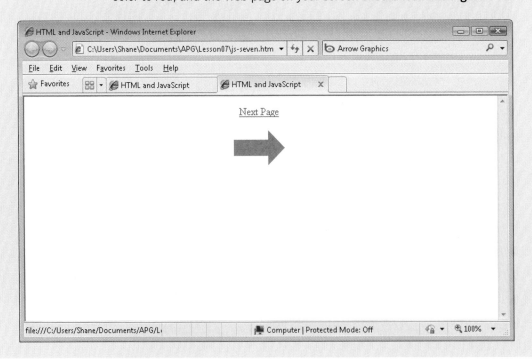

If you are an astute observer, you noticed that the JavaScript code in the js-seven.html HTML document is exactly the same as in the js-six.html file. It is important that you have a solid understanding of the changes that were made in the HTML body and how these changes relate to the JavaScript code.

First, the <a> and </a> anchor tags no longer enclose the <img> tag, so the arrow image is no longer part of the hyperlink reference. Instead, the anchor tags now enclose the newly added "Next Page" text. This means that the *onMouseOver* and *onMouseOut* events fire when the mouse pointer rolls over the new "Next Page" hyperlink instead of when it rolls over the arrow image. However, the action performed by JavaScript code is the same as before, so the image changes color just like it did before.

Although it was not technically necessary to include the <p> and </p> paragraph tags around the arrow image, it was done to improve the look of the page. The <p> tag causes the arrow image to display below the Next Page link rather than to the right of it.

Did you notice that the arrow image was surrounded by a blue rectangle in the previous step-by-step when you viewed the file js-six.html but not when you viewed the file js-seven.html? In Step-by-Step 7.1, in file js-six.html, the image is defined as a hyperlink, and the hyperlink images are normally displayed with a blue border by a Web browser. The blue border is still visible when the arrow image is changed from blue to red. But when you view the file js-seven.html as a Web page in Step-by-Step 7.2, the image is not defined as a hyperlink, so the blue border is gone. Instead, the Next Page text is defined as the hyperlink, so it is displayed as blue and underlined, regardless of the color of the arrow image.

> **EXTRA FOR EXPERTS**
>
> **Using JavaScript Events.** All of the activities in this lesson make use of one or more JavaScript events. However, several JavaScript events are not discussed in this lesson. But that doesn't mean you can't do a little independent study and learn how to use them on your own. Table 7-1 provides an alphabetical list of JavaScript events, along with a brief description of the condition that will trigger each event.

TABLE 7–1 JavaScript events

EVENT NAME	EVENT TRIGGER
onAbort	The user aborted the loading of a Web page.
onBlur	The user deactivated an object (the object lost focus).
onChange	The user changed the object in some way.
onClick	The user clicked the mouse pointer on an object.
onError	The JavaScript interpreter encountered a script error.
onFocus	The user activated an object (the object received focus).
onLoad	The Web browser finished loading a page.
onMouseOver	The mouse pointer passed over an object.
onMouseOut	The mouse pointer moved off an object.
onSelect	The user selected (highlighted) the contents of an object.
onSubmit	The user submitted an HTML form.
onUnload	The Web browser unloaded a page from memory.

Creating a Cycling Banner

When you surf the Web, you typically encounter commercial Web sites that contain advertisements that are constantly changing. As it turns out, these cycling banners (also known as *ad banners*) can be created in various ways using different Internet technologies. However, one of the easiest and most efficient ways to create advertisements that are able to cycle or change continuously is by using JavaScript events and functions.

A *cycling banner* is really nothing more than a sequence of graphic images that are displayed one after another with a small pause between each image. After all of the images in the sequence have been displayed, the browser will cycle back to the first image and start the sequence all over again. This is the reason why this particular Web page effect is called a cycling banner.

You might think that creating a cycling banner takes a lot of time and effort, but this is not the case with JavaScript. In this next step-by-step, you enter the simple code to integrate an effective ad display into your Web page. By utilizing a single JavaScript event and by defining one simple JavaScript function, you are well on your way to fame and fortune in the world of cycling banner design. Are you ready for this?

VOCABULARY

ad banner

cycling banner

WARNING

To complete this next step-by-step, you need access to the following Data files that your instructor will have given you: **lions.gif, tigers.gif, bears.gif,** and **ohmy.gif**. These files must be stored in the folder where you have been saving your HTML files for this book. Ask your teacher for assistance if necessary.

Step-by-Step 7.3

In this next step-by-step, you make use of a JavaScript array and a timeout function to create a cycling banner. Each image in the sequence displays after a two-second delay, and then the sequence cycles back to the beginning after the last image is displayed.

1. Make sure that the image files **lions.gif**, **tigers.gif**, **bears.gif**, and **ohmy.gif** are properly saved in the same folder where you have been saving your Web pages for these lessons.

2. Open Notepad, SimpleText, or your favorite text editor if it is not already open, click **File** on the menu bar, and then click **New** to create a new blank document.

3. Enter the HTML and JavaScript text exactly as shown in **Figure 7–7**.

FIGURE 7–7   js-eight.html file

```
<html>

<head>
<title>HTML and JavaScript</title>
<script>
var imgArray = new Array(4);
var index = 0;
```

Continued on next page »

FIGURE 7–7   js-eight.html file

《 *Continued from previous page*

```
function cycle()
{
   document.banner.src = imgArray[index].src;
   index++;
   if (index > 3)
   {
      index = 0;
   }
   setTimeout("cycle()", 2000);
   return;
}

function startup()
{
   imgArray[0] = new Image;
   imgArray[0].src = "lions.gif";
   imgArray[1] = new Image;
   imgArray[1].src = "tigers.gif";
   imgArray[2] = new Image;
   imgArray[2].src = "bears.gif";
   imgArray[3] = new Image;
   imgArray[3].src = "ohmy.gif";
   cycle();
   return;
}
</script>
</head>

<body onLoad="startup()">
   <div align="center">
      <img name="banner" src="lions.gif">
   </div>
</body>

</html>
```

Line 23 – Line 30

4. Save your newly created file as **js-eight.html** or **js-eight.htm** in the same folder where you have been saving the files for this book.

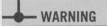

WARNING

If your browser displays the message, "To help protect your security, Internet Explorer has restricted this webpage from running scripts or ActiveX controls that could access your computer. Click here for options." click the message bar, click Allow Blocked Content, and then click Yes in the Security Warning dialog box.

5. Start your favorite Web browser and open the **js-eight.html** or **js-eight.htm** file to view the file as a Web page. The resulting Web page should initially look like **Figure 7–8**. After successive two-second delays, the image should change to look like **Figure 7–9**, **Figure 7–10**, and **Figure 7–11**. Then, the entire sequence should repeat.

FIGURE 7–8
Initial Web page

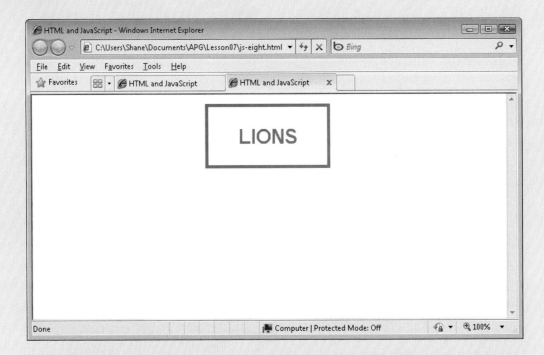

FIGURE 7–9
Web page after two-second delay

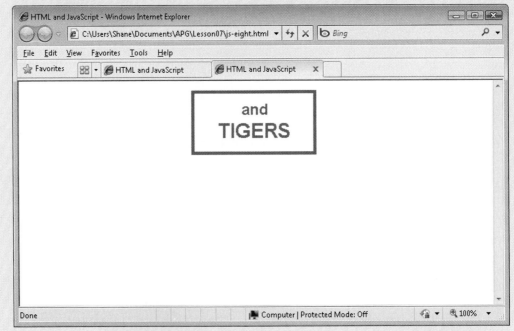

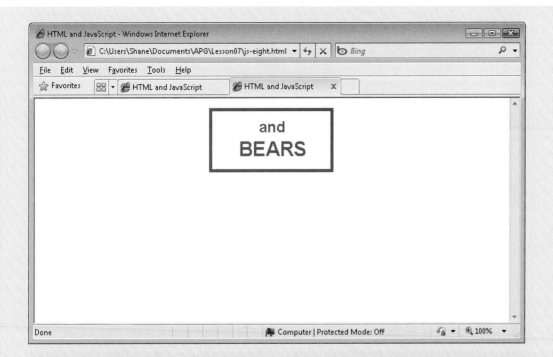

FIGURE 7–10
Web page after four-second delay

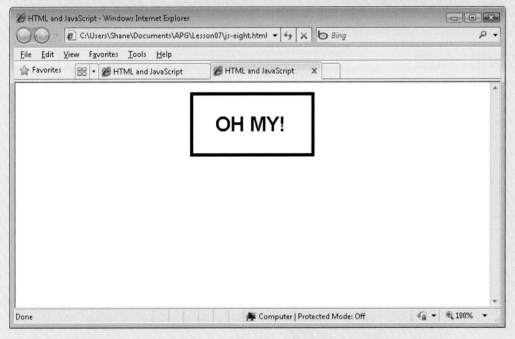

FIGURE 7–11
Web page after six-second delay

The preceding step-by-step introduced several important JavaScript concepts within a relatively small amount of source code. Take the time to carefully review the source code listing in Figure 7-7 to make sure you understand exactly how the code created the cycling effect.

First, take a look at Line 6 (`var imgArray = new Array(4);`). This line includes a JavaScript object that you have not used before: an array. An *array* is a collection of similar objects that can be accessed by means of a variable name and an index. An *index* is an integer variable that identifies which element of an array is being referenced. Arrays are available in virtually every modern computer language, so it's important for you to become familiar with them. In this case, the array is defined to contain a maximum of four (4) elements, and its variable name is *imgArray*. This array contains four Image objects, but arrays can contain any other type of JavaScript object as well.

▶ **VOCABULARY**
array

index

imgArray

Second, consider the JavaScript statements in Lines 23 through 30 in the startup() function. These statements should look familiar to you because you used similar statements in the startup() function of Step-by-Step 7.1 and Step-by-Step 7.2. Line 23 creates a new Image object and assigns it to the image array at index 0. Line 24 then sets the **src** (source) property of this new image object to contain the contents of the file called **lions.gif**. Similarly, the JavaScript statements in Lines 25 and 26 create a new image object and set its source property to contain the contents of **tigers.gif**. Lines 27 and 28 then perform the same task for **bears.gif**, and Lines 29 and 30 do likewise for **ohmy.gif**.

Third, after initializing the appropriate image objects, the startup() function calls the cycle() function. As its name implies, the cycle function contains the logic that makes the images display in a cyclic fashion on the Web page. The **index** variable (initialized to a value of **0** on Line 7) determines which element in the **imgArray** array displays on the screen. The Web page image object was given the name **banner** as specified by the **name** attribute of the <img> tag. Then, the index is *incremented* by 1 (index++) and checked to make sure it does not exceed a value of 3 (because the valid indices for a four-element array in JavaScript are 0, 1, 2, and 3). Finally, the cycle() function goes to sleep for two seconds (**2000** milliseconds as specified in the **setTimeout()** method) and then calls the cycle() function again to move to the next image in the cycle. Is the program making sense to you now?

▶ **VOCABULARY**

increment

TECHNOLOGY TIMELINE

Programming with Arrays

Arrays were invented to help programmers access a potentially large number of data elements with a single variable name. Nearly every programming and scripting language supports the concept of arrays, but they don't all implement array indexing the same way. If you define a 10-element array in some programming languages, such as Basic, Fortran, or Pascal, you would use index values of 1, 2, 3, ...10 to access those 10 elements. But other languages (including C, C++, and Java) do not use this one-based indexing technique. Instead, they implement a zero-based method that makes the valid array indices for a 10-element array 0, 1, 2, ...9. At first glance, you might think that the one-based approach makes more sense because it is easier for novice programmers to understand. However, if you were to look at the low-level machine code generated by different language compilers, you would see that the one-based approach is slightly less efficient for the computer hardware to process. This is one reason why many professional programmers prefer to use zero-based languages for their software development projects.

Displaying Random Images

In the previous step-by-step, you learned how to display a sequence of graphic images in a specific order. There are also times when Web page designers want their images to appear in a random order. This approach is normally used when a particular Web site contains a large collection of graphic images and the site owner would like the system to randomly select an image for display.

At first, you might assume that displaying images in a fixed sequence is much easier than displaying them in a random order. But this is not the case when you are working with JavaScript. In fact, it actually requires fewer lines of code to display random images than it does to create a cycling banner. This is primarily due to JavaScript's built-in support of random number generation.

Because much of the source code for this activity is the same as for the previous activity, you'll be able to start with the js-eight.html file you created in the previous step-by-step and just make a few changes. In fact, all you need to do is replace the cycle() function with a similar function called select(). You don't even need to worry about acquiring new graphic files because we will use the same images as in the previous activity.

Step-by-Step 7.4

In this step-by-step, you create a JavaScript function that displays images in a random order. To make the images in your Web page display randomly rather than in a specified sequence, you only need to replace the cycle() function with a new function that we call select().

1. Open Notepad, SimpleText, or your favorite text editor if it is not already open.

2. If the **js-eight.html** or **js-eight.htm** file is not already open in the text editor, click **File** on the menu bar and then click **Open** to open the **js-eight.html** or **js-eight.htm** file you created in Step-by-Step 7.3.

3. Click **File** on the menu bar, click **Save As**, and then save the Web document as **js-nine.html** or **js-nine.htm** in the same folder that you have been saving all the files for this book to preserve the js-eight.html file.

4. Change the HTML code from the cycle() function to the select() function exactly as shown in bold in this step and in **Figure 7–12**.

```
function select()
{
    index = Math.floor(Math.random() * 4);
    document.banner.src = imgArray[index].src;
    setTimeout("select()", 2000);
    return;
}

function startup()
{
    imgArray[0] = new Image;
    imgArray[0].src = "lions.gif";
    imgArray[1] = new Image;
    imgArray[1].src = "tigers.gif";
    imgArray[2] = new Image;
    imgArray[2].src = "bears.gif";
    imgArray[3] = new Image;
    imgArray[3].src = "ohmy.gif";
    select();
    return;
}
```

FIGURE 7–12   js-nine.html file

```
<html>

<head>
<title>HTML and JavaScript</title>
<script>
var imgArray = new Array(4);
var index = 0;

function select()
{
  index = Math.floor(Math.random() * 4);
  document.banner.src = imgArray[index].src;
  setTimeout("select()", 2000);
  return;
}

function startup()
{
  imgArray[0] = new Image;
  imgArray[0].src = "lions.gif";
  imgArray[1] = new Image;
  imgArray[1].src = "tigers.gif";
  imgArray[2] = new Image;
  imgArray[2].src = "bears.gif";
  imgArray[3] = new Image;
  imgArray[3].src = "ohmy.gif";
  select();
  return;
}
</script>
</head>

<body onLoad="startup()">
  <div align="center">
    <img name="banner" src="lions.gif">
  </div>
</body>

</html>
```

5. Save the changes to the file **js-nine.html** or **js-nine.htm**.

6. Start your favorite Web browser and then open the **js-nine.html** or **js-nine.htm** file to view the file as a Web page in the browser. The resulting Web page should look like Figure 7–8, Figure 7–9, Figure 7–10, or Figure 7–11. The image should change every two seconds in a random pattern.

The JavaScript code used to create the random image effects in this step-by-step should make sense to you because it is similar to the code that was used to create the sequential cycling of images in the previous step-by-step. However, there are a few new concepts that might need some explaining.

First, you changed the function name from cycle() to select() because it more accurately reflects the purpose and behavior of the function. As a result of this name change, you had to modify the call in the startup() function so that it invoked the proper function name. If you failed to make this change, the Web browser would have responded with a script error.

Second, you included the appropriate JavaScript code to generate a random number and then converted that number into a valid array index in the range 0 to 3. The JavaScript method **random**(), which is part of the **Math** object, is guaranteed to return a real number that is greater than or equal to 0.0 and less than 1.0. A *real number* (also called a *floating-point number*) is a numerical value that includes a decimal portion. Because the numbers in this restricted range are not usable as array indices (which must always be integers), you need to scale them to the proper range. In this case, you have four elements in the array, so you multiply (with the * operator) the random value by 4. Now, you have a real number that is guaranteed to be greater than or equal to 0.0 and less than 4.0. The final step is to invoke the **floor**() method of the **Math** object, which eliminates the decimal part of the resulting number. This means that the only possible values remaining are the integers 0, 1, 2, and 3, and these are exactly the values you need to use as array indices.

Just to be sure you feel comfortable with this process, look at another example. Suppose that the first three times the select() function is called, the Math.random() method generates random values of 0.137, 0.8312, and 0.54. When the code multiplies these numbers by 4, the resulting values are 0.548, 3.3248, and 2.16, respectively. Then, when you run these new real numbers through the Math.floor() method, the final numbers stored in the **index** variable will be 0, 3, and 2. These are all valid array index values, so the images displayed are the contents of the files lions.gif, followed by ohmy.gif, and, finally, bears.gif. Or in other words, you would see Figure 7–8, followed by Figure 7–11, and, finally, Figure 7–10 on your screen.

Creating a JavaScript Slide Show

In the previous two step-by-steps, you created HTML files that included JavaScript functions that automatically changed the image on the screen every two seconds. But sometimes it is more desirable to let users decide when they want the image to change. Allowing the user to change the image by clicking his or her choice of Web page objects constitutes an electronic *slide show*.

In the next step-by-step, you write JavaScript code that provides the user with two hyperlinks labeled Back and Next. When the user clicks either one of these links, the image displayed in the Web page changes appropriately. For the sake of simplicity, you use the same graphic images as in the previous two exercises.

> **VOCABULARY**
> **real number**
> **floating-point number**
> **slide show**

EXTRA FOR EXPERTS

Watch Your Case! HTML is not case sensitive. The browser will interpret the tags <IMG>, <Img>, and <img> in exactly the same way. However, this is not true of many programming and scripting languages such as JavaScript. When naming JavaScript objects, variables, or functions, you must make certain to use the same case each time. The JavaScript interpreter will treat INDEX, Index, and index as three different variable names. This will often cause your code to function incorrectly or crash with a script error.

Step-by-Step 7.5

In this step-by-step, you modify the Web document you created in the previous step-by-step. You remove the select() function and insert two new functions named doBack() and doNext() that respond to the user's input. You also add some additional HTML code to make the Web page look nicer.

1. Open Notepad, SimpleText, or your favorite text editor if it is not already open.

2. If the **js-nine.html** or **js-nine.htm** file is not already open in the text editor, click **File** on the menu bar and then click **Open** to open the **js-nine.html** or **js-nine.htm** file you created in the previous step-by-step.

3. Click **File** on the menu bar, click **Save As**, and then save the file as **js-ten.html** or **js-ten.htm** in the same folder to preserve the js-nine.html file.

4. Replace the select() function with the doBack() and doNext() functions in the JavaScript code exactly as shown in this step and in bold in **Figure 7–13**.

```
function doBack()
{
  if (index > 0)
  {
    index--;
    document.slideshow.src =
      imgArray[index].src;
  }
  return;
}

function doNext()
{
  if (index < 3)
  {
    index++;
    document.slideshow.src =
      imgArray[index].src;
  }
  return;
}
```

5. Add the Web page enhancing HTML code between the <div> </div> tags exactly as shown in this step and in bold in **Figure 7–13**.

```
<h2>My JavaScript Slide Show</h2>
<p>
  <img name="slideshow" src="lions.gif">
</p>
<p>
  <a href="javascript:doBack()">Back</a>
     
  <a href="javascript:doNext()">Next</a>
</p>
```

FIGURE 7–13   js-ten.html file

```
<html>

<head>
<title>HTML and JavaScript</title>
<script>
var imgArray = new Array(4);
var index = 0;

function doBack()
{
  if (index > 0)
  {
    index--;
    document.slideshow.src = imgArray[index].src;
  }
  return;
}

function doNext()
{
  if (index < 3)
  {
    index++;
    document.slideshow.src = imgArray[index].src;
  }
  return;
}

function startup()
{
  imgArray[0] = new Image;
  imgArray[0].src = "lions.gif";
  imgArray[1] = new Image;
  imgArray[1].src = "tigers.gif";
  imgArray[2] = new Image;
  imgArray[2].src = "bears.gif";
  imgArray[3] = new Image;
  imgArray[3].src = "ohmy.gif";
  return;
```

Continued on next page 》

FIGURE 7–13   js-ten.html file

« *Continued from previous page*

```
}
</script>
</head>

<body onLoad="startup()">
  <div align="center">
    <h2>My JavaScript Slide Show</h2>
    <p>
      <img name="slideshow" src="lions.gif">
    </p>
    <p>
      <a href="javascript:doBack()">Back</a>         Line 52
         
      <a href="javascript:doNext()">Next</a>
    </p>
  </div>
</body>

</html>
```

6. Save the changes to the **js-ten.html** or **js-ten.htm** file.

7. Start your favorite Web browser and then open the **js-ten.html** or **js-ten.htm** file to view the file as a Web page in your browser. The resulting Web page should look like **Figure 7–14**.

FIGURE 7–14
JavaScript slide show

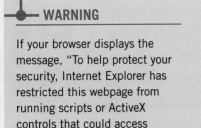

WARNING

If your browser displays the message, "To help protect your security, Internet Explorer has restricted this webpage from running scripts or ActiveX controls that could access your computer. Click here for options." click the message bar, click Allow Blocked Content, and then click Yes in the Security Warning dialog box.

8. Click the **Back** and **Next** hyperlinks to make sure the slide show image changes appropriately.

Once again, you learned some new JavaScript concepts in the previous step-by-step, so take a moment to run through the new code to make sure you understand how the slide show worked. The code in the startup() function is the same as in the two previous step-by-steps, so you should feel comfortable with how this code works by now. But, you might not be completely familiar with the doBack() and doNext() functions.

The first job of the doBack() function is to test the value of the index variable. If it is greater than 0, you know the active slide show image is not the first image, so the browser needs to "back up" to the previous image in the sequence. This is done by decrementing the value stored in index (`index--`) and then loading a new image source into the slide show image object of our HTML document. As you might expect, the term *decrement* means to subtract 1 from the current value of a variable. If the current value of index is 0, the doBack() function performs no action.

The content of the doNext() function is, of course, very similar to that of the doBack() function. The code first checks the value of index to ensure that its current value is less than 3. If it is, you know the browser is not displaying the last image in the slide show, so it needs to change the image on the screen. This is done by incrementing the **index** variable and then setting the **src** property of the slide show object to the next image in the list. If the value of index is 3, the doNext() function performs no action.

If you have a firm understanding of the material presented in Unit 1, you should feel perfectly comfortable with most of the HTML code contained within the body tags of this js-ten.html Web page. However, there are a couple of HTML items that you have not used before that you might not fully understand.

You should notice that the **href** attribute of the Back hyperlink does not include a reference to another HTML document. Instead, it contains a reference to a JavaScript function named **doBack()**. This means that when the user clicks on this hyperlink, the browser will execute the specified function rather than load a new HTML page. The href attribute of the Next hyperlink is, of course, analogous.

You probably also noticed the three cryptic letters and symbols ** ** that occur on Line 52 of the source code listing in the file js-ten.html shown in Figure 7–13. Technically speaking, this symbol is called an *entity code*, and it represents a "**n**on-**b**reaking **sp**ace," which forces the Web browser to insert a space character into your Web page. There are, of course, many other entity codes, but you do not need to worry about them now. Just be aware that these codes simply insert a little extra space between the Back and Next hyperlinks and can be deleted without affecting the behavior of the Web page.

▶ **VOCABULARY**

decrement

entity code

◗ **INTERNET**

JavaScript Copyright Infringement. We mentioned in Lesson 3 that it is very unethical for Web page developers to download copyrighted images from commercial Web sites and then use those images for their own purposes. This obviously holds true whether the images are used in standard HTML pages or in JavaScript pages. But when you start developing JavaScript enhanced Web pages, you should also be aware that script piracy is just as unethical as picture piracy. In fact, it is not just unethical, it is also illegal! Although downloading and studying script that has been created by other people is sometimes a great way to learn JavaScript, you must keep in mind that the copyright laws still apply. You should feel free to use publicly accessible JavaScript code for educational purposes, but you should not simply copy scripts from someone else's Web site to use on your own unless you receive the owner's permission to do so.

SUMMARY

In this lesson, you learned:

- How to use JavaScript events.
- How to create an image rollover.
- How to create a hyperlink rollover.

- How to create a cycling banner.
- How to display random images.
- How to create a JavaScript slide show.

■ VOCABULARY REVIEW

Define the following terms:

ad banner	event	increment
array	floating-point number	index
cycling banner	function	real number
decrement	hyperlink rollover	slide show
entity code	image rollover	variable

■ REVIEW QUESTIONS

TRUE / FALSE

Circle T if the statement is true or F if the statement is false.

T F **1.** All JavaScript events are triggered by user input.

T F **2.** JavaScript event names are used within HTML tags rather than in JavaScript code.

T F **3.** <script></script> tags can appear in the header section and/or the body section of an HTML document.

T F **4.** JavaScript events are fired when the user clicks the mouse, but not when the mouse pointer moves.

T F **5.** HTML objects with names can be referenced within JavaScript code.

T F **6.** An image on a Web page can only change if it is defined as an image rollover.

T F **7.** A hyperlink rollover can contain an image or standard text or both.

T F **8.** JavaScript arrays can only contain JavaScript Image objects.

T F **9.** The index of the first element in a JavaScript array is always 1.

T F **10.** The JavaScript Math.random() method always returns an integer value.

FILL IN THE BLANK

Complete the following sentences by writing the correct word or words in the blanks provided.

1. A JavaScript _____ is triggered by user input or by system-level functions.

2. The JavaScript _____ event is invoked when a Web page is loaded by the Web browser.

3. A JavaScript _____ is similar to a method but is not attached to a JavaScript object.

4. An image or hypertext _____ is created by using the JavaScript *onMouseOver* and *onMouseOut* events.

5. A JavaScript _____ is nothing more than a name that is associated with a constant value or object.

6. A JavaScript _____ is an object capable of containing multiple data elements.

7. A particular data element in an array is accessed by means of a(n) _____.

8. An ad banner is also known as a(n) _____ banner.

9. The JavaScript methods random() and floor() are part of the _____ object.

10. The JavaScript _____ method always returns a real number between 0.0 (inclusive) and 1.0 (exclusive).

WRITTEN QUESTIONS

Write a short answer to each of the following questions:

1. What is a JavaScript event? How are events generated?

2. What is a JavaScript function? How does a function differ from a method?

3. What is a cycling banner? Why is it called "cycling"?

4. What is the purpose of the Math object methods random() and floor()?

5. What is a JavaScript electronic slide show?

■ PROJECTS

PROJECT 7–1: JAVASCRIPT MAINTENANCE

In this project, GreatApplications, Inc., has just hired you to replace a JavaScript programmer who recently left the company. Unfortunately, your predecessor left an important project unfinished. You must fix the script created in Step-by-Step 7.1 (js-six.html). You might have noticed that if you click the mouse when your mouse pointer is over the arrow image, your Web browser displays an error message. Your first task as a new GreatApplications employee is to find the source of this problem and to correct it.

Go ahead and create an appropriate HTML page and save it with the name **webpage.html**. Then, view your js-six.html page again and verify that your browser will display your new page by clicking the arrow image as it changes color. Don't forget that your new HTML Web page file must be saved in the same folder as your js-six.html file.

PROJECT 7–2: TEAMWORK PROJECT

The management team of GreatApplications, Inc., has decided that they want to create an Electronic Zoo, and they want to make it available to the public on their corporate Web site. Consequently, they have given your team the assignment of creating a JavaScript ad banner that contains the images of four different animals. Form and organize teams of three or four members. Each member should spend some time searching the Web for suitable animal images (noncopyrighted images), and then you must create a JavaScript banner program to display them. Start with the source code listed in Figure 7–7 (js-eight.html), and then make the necessary modifications to get the program to display the animal images that you have collected. Some things you might want to do include:

■   Add a Web page title.

■   Change the image filenames.

■   Adjust the image display size.

■   Make sure the images are not copyrighted!

Save your team's work as **Project 7-2.html** or **Project 7-2.htm**.

PROJECT 7–3: WEB PROJECT

The management team of GreatApplications, Inc., has decided that they want to change their animal ad banner into a slide show. They also want to increase the number of animal images from four to eight. Here are some things you need to do to accomplish this assignment:

- Review Step-by-Step 7.5 and identify the critical components of a slide show.

- Make the slide show functional with four animal images.

- Increase the size of your image array to 8, and add four new animal images.

- Modify your doBack() and doNext() functions to handle index values in the range 0 to 7.

- Make sure the images are not copyrighted!

Save your work as **Project 7-3.html** or **Project 7-3.htm**.

 # CRITICAL THINKING

ACTIVITY 7–1: IMAGE AND HYPERLINK ROLLOVERS

In Step-by-Step 7.1, you learned how to create a rollover that reacts when the mouse pointer passes over an image. In Step-by-Step 7.2, you learned how to create a rollover that changes the color of the arrow when the mouse pointer passes over a hyperlink. This activity tests if you know how to create a rollover that can react to either condition.

Modify your **js-seven.html** file so that the arrow image changes color when the mouse pointer passes over either the hyperlink or the arrow. Only one small modification is required to accomplish this. Save your work as **Activity 7-1.html** or **Activity 7-1.htm**.

ACTIVITY 7–2: AD BANNERS

In Step-by-Step 7.3, you learned how to create a cycling banner, or ad banner, as it is often called. As you might have noticed, many commercial Web sites include ad banners, usually at the top or on the right side of their Web pages. The reason there are so many sites like this online boils down to a monetary issue. The owner of the site charges companies a certain amount to include their advertisements on the host Web pages. In this way, many Web sites can provide services to their users for free but still cover their own operating costs. Analyze several of these Web sites and consider the following questions:

1. What types of businesses might choose to pay Web site owners to host their ad banners?

2. What types of products and services are most likely to be advertised in this manner?

3. Why do you suppose most ad banners are defined as hyperlinks?

4. What types of Web sites are most likely to host ad banners?

CAPSTONE SIMULATION

In this lesson, you learned many valuable JavaScript skills that allow you to create cycling banners, random image displays, and electronic slide shows. You should recognize, however, that these techniques are not mutually exclusive. In other words, you do not necessarily have to choose only one of these techniques for a given Web page. If you want, you can use all three techniques together. Demonstrate that you have mastered all of the concepts presented in this lesson by creating a Web page that uses all three of these JavaScript image techniques. When you are finished, your Web page should look similar to Figure 7–15.

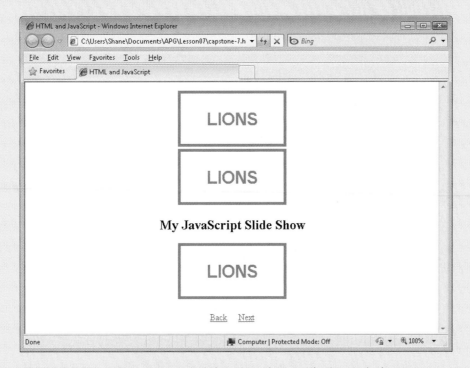

FIGURE 7–15   Web page containing three image display techniques

Project Requirements:

- Use the same image files you used in Step-by-Steps 7.3, 7.4, and 7.5.
- Create a cycling banner in the upper third of your Web page.
- Create a random image display in the middle third of your Web page.
- Create a slide show in the lower third of your Web page.
- Use different names for your two banner images.
- Use different names for your three array index variables.
- Name your resulting Web page **capstone-7.html** or **capstone-7.htm**.

LESSON 8

Creating Forms with JavaScript

■ OBJECTIVES

Upon completion of this lesson, you should be able to:

- Create an HTML form.
- Make a form submission button functional.
- Make a form clearing button functional.
- Validate text fields with JavaScript.
- Validate radio buttons with JavaScript.

In Lesson 3, you received a brief introduction to HTML forms. In this lesson, you begin by reviewing the information presented in Lesson 3 and then you learn how to use JavaScript to enhance the capabilities of HTML forms. There are several JavaScript events that can be used to add some "intelligence" to simple HTML form components.

■ VOCABULARY

check box

components

controls

data validation

radio button

text field

Making HTML Forms More Functional

You begin the process of creating a fully functional, robust form by defining the general layout of the form on a Web page. This first step is accomplished by using the appropriate HTML tags described in Lesson 3. The next step is to identify the various objects in the HTML form with which the users interact. You have to give each of these interactive objects (also called *controls* or *components*) a name so that they can be referenced within JavaScript code. The final step is to write the JavaScript functions that are invoked when the user triggers a specific JavaScript event.

One of the most important concepts you learn in this lesson is the idea of data validation. *Data validation* is the process of checking user input data to make sure that it is complete and accurate. Although it is not always possible to catch every error a user could make when filling out a form, there are many kinds of mistakes that can be detected. For example, if the user forgets to fill out a portion of a form, it is an easy task for JavaScript to detect the absence of required data and alert the user accordingly.

For you to learn these JavaScript form-processing concepts effectively, the lesson is based on a fictitious case. You pretend that you work for a newly established pizza company, the JavaScript Pizza Parlor. As an employee of this new company, your job is to create a Web page that allows customers to place their pizza orders over the Internet. As you work through the following step-by-steps, you learn how to make the Web-based order form better for users who want to order pizza and better for the owners of the company who want to sell more pizza.

Creating a Pizza Order Form

The first step in creating an effective order form for the JavaScript Pizza Parlor is to define its appearance on the Web page with the appropriate HTML tags. In the following step-by-step, you use several tags and attributes that were introduced in Lesson 3 to make your form appealing and well organized. The completed form consists of nothing more than headings, labels, and user input controls, but it takes time and practice to make these elements look good on the screen. Take note of the ways in which the heading, font, and break tags are used to control the final appearance of the pizza order form.

You should also pay close attention to the **name** attribute that appears in several of the HTML tags used in Step-by-Step 8.1. Although these names do not affect the appearance of the form at all, they are critical elements of the document. They are used extensively by the JavaScript functions you create in subsequent step-by-steps in this lesson as you continue to enhance the form.

▶ **VOCABULARY**

controls

components

data validation

─┼── **WARNING**

Your particular Web browser might display various warning messages as you try to work through the following JavaScript activities. If you see such a warning, simply click the option to enable JavaScript. None of the activities in this book are capable of damaging your computer system in any way.

Step-by-Step 8.1

In this step-by-step, you create a simple pizza order form for the fictitious JavaScript Pizza Parlor. You use text field, radio button, and check box controls to define the form's appearance and basic functionality.

1. Open Notepad, SimpleText, or your favorite text editor.

2. Create a new blank document, if necessary.

3. Enter the HTML text exactly as shown in **Figure 8–1**.

FIGURE 8–1   js-eleven.html file

```html
<html>

<head>
  <title>HTML and JavaScript</title>
</head>

<body>
  <form name="PizzaForm">
    <h1>The JavaScript Pizza Parlor</h1>
    <p>
      <h4>Step 1: Enter your name, address, and phone number:</h4>
      <font face="Courier New">
        Name:    <input name="customer" size="50"
        type="text"><br>
        Address: <input name="address" size="50" type="text"><br>
        City:    <input name="city" size="15" type="text">
        State: <input name="state" size="2" type="TEXT">
        Zip: <input name="zip" size="5" type="text"><br>
        Phone:   <input name="phone" size="50" type="text"><br>
      </font>
    </p>
    <p>
      <h4>Step 2: Select the size of pizza you want:</h4>
      <font face="Courier New">
        <input name="sizes" type="radio">Small
        <input name="sizes" type="radio">Medium
        <input name="sizes" type="radio">Large<br>
      </font>
    </p>
    <p>
      <h4>Step 3: Select the pizza toppings you want:</h4>
      <font face="Courier New">
        <input name="toppings" type="checkbox">Pepperoni
        <input name="toppings" type="checkbox">Canadian Bacon
        <input name="toppings" type="checkbox">Sausage<br>
        <input name="toppings" type="checkbox">Mushrooms
        <input name="toppings" type="checkbox">Pineapple
        <input name="toppings" type="checkbox">Black Olives<br>
      </font>
    </p>
    <input type="button" value="Submit Order">
    <input type="button" value="Clear Entries">
  </form>
</body>

</html>
```

4. Save your newly created file as **js-eleven.html** or **js-eleven.htm** in the same folder you saved the files from the previous lessons.

5. Start your favorite Web browser, and then open the **js-eleven.html** or **js-eleven.htm** file to view the file as a Web page. The Web page on your screen should look like the one shown in **Figure 8–2**.

FIGURE 8–2
Pizza order form

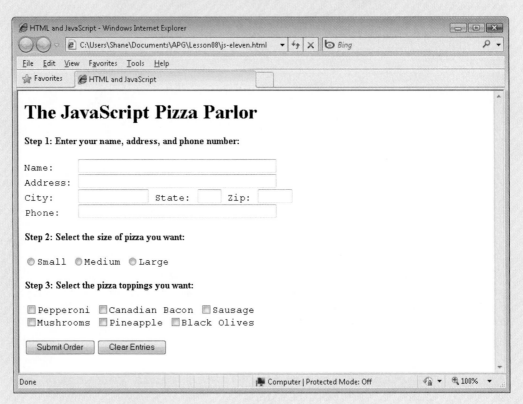

As indicated before, the HTML tags used in Step-by-Step 8.1 were previously introduced in Lesson 3. But, to make sure you understand how these tags work, you should review some of these concepts before continuing to the JavaScript portion of this lesson. Because the form is divided into three sections (or steps), take a closer look at each section to see exactly how it works.

The section identified as Step 1 consists of a heading and six labeled text fields. A ***text field*** is an input control that allows the user to enter a string value into a specific location on the Web page. Each text field is assigned a name and a size. The * * symbols are used to align the left edges of the Name, Address, City, and Phone fields.

The Step 2 section is composed of a heading and three labeled radio buttons. A ***radio button*** (also called an option button) is an input control that allows the user to select just one option from a set of options. In this case, the radio buttons are labeled Small, Medium, and Large to correspond to the available pizza sizes. The Web browser treats these three options as a set because they all have been given the same name *sizes*.

The final section, identified as Step 3, consists of the heading and six labeled check boxes. A ***check box*** is an input control that allows the user to select any number of options from a set of options. As is the case with Step 2, these check boxes were given labels that correspond to the six kinds of pizza toppings available. The Web browser also treats these six options as a set because they all have been assigned the name *toppings*.

▶ **VOCABULARY**

text field

radio button

check box

The final part of this pizza order form contains two buttons that are located at the bottom of the page, labeled Submit Order and Clear Entries. These input controls are defined with the <input> tag just like the other controls, but the **type** attribute is set to "button" rather than "text," "radio," or "checkbox." If you try to click either of these controls, you will find that they currently do not perform any action. You enter the code necessary to make these buttons functional as you work through the next two step-by-steps.

Making the Submit Order Button Functional

Now that you have a solid HTML foundation for the pizza order form, you can start adding some extra functionality with JavaScript. The first task is to add a JavaScript function that will be invoked (called) when the user clicks the Submit Order button. In this case, you enter the code to simply display an alert box to let the user know that his or her pizza order has been submitted to the JavaScript Pizza Parlor. This is an important part of our form because it is usually a good idea to let users know what the program is doing. You also want them to know that their pizza is on the way!

To get the Submit Order button to call a JavaScript function when it is clicked, you need to make use of a JavaScript event. As you might expect, this event is called *onClick*, and it is triggered whenever an input control of type **button** is clicked.

EXTRA FOR EXPERTS

What is a string? *String* is a term that is well understood by experienced programmers and Web developers but might be new to beginners. In the context of HTML and JavaScript, a string is nothing more than a sequence of one or more characters. A string can consist of a single word, a complete sentence, or an entire chapter of a book. Normally, strings contain meaningful text, but this is not a requirement. A meaningless sequence of gibberish or cryptic symbols can also be a string, and there is virtually no limit to the length of a string.

Step-by-Step 8.2

In this step-by-step, you add an *onClick* event to a button input tag. You also add a JavaScript function to the header section of your HTML document.

1. Open Notepad, SimpleText, or your favorite text editor if it is not already open.

2. If the **js-eleven.html** or **js-eleven.htm** file is not already open in the text editor, click **File** on the menu bar, click **Open**, browse to the folder that contains your files for this book, and then open the **js-eleven.html** or **js-eleven.htm** file you created in the previous step-by-step.

3. Click **File** on the menu bar, click **Save As**, and then save the HTML file as **js-twelve.html** or **js-twelve.htm** in the same folder to preserve the js-eleven.html file.

4. Add the **doSubmit()** function to the header section of your HTML file, as shown in this step and in bold in **Figure 8–3**.

```
<script>
function doSubmit()
{
  alert("Your pizza order has been submitted.");
  return;

}

</script>
```

5. Add the *onClick* event to the Submit Order <input> tag, as shown in this step and in bold in **Figure 8–3**.

```
<input type="button" value="Submit Order"
onClick="doSubmit()">
```

FIGURE 8–3   js-twelve.html file

```
<html>

<head>
<title>HTML and JavaScript</title>
<script>
function doSubmit()
{
  alert("Your pizza order has been submitted.");
  return;
}
</script>
</head>

<body>
  <form name="PizzaForm">
    <h1>The JavaScript Pizza Parlor</h1>
    <p>
      <h4>Step 1: Enter your name, address, and phone number:</h4>
      <font face="Courier New">
        Name:    <input name="customer" size="50"
        type="text"><br>
        Address: <input name="address" size="50" type="text"><br>
        City:    <input name="city" size="15" type="text">
        State: <input name="state" size="2" type="TEXT">
        Zip: <input name="zip" size="5" type="text"><br>
        Phone:   <input name="phone" size="50" type="text"><br>
      </font>
    </p>
    <p>
      <h4>Step 2: Select the size of pizza you want:</h4>
      <font face="Courier New">
        <input name="sizes" type="radio">Small
        <input name="sizes" type="radio">Medium
        <input name="sizes" type="radio">Large<br>
      </font>
    </p>
```

Continued on next page ≫

FIGURE 8–3   js-twelve.html file

《 *Continued from previous page*

```html
    <p>
      <h4>Step 3: Select the pizza toppings you want:</h4>
      <font face="Courier New">
        <input name="toppings" type="checkbox">Pepperoni
        <input name="toppings" type="checkbox">Canadian Bacon
        <input name="toppings" type="checkbox">Sausage<br>
        <input name="toppings" type="checkbox">Mushrooms
        <input name="toppings" type="checkbox">Pineapple
        <input name="toppings" type="checkbox">Black Olives<br>
      </font>
    </p>
    <input type="button" value="Submit Order" onClick="doSubmit()">
    <input type="button" value="Clear Entries">
  </form>
</body>

</html>
```

6. Save the changes to the file **js-twelve.html** or **js-twelve.htm**.

7. Start your favorite Web browser and then open the **js-twelve.html** or **js-twelve.htm** file to view the file as a Web page in the browser. The Web page on your screen should look like the one shown in **Figure 8–2**.

8. Click the **Submit Order** button and verify that the resulting Web page looks like **Figure 8–4**.

9. Click **OK** in the alert box to close it.

⊶— WARNING

If your browser displays the message, "To help protect your security, Internet Explorer has restricted this webpage from running scripts or ActiveX controls that could access your computer. Click here for options." click the message bar, click Allow Blocked Content, and then click Yes in the Security Warning dialog box.

FIGURE 8–4
Web page with Submit
Order button clicked

Your browser might
display a different
message in
the title bar

Alert box

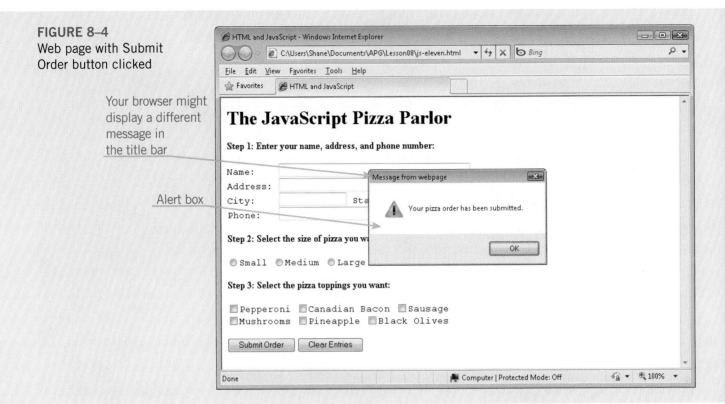

If you think about the code you just entered for a moment, you should recognize that there is very little new material, as much of the code was introduced in previous lessons. The **doSubmit()** function you just added does nothing more than invoke the JavaScript **alert()** method, which you used in the step-by-steps in Lesson 6. The concept of defining a JavaScript function was covered in detail in Lesson 7. Consequently, you should have a good understanding of how this part of the program works.

As for the *onClick* event you added to the submit button <input> tag, it also looks and acts just like the *onMouseOver*, *onMouseOut*, and *onLoad* events you used in Lesson 7. In other words, you should be quite familiar with the concepts presented in this step-by-step.

Making the Clear Entries Button Functional

You probably know from personal experience that it is very common for people to make mistakes while filling out paper forms. If using a pen, forms can get quite messy; if using a pencil, even erasers create messy forms. People also make mistakes when entering data in forms online or electronically, especially when the forms require that a person enter a large amount of information. Fortunately, there are simple features that can be built into electronic forms to help people correct errors while they fill out forms. In addition to using the Backspace or Delete key to correct mistakes, it is customary for Web page designers to include some type of clear button that allows the user to erase all form entries with a single click and start over.

Clearing forms is not only helpful in correcting errors. In the case of the pizza order form, it would be nice to give the customer the ability to clear the form after an order has been submitted. Then, a second order could be placed without having to change all of the existing data one field at a time.

To accomplish this task, you need to add the **doClear()** function to your HTML/JavaScript document. You must also add an *onClick* event to the <input> tag of the Clear Entries button, just as you did for the Submit Order button in the previous step-by-step. This event will call the *doClear()* function to erase any existing form data.

TECHNOLOGY TIMELINE

Over the past two or three decades, many software developers have learned the importance of giving users adequate feedback. In other words, it is essential for programmers to give the user some kind of visual (or sometimes audio) clue as to what the program is doing or when it has completed its operation. Think about it for a minute. What do you suppose an average computer user would do if he or she clicked the Submit Order button on an electronic form and nothing happened?

Unless a message appears to confirm that the order has actually been submitted, a user would probably click the button again. Maybe the customer might click it several more times in hopes of receiving some response. Other users might even erroneously conclude that their computer stopped responding and needs to be rebooted!

This is an especially significant issue when a program has to perform an operation that takes a long time to complete. When your Web browser is downloading large graphic images over a slow Internet connection, for example, it is essential for the JavaScript program to give some kind of visual feedback to let you know it is actually doing something. Otherwise, you would see a lot of impatient users submitting multiple orders or maybe even rebooting their computers for no reason. So, please be considerate of users and design your JavaScript programs to give lots of appropriate feedback.

Step-by-Step 8.3

In this step-by-step, you add another *onClick* event to a second button input tag. You also add a new JavaScript function to the header section of your HTML document.

1. Open Notepad, SimpleText, or your favorite text editor if it is not already open.

2. If the **js-twelve.html** or **js-twelve.htm** file is not already open in the text editor, click **File** on the menu bar, click **Open**, browse to the folder that contains your files for this book, and then open the **js-twelve.html** or **js-twelve.htm** file you created in Step-by-Step 8.2.

3. Click **File** on the menu bar, click **Save As**, and then save the HTML file as **js-thirteen.html** or **js-thirteen.htm** in the same folder to preserve the js-twelve.html file.

4. Add the **doClear()** function to the header section of your HTML file, as shown in this step and in bold in **Figure 8–5**.

```
<script>
function doClear()
{
  document.PizzaForm.customer.value = "";
  document.PizzaForm.address.value = "";
  document.PizzaForm.city.value = "";
  document.PizzaForm.state.value = "";
  document.PizzaForm.zip.value = "";
  document.PizzaForm.phone.value = "";
```

```
                         document.PizzaForm.sizes[0].checked = false;
                         document.PizzaForm.sizes[1].checked = false;
                         document.PizzaForm.sizes[2].checked = false;

                         document.PizzaForm.toppings[0].checked = false;
                         document.PizzaForm.toppings[1].checked = false;
                         document.PizzaForm.toppings[2].checked = false;
                         document.PizzaForm.toppings[3].checked = false;
                         document.PizzaForm.toppings[4].checked = false;
                         document.PizzaForm.toppings[5].checked = false;
                         return;
                       }

                       function doSubmit()
                       {
                         alert("Your pizza order has been submitted.");
                         return;
                       }
                       </script>
```

5. Add the *onClick* event to the Clear Entries `<input>` tag, as shown in this
   step and in bold in **Figure 8–5**.

```
<input type="button" value="Clear Entries"
onClick="doClear()">
```

FIGURE 8–5   js-thirteen.html file

```
<html>

<head>
<title>HTML and JavaScript</title>
<script>
function doClear()
{
  document.PizzaForm.customer.value = "";
  document.PizzaForm.address.value = "";
  document.PizzaForm.city.value = "";
  document.PizzaForm.state.value = "";
  document.PizzaForm.zip.value = "";
  document.PizzaForm.phone.value = "";

  document.PizzaForm.sizes[0].checked = false;
  document.PizzaForm.sizes[1].checked = false;
  document.PizzaForm.sizes[2].checked = false;
```

Continued on next page ⟫

FIGURE 8–5   js-thirteen.html file

《 Continued from previous page

```html
    document.PizzaForm.toppings[0].checked = false;
    document.PizzaForm.toppings[1].checked = false;
    document.PizzaForm.toppings[2].checked = false;
    document.PizzaForm.toppings[3].checked = false;
    document.PizzaForm.toppings[4].checked = false;
    document.PizzaForm.toppings[5].checked = false;
    return;
}

function doSubmit()
{
    alert("Your pizza order has been submitted.");
    return;
}
</script>
</head>

<body>
    <form name="PizzaForm">
        <h1>The JavaScript Pizza Parlor</h1>
        <p>
            <h4>Step 1: Enter your name, address, and phone number:</h4>
            <font face="Courier New">
                Name:    <input name="customer" size="50"
                type="text"><br>
                Address: <input name="address" size="50" type="text"><br>
                City:    <input name="city" size="15" type="text">
                State: <input name="state" size="2" type="TEXT">
                Zip: <input name="zip" size="5" type="text"><br>
                Phone:   <input name="phone" size="50" type="text"><br>
            </font>
        </p>
        <p>
            <h4>Step 2: Select the size of pizza you want:</h4>
            <font face="Courier New">
                <input name="sizes" type="radio">Small
                <input name="sizes" type="radio">Medium
                <input name="sizes" type="radio">Large<br>
            </font>
        </p>
        <p>
            <h4>Step 3: Select the pizza toppings you want:</h4>
            <font face="Courier New">
                <input name="toppings" type="checkbox">Pepperoni
                <input name="toppings" type="checkbox">Canadian Bacon
                <input name="toppings" type="checkbox">Sausage<br>
```

Continued on next page 》

FIGURE 8–5   js-thirteen.html file

《 *Continued from previous page*

```
        <input name="toppings" type="checkbox">Mushrooms
        <input name="toppings" type="checkbox">Pineapple
        <input name="toppings" type="checkbox">Black Olives<br>
      </font>
    </p>
    <input type="button" value="Submit Order" onClick="doSubmit()">
    <input type="button" value="Clear Entries" onClick="doClear()">
  </form>
</body>

</html>
```

WARNING

If your browser displays the message, "To help protect your security, Internet Explorer has restricted this webpage from running scripts or ActiveX controls that could access your computer. Click here for options." click the message bar, click Allow Blocked Content, and then click Yes in the Security Warning dialog box.

6. Save the changes to the file **js-thirteen.html** or **js-thirteen.htm**.

7. Start your favorite Web browser, and then open the **js-thirteen.html** or **js-thirteen.htm** file to view the file as a Web page. The Web page should initially look like **Figure 8–2**.

8. Type your first name into the Name field in the form, click one of the **option buttons** to select the size of the pizza, click two of the **check boxes** to select your toppings, and then click the **Clear Entries** button. The form entries should disappear, and the Web page should again look like **Figure 8–2**.

As you can see, the code required to make the Clear Entries button functional is very similar to the code you used to make the Submit Order button active. However, some new concepts are introduced in the **doClear()** function that are important for you to understand. So take a closer look at what these JavaScript statements are doing.

The first statement of the doClear() function makes use of the *value* property of the **text** input control object. In this particular case, the text control is assigned the name *customer*, and it is an element within the **form** object that you named *PizzaForm*. The form object, in turn, is contained with the document object that was first introduced in Lesson 6. Therefore, you can easily clear the value stored in that text field by assigning an empty string ("") to the *document.PizzaForm.customer.value* property.

The next five statements of the doClear() function perform essentially the same action, except that they reference the text control objects named *address*, *city*, *state*, *zip*, and *phone*. Because these five controls also belong to the form object within the HTML document, they are referenced with a *document.PizzaForm* prefix. In addition, you clear these five controls by assigning an empty string to their value property, just like you did with the customer field.

Clearing the pizza size value in Step 2 is performed in a similar fashion, but there's a new concept at work here. Because you gave all three **radio** input controls the same name (*sizes*), the JavaScript interpreter treats them as an array of objects.

This means that you must use an index value to indicate which radio button you want to access. The index values assigned to the array elements always start at 0, and they increase sequentially for each new element encountered. In this case, the radio buttons labeled *Small*, *Medium*, and *Large* are assigned index values of 0, 1, and 2, respectively. Each of these objects contains a property called *checked* that indicates whether the option is selected or not. You can clear all of these options simply by setting their checked property to the logical value *false*.

The pizza topping options of Step 3 work just like the pizza size options of Step 2. Because you defined six of these **checkbox** objects with the same name (*toppings*), they are treated as a six-element array. Their index values are, of course, assigned as 0 through 5, and they are cleared when their **checked** property is set to *false*.

TECHNOLOGY CAREERS

As you work through the various activities in this lesson, you might wonder how an actual pizza business would receive orders by means of a Web page. After all, the JavaScript code in these programs does nothing more than display various items of information on the screen. There are no programmed instructions included in these examples that would actually cause the data entered into the form to be sent to another location. So how does this work? Well, you can rest assured that JavaScript is capable of sending information to another location. This data transfer normally travels through an HTTP connection, eventually arriving at a Web server somewhere. When the server receives the form data, it is processed by another program that is typically written in ASP, JSP, PHP, or some other server-side scripting/programming language.

Server-side script looks a lot like JavaScript code, and it is processed in a similar fashion. Server-script programs are capable of many different functions, but they are most frequently used to update a database system. This means that the pizza company, or any other type of business for that matter, can use any number of software packages to collect information from electronic forms that are distributed over the Web. Server-script programs do not appear out of thin air. Someone has to write them, and that someone could be you! Individuals who can add knowledge of server scripting to their JavaScript coding skills should have a relatively easy time finding a job in the software field.

Validating Text Fields

Practically every business that provides its customers with electronic forms that collect data has the need to validate the data to ensure that customers have entered appropriate and complete information. Consider the JavaScript Pizza Parlor, for example. What might happen if a customer ordering a delivery from a pizza business completed and sent an order form with the address field left blank? How could they possibly deliver a pizza to an unknown address? Or even worse, what if an inconsiderate prankster decided to submit dozens of pizza orders that were to be delivered to a phony address? Scenarios like these would cause the business more harm than good.

To complete the next step-by-step, assume that the owner of the JavaScript Pizza Parlor would like your JavaScript program to accept only orders that have data in the customer, address, city, and phone fields. If a customer attempts to submit an order with any one of these fields left blank, the program will display an appropriate error message. Please note that this is very basic data validation. It is possible to perform validation that is much more extensive and sophisticated, but that is beyond the scope of this lesson.

Step-by-Step 8.4

In this step-by-step, you create a new JavaScript function that will validate the text fields in Step 1 of your pizza order form. You also add an if statement to the doSubmit() function to call the new function.

1. Open Notepad, SimpleText, or your favorite text editor if it is not already open.

2. If the **js-thirteen.html** or **js-thirteen.htm** file is not already open in the text editor, click **File** on the menu bar, click **Open**, browse to the folder with your saved files, and then open the **js-thirteen.html** or **js-thirteen. htm** file you created in Step-by-Step 8.3.

3. Click **File** on the menu bar, click **Save As**, and then save the Web document as **js-fourteen.html** or **js-fourteen.htm** in the same folder to preserve the js-thirteen.html file.

4. Add an **if** statement to the doSubmit() function, as shown in this step and in bold in **Figure 8–6**.

```
function doSubmit()
{
   if (validateText() == false)
   {
     alert("Required data missing in Step 1");
     return;
   }
   alert("Your pizza order has been submitted.");
   return;
}
```

5. Add the validateText() function to the script section of your Web document, as shown in this step and in bold in **Figure 8–6**.

```
function validateText()
{
   var customer = document.PizzaForm.customer.
   value;
   if (customer.length == 0) return false;
   var address = document.PizzaForm.address.
   value;
   if (address.length == 0) return false;
   var city = document.PizzaForm.city.value;
   if (city.length == 0) return false;
   var phone = document.PizzaForm.phone.value;
   if (phone.length == 0) return false;
   return true;
}
```

FIGURE 8–6   js-fourteen.html file

```
<html>

<head>
<title>HTML and JavaScript</title>
<script>
function doClear()
{
  document.PizzaForm.customer.value = "";
  document.PizzaForm.address.value = "";
  document.PizzaForm.city.value = "";
  document.PizzaForm.state.value = "";
  document.PizzaForm.zip.value = "";
  document.PizzaForm.phone.value = "";

  document.PizzaForm.sizes[0].checked = false;
  document.PizzaForm.sizes[1].checked = false;
  document.PizzaForm.sizes[2].checked = false;

  document.PizzaForm.toppings[0].checked = false;
  document.PizzaForm.toppings[1].checked = false;
  document.PizzaForm.toppings[2].checked = false;
  document.PizzaForm.toppings[3].checked = false;
  document.PizzaForm.toppings[4].checked = false;
  document.PizzaForm.toppings[5].checked = false;
  return;
}

function doSubmit()
{
  if (validateText() == false)
  {
    alert("Required data missing in Step 1");
    return;
  }
  alert("Your pizza order has been submitted.");
  return;
}

function validateText()
{
  var customer = document.PizzaForm.customer.value;
  if (customer.length == 0) return false;
  var address = document.PizzaForm.address.value;
  if (address.length == 0) return false;
  var city = document.PizzaForm.city.value;
  if (city.length == 0) return false;
```

Continued on next page 》》

FIGURE 8–6   js-fourteen.html file

《 *Continued from previous page*

```
    var phone = document.PizzaForm.phone.value;
    if (phone.length == 0) return false;
    return true;
}
</script>
</head>

<body>
  <form name="PizzaForm">
    <h1>The JavaScript Pizza Parlor</h1>
    <p>
      <h4>Step 1: Enter your name, address, and phone number:</h4>
      <font face="Courier New">
        Name:    <input name="customer" size="50"
        type="text"><br>
        Address: <input name="address" size="50" type="text"><br>
        City:    <input name="city" size="15" type="text">
        State: <input name="state" size="2" type="TEXT">
        Zip: <input name="zip" size="5" type="text"><br>
        Phone:   <input name="phone" size="50" type="text"><br>
      </font>
    </p>
    <p>
      <h4>Step 2: Select the size of pizza you want:</h4>
      <font face="Courier New">
        <input name="sizes" type="radio">Small
        <input name="sizes" type="radio">Medium
        <input name="sizes" type="radio">Large<br>
      </font>
    </p>
    <p>
      <h4>Step 3: Select the pizza toppings you want:</h4>
      <font face="Courier New">
        <input name="toppings" type="checkbox">Pepperoni
        <input name="toppings" type="checkbox">Canadian Bacon
        <input name="toppings" type="checkbox">Sausage<br>
        <input name="toppings" type="checkbox">Mushrooms
        <input name="toppings" type="checkbox">Pineapple
        <input name="toppings" type="checkbox">Black Olives<br>
      </font>
    </p>
    <input type="button" value="Submit Order" onClick="doSubmit()">
    <input type="button" value="Clear Entries" onClick="doClear()">
  </form>
</body>

</html>
```

6. Save your changes to the **js-fourteen.html** or **js-fourteen.htm** file.

7. Start your favorite Web browser and open the **js-fourteen.html** or **js-fourteen.htm** file to view the file as a Web page.

8. Click the **Submit Order** button before entering any data into the form. Verify that the alert box with the text "Required data missing in Step 1" opens on your screen and the Web page looks like **Figure 8–7**.

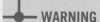
WARNING

If your browser displays the message, "To help protect your security, Internet Explorer has restricted this webpage from running scripts or ActiveX controls that could access your computer. Click here for options." click the message bar, click Allow Blocked Content, and then click Yes in the Security Warning dialog box.

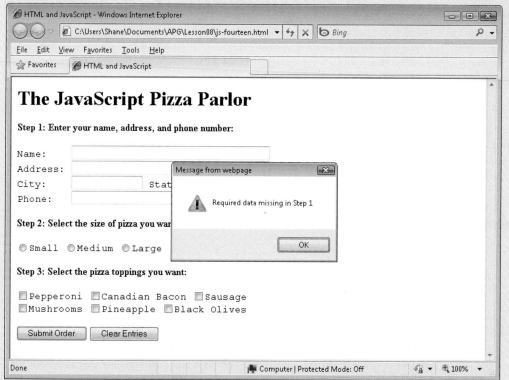

FIGURE 8–7
Data validation – text fields

9. Click **OK** to close the alert box.

You added a relatively small amount of JavaScript code to the Web page to validate the entry in the form. This code illustrates some important concepts.

First, the **validateText()** function is slightly different from any other function you have entered up to now because it returns a value. Returning a value means that whenever any other function calls this function (the doSubmit() function in this case), its name is essentially replaced by the value it returns. The validateText() function can only return one of two possible values: *false* or *true*. The false value is returned if the value property of the **customer** object, the **address** object, the **city** object, or the **phone** object is an empty string. That is, nothing was entered in the field. The false value is returned if the **length** of any one of these fields is 0. If none of the required text fields are blank, meaning a user entered something in each of the fields, the function returns the true value.

Second, the return value of the **validateText()** function is compared with the value **false** by the new `if` statement in the doSubmit() function. If the return value is false, the doSubmit() function displays an alert box to let the user know that he or she has left a required text field blank. Otherwise, the user will see a different alert box confirming that the pizza order has been submitted.

TECHNOLOGY TIMELINE

Assignment vs. Comparison

You might have noticed that many of the JavaScript statements in this lesson use a single equal sign (=), whereas others use two equal signs (==). All programming languages must make a distinction between assigning a value to a variable and comparing the content of a variable to some other value. In the case of C, C++, Java, and JavaScript, the assignment operation is accomplished with the "=" character, whereas the comparison operation is performed by two "= =" characters.

So what happens if you confuse these two operators? Well, the answer depends on the language you're using. For many years, the C and C++ languages have been criticized because they allow the programmer to easily confuse the assignment operator with the comparison operator. This type of mistake is usually difficult to find because the program will compile and run just fine, but it will yield unexpected and/or incorrect results.

The Java language designers, however, took this common pitfall into account when they defined its syntax rules. As a result, you'll see a compilation error if you attempt to use the wrong operator. Unfortunately, the architects of JavaScript did not follow the Java experts in this regard. Like C and C++, JavaScript will use the wrong operator without a single complaint. Unexpected or erratic program behavior is the only clue you will get when you make this kind of mistake, so please use caution when you are programming using these operators!

Validating Radio Buttons

Now that you know how to check for blank text fields, consider another type of data validation. In Step 2 of the pizza order form, the customer has to select the size of pizza he or she wants. What will happen if the customer fails to do this and does not select any of the options? As the JavaScript code currently stands, the order will be submitted whether or not a customer selects a size. This means that the clerk who receives the order at the JavaScript Pizza Parlor will have no idea what size of pizza the customer wants.

Fortunately, you add some new JavaScript code in the next step-by-step that prevents this situation from occurring. To ensure that a customer's order includes a selection of pizza size, all you have to do is add another data validation function to the program and a new if statement to the existing doSubmit() function.

TECHNOLOGY TIMELINE

The term *radio button* has been around the software industry ever since Microsoft introduced its Windows operating system in the late 1980s. But few people know where the term originated or exactly what it means. The Microsoft programmers who designed the Windows interface recognized that it is often necessary to treat a set of options as mutually exclusive. In other words, only one option can be selected at any given time. They also wanted to give this type of action a special name that would help the user understand this behavior. The term they chose to use was *radio button* because the behavior of these options is similar to the function selection buttons found on old-style stereo systems. These stereos typically contained several buttons labeled AM, FM, FM STEREO, PHONO, TAPE, and AUX that allowed the user to select the music source. Because it was possible to listen to only one music source at a time, pushing any one of these buttons caused any other selected button to pop out. These mechanical radio buttons were usually round, so the Windows programmers gave a round shape to their radio buttons.

Step-by-Step 8.5

In this step-by-step, you add a new JavaScript function that will validate the radio buttons in Step 2 of your pizza order form. You also add a second if statement to the doSubmit() function to call the new function.

1. Open Notepad, SimpleText, or your favorite text editor if it is not already open.

2. If the **js-fourteen.html** or **js-fourteen.htm** file is not already open in the text editor, click **File** on the menu bar, click **Open**, browse to the folder with your saved files, and then open the **js-fourteen.html** or **js-fourteen. htm** file you created in Step-by-Step 8.4.

3. Click **File** on the menu bar, click **Save As**, and then save the HTML file as **js-fifteen.html** or **js-fifteen.htm** to preserve the js-fourteen.html file.

4. Add a new **if** statement to the doSubmit() function, as shown in this step and in bold in **Figure 8–8**.

```
function doSubmit()
{
  if (validateText() == false)
  {
    alert("Required data missing in Step 1");
    return;
  }
  if (validateRadio() == false)
  {
    alert("Required data missing in Step 2");
    return;
  }
  alert("Your pizza order has been submitted.");
  return;
}
```

5. Add the **validateRadio()** function to the script section of your Web document, as shown in this step and in bold in **Figure 8–8**.

```
function validateRadio()
{
  if (document.PizzaForm.sizes[0].checked) return
true;
  if (document.PizzaForm.sizes[1].checked) return
true;
  if (document.PizzaForm.sizes[2].checked) return
true;
  return false;
}
```

FIGURE 8–8   js-fifteen.html file

```
<html>

<head>
<title>HTML and JavaScript</title>
<script>
function doClear()
{
  document.PizzaForm.customer.value = "";
  document.PizzaForm.address.value = "";
  document.PizzaForm.city.value = "";
  document.PizzaForm.state.value = "";
  document.PizzaForm.zip.value = "";
  document.PizzaForm.phone.value = "";

  document.PizzaForm.sizes[0].checked = false;
  document.PizzaForm.sizes[1].checked = false;
  document.PizzaForm.sizes[2].checked = false;

  document.PizzaForm.toppings[0].checked = false;
  document.PizzaForm.toppings[1].checked = false;
  document.PizzaForm.toppings[2].checked = false;
  document.PizzaForm.toppings[3].checked = false;
  document.PizzaForm.toppings[4].checked = false;
  document.PizzaForm.toppings[5].checked = false;
  return;
}

function doSubmit()
{
  if (validateText() == false)
  {
```

Continued on next page ≫

FIGURE 8–8   js-fifteen.html file

《 *Continued from previous page*

```
      alert("Required data missing in Step 1");
      return;
  }
  if (validateRadio() == false)
  {
      alert("Required data missing in Step 2");
      return;
  }
  alert("Your pizza order has been submitted.");
  return;
}

function validateText()
{
  var customer = document.PizzaForm.customer.value;
  if (customer.length == 0) return false;
  var address = document.PizzaForm.address.value;
  if (address.length == 0) return false;
  var city = document.PizzaForm.city.value;
  if (city.length == 0) return false;
  var phone = document.PizzaForm.phone.value;
  if (phone.length == 0) return false;
  return true;
}

function validateRadio()
{
  if (document.PizzaForm.sizes[0].checked) return true;
  if (document.PizzaForm.sizes[1].checked) return true;
  if (document.PizzaForm.sizes[2].checked) return true;
  return false;
}
</script>
</head>

<body>
  <form name="PizzaForm">
    <h1>The JavaScript Pizza Parlor</h1>
    <p>
      <h4>Step 1: Enter your name, address, and phone number:</h4>
      <font face="Courier New">
        Name:    <input name="customer" size="50"
        type="text"><br>
        Address: <input name="address" size="50" type="text"><br>
        City:    <input name="city" size="15" type="text">
```

Continued on next page 》

FIGURE 8–8   js-fifteen.html file

《 *Continued from previous page*

```
             State: <input name="state" size="2" type="TEXT">
             Zip: <input name="zip" size="5" type="text"><br>
             Phone:   <input name="phone" size="50" type="text"><br>
         </font>
      </p>
      <p>
         <h4>Step 2: Select the size of pizza you want:</h4>
         <font face="Courier New">
             <input name="sizes" type="radio">Small
             <input name="sizes" type="radio">Medium
             <input name="sizes" type="radio">Large<br>
         </font>
      </p>
      <p>
         <h4>Step 3: Select the pizza toppings you want:</h4>
         <font face="Courier New">
             <input name="toppings" type="checkbox">Pepperoni
             <input name="toppings" type="checkbox">Canadian Bacon
             <input name="toppings" type="checkbox">Sausage<br>
             <input name="toppings" type="checkbox">Mushrooms
             <input name="toppings" type="checkbox">Pineapple
             <input name="toppings" type="checkbox">Black Olives<br>
         </font>
      </p>
      <input type="button" value="Submit Order" onClick="doSubmit()">
      <input type="button" value="Clear Entries" onClick="doClear()">
   </form>
</body>

</html>
```

WARNING

If your browser displays the message, "To help protect your security, Internet Explorer has restricted this webpage from running scripts or ActiveX controls that could access your computer. Click here for options." click the message bar, click Allow Blocked Content, and then click Yes in the Security Warning dialog box.

6. Save your changes to the **js-fifteen.html** or **js-fifteen.htm** file.

7. Start your favorite Web browser and open the **js-fifteen.html** or **js-fifteen.htm** file to view it as a Web page.

8. Enter your first name, street address, city, state, zip, and phone number into the required text fields in Step 1 of the pizza order form. (*Hint*: You can press the Tab key to move from field to field.)

9. Click the **Submit Order** button without selecting a pizza size. The alert box opens, and the resulting Web page should look like **Figure 8–9**.

10. Click **OK** to close the alert box.

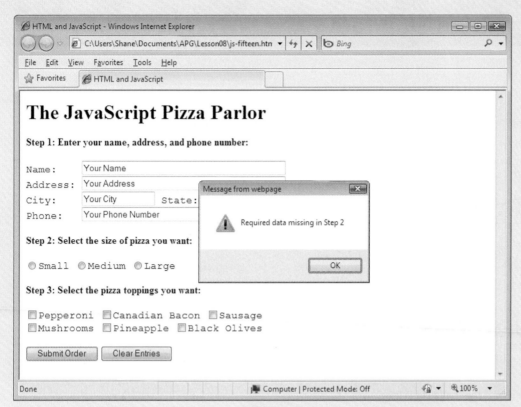

FIGURE 8–9
Data validation – radio buttons

The main idea behind the step-by-step you just completed is similar to the previous step-by-steps, but it is important that you understand the subtle differences.

To validate the contents of a text field, the program checks the contents of the object's *value* property to see if it contains an empty string. To validate a set of radio buttons, you need to test the value of each object's *checked* property to see if it is set to *true* or *false*. Consequently, the **validateRadio()** function subsequently tests the value of each checked property in the object set and returns a *true* value if it encounters a selected radio button. However, if none of the radio buttons in the set is selected, the function returns a *false* value.

The true/false value returned by the validateRadio() function is evaluated by the doSubmit() function, just as it was for the validateText() function. If the return value is false, the user will see an appropriate alert box to let him or her know that Step 2 was not completed correctly. The end result of this activity is that customers will not be able to submit an order to the JavaScript Pizza Parlor without selecting a pizza size first.

EXTRA FOR EXPERTS

The logical NOT operator. Like C, C++, and Java, JavaScript gives you the ability to invert the value of a logical variable with the NOT operator (!). You can invert a true value to false or a false value to true by placing a single ! in front of the variable. This operator is most commonly used when the programmer wants to test for a false condition. Whenever a variable (or function return value) is being compared to the false value (== false), the comparison can be shortened by using the ! operator instead. Here's a specific example:

```
if (validateText() ==
false) is equivalent to if
(!validateText())
```

The preferred way of testing for a false value is a matter of personal taste. However, it is very common to see novice programmers use the former approach, whereas professional coders tend to use the latter technique. Either way will work just fine.

SUMMARY

In this lesson, you learned:

- How to create an HTML form.
- How to make a form submission button functional.
- How to make a form clearing button functional.

- How to validate text fields with JavaScript.
- How to validate radio buttons with JavaScript.

■ VOCABULARY REVIEW

Define the following terms:

check box	controls	radio button
components	data validation	text field

■ REVIEW QUESTIONS

TRUE / FALSE

Circle T if the statement is true or F if the statement is false.

T   F   **1.**   Data validation is the process of checking user input data to make sure it is complete and accurate.

T   F   **2.**   Forms that are validated with JavaScript must be defined in a completely different way than standard HTML forms.

T   F   **3.**   The **name** attribute helps to define selection options in HTML forms.

T   F   **4.**   Each input control in a radio button set must be assigned a unique name.

T   F   **5.**   The term *radio button* is derived from the word *radial*, which means *round*.

T   F   **6.**   The only difference in HTML code between a radio button control and a checkbox control is the value of the type attribute used in the <input> tag.

T   F   **7.**   To get a button to call a JavaScript function when it is clicked, you need to make use of the *onClick* event.

T   F   **8.**   Some JavaScript functions return a value, whereas others do not.

T   F   **9.**   Because today's users now have so much Web experience, it is considered unnecessary for JavaScript programmers to provide visual or audio feedback regarding form errors.

T   F   **10.**   In JavaScript, it is impossible to determine if a user has selected a particular radio button.

FILL IN THE BLANK

Complete the following sentences by writing the correct word or words in the blanks provided.

1. Text fields, radio buttons, and check boxes are examples of input _____.

2. An HTML form can be accessed in JavaScript by using its _____ attribute.

3. A JavaScript function can be called from a button by using the _____ event.

4. A text field can be cleared by setting its _____ property to an empty string ("").

5. Radio buttons and check boxes can be cleared by setting their _____ property to false.

6. A text field is empty if the _____ of its value property is 0.

7. A radio button or check box is selected if its checked property is set to _____.

8. If two or more input controls are given the same name, JavaScript creates a(n) _____.

9. A set of JavaScript _____ is mutually exclusive, meaning that only one of the set can be selected.

10. A set of JavaScript _____ is not mutually exclusive, meaning that zero or more can be selected.

WRITTEN QUESTIONS

Write a short answer to each of the following questions:

1. How is an HTML form defined for use with JavaScript?

2. What is user feedback? Why is it important?

3. Describe how to clear text fields with JavaScript.

4. Explain how to set or clear radio buttons and check boxes.

5. What is data validation? Why is it important?

■ PROJECTS

PROJECT 8-1: FOUR CORNERS PIZZA

GreatApplications, Inc., has just won a major business contract with a pizza company called The Four Corners Pizza Palace. This company wants GreatApplications to create a Web-based pizza order form like the one you created for the JavaScript Pizza Parlor in this lesson.

The Four Corners Pizza Palace does business in the famous "Four Corners" area of the United States. The Four Corners is a geographical area located where the four states Arizona (AZ), Colorado (CO), New Mexico (NM), and Utah (UT) meet. Therefore, The Four Corners Pizza Palace will need a drop-down list that contains two-letter abbreviations for each of the states. This information will help the company tabulate the sales tax for each state. You are to create a pizza order form and add the state code drop-down list selection box. (If you don't remember how to create a drop-down list control, refer to Step-by-Step 3.5 in Lesson 3.) Make sure the user selects a state when placing an order, and make sure the state control is cleared when the Clear Entries button is clicked.

Save your work as **Project 8-1.html** or **Project 8-1.htm**.

PROJECT 8-2: WEB PROJECT

The management team of GreatApplications, Inc., has decided that they need you to enhance the pizza form you created for the JavaScript Pizza Parlor. Complete the following changes to the form:

■ Add a new text field labeled **Email** directly below the **Phone** field.

■ Add a new pizza size called **Jumbo** to the right of the **Large** size.

■ Add two new toppings on a new line on the form. Label the toppings **Green Peppers** and **Extra Cheese**.

Make sure your new form components clear properly when the Clear Entries button is clicked. Save your work as **Project 8-2.html** or **Project 8-2.htm**.

PROJECT 8–3: TEAMWORK PROJECT

The pizza order form you create in this lesson is obviously designed for educational, rather than business, purposes. Nevertheless, do you think there might be some pizza companies out there that really do accept pizza orders on the Web? As a team, make a list of all the pizza stores you can think of in your local area. Then, use your favorite search engine to research the pizza stores on the Web and determine how many (if any) offer a Web-based order form. See how many ideas you can get from these sites that you could use to improve your own order form.

CRITICAL THINKING

ACTIVITY 8–1: DATA VALIDATION

In this lesson, we have discussed the concept of data validation at length. In Step-by-Steps 8.4 and 8.5, you learned to implement simple validation techniques. But what if you were asked to explain the concept to a fellow student, including reasons why it is important to use these techniques? Could you do it? Data validation is a fundamental part of virtually every professional computer program, no matter what type of program it is or in what programming language it is written. So, it is essential that you attain a solid understanding of the concept. To help make sure you do, answer the following questions:

1. What types of data must be validated for a typical form?

2. Is checking for blank fields always sufficient for text validation? Explain.

3. Is it always possible for a computer program to validate every field on the form? Why or why not?

ACTIVITY 8–2: BETTER FEEDBACK

Your supervisor at GreatApplications, Inc., is still not completely satisfied with the JavaScript Pizza Parlor form because it does not give sufficiently detailed feedback. Modify the **doSubmit()** function of your Web document so that it identifies the specific text field that is missing data (if appropriate). The feedback message for Step 2 should also be modified to indicate that the user must select a pizza size if he or she failed to do so. Save your work as **Activity 8-2.html** or **Activity 8-2.htm**.

■ CAPSTONE SIMULATION

If you have gained a firm understanding of the material presented in this lesson, you should be able to create a professional-looking order form for almost any situation. Demonstrate that you have mastered the concepts of Lesson 8 by creating an order form for the fictitious JavaScript Computer Company. This company wants you to build a JavaScript-enabled Web page that allows customers to order a custom computer system containing the exact components they want. Create a computer order form that looks like the one in Figure 8-10.

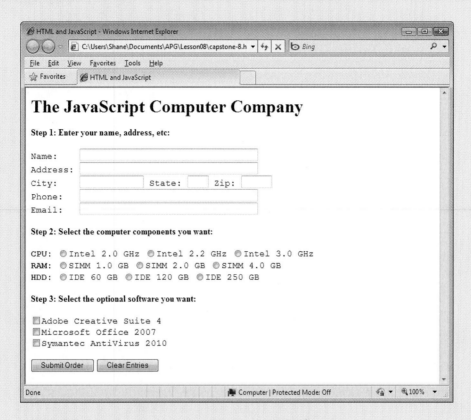

FIGURE 8–10   A sample computer system order form

Project Requirements:

- Create an appropriate title.
- Create text fields to collect customer information.
- Use radio buttons to represent required computer component options.
- Use check boxes to represent optional software options.
- Name your resulting Web page **capstone-8.html** or **capstone-8.htm**.

LESSON 9

Using JavaScript with Frames

■ OBJECTIVES

Upon completion of this lesson, you should be able to:

- Create a JavaScript function with a parameter list.
- Create JavaScript-enabled hyperlinks that affect frames.
- Create JavaScript-enabled buttons that affect frames.
- Create top-level JavaScript functions.

In Lesson 4, you learned how to create HTML frames to better organize information on a Web page. In this lesson, you learn how to create JavaScript functions that can access information across frames within a frameset. It is important that the information displayed in one frame is properly associated with the information in another frame. JavaScript is one technology that can help you do this.

■ VOCABULARY

child document

function parameter

parameter list

parent document

parent object

top object

Advanced JavaScript Programming

The JavaScript code you wrote to create the Web pages in Lessons 5, 6, and 7 was limited to a single HTML document. As you learned from the Web pages you created in Lesson 4, not all Web pages consist of just one HTML file. In fact, any Web page that contains a frameset is always composed of multiple files. There must be one file that defines the frameset and two or more additional files that define the frames within that frameset. The frameset file is known as the ***parent document***, and the frame files contained within the frameset are known as ***child documents***.

So the question becomes, is it possible for a Web user to perform an action in one frame that affects the appearance of a different frame? The answer is yes. All frames that make up a Web page can communicate with each other by means of JavaScript functions because the Web browser provides a common environment in which frames can interact. The JavaScript code that accomplishes such cross-frame cooperation is a little more complicated than single-document code, but it is still well within your abilities as a new JavaScript programmer.

Before you can write JavaScript code that allows different frames to interact, you must create HTML documents that define a frameset. In the first step-by-step in this lesson, you learn how to create a frameset that contains an image in one frame and a standard HTML table in another frame. The table initially contains nonfunctional filenames, which you later convert into hyperlinks. But for now, the goal is simply to create an appropriate frame-based Web page.

To complete this next step-by-step, you need access to the following Data files that your instructor will have given you: **lions.gif**, **tigers.gif**, **bears.gif**, and **ohmy.gif**. These files must be stored in the folder where you have been saving your HTML files for this book. Ask your teacher for assistance if necessary.

VOCABULARY
parent document

child document

WARNING

To complete the step-by-step exercises in this lesson, you need to get a copy of the Data files for this lesson from your instructor. These files include **lions.gif**, **tigers.gif**, **bears.gif**, and **ohmy.gif**. You must save these files in the folder where you have been saving your HTML files for this book. Ask your teacher for assistance if necessary.

Step-by-Step 9.1

In this step-by-step, you create a simple HTML frameset. One frame contains an image, and the other frame contains a simple table.

1. Open Notepad, SimpleText, or your favorite text editor.

2. Create a new blank document, if necessary.

3. Enter the HTML text exactly as shown in **Figure 9–1**.

FIGURE 9–1   js-sixteen.html file

```
<html>

<head>
  <title>HTML and JavaScript</title>
</head>

<frameset rows="150,*">
  <frame name="UpperFrame" src="upper1.html">
  <frame name="LowerFrame" src="lower1.html">
</frameset>

</html>
```

4. Save your newly created file as **js-sixteen.html** or **js-sixteen.htm** in the same folder where you saved the files from the previous lessons.

5. Click **File** on the menu bar, and then click **New** to create a new blank document.

6. Enter the HTML text exactly as shown in **Figure 9–2**.

FIGURE 9–2 upper1.html file

```
<html>

<head>
   <title>HTML and JavaScript</title>
</head>

<body>
   <div align="center">
     <img name="UpperImage" src="lions.gif">
   </div>
</body>

</html>
```

7. Save your newly created file as **upper1.html** or **upper1.htm** in the same folder where you saved the files from the previous lessons.

8. Click **File** on the menu bar, and then click **New** to create a new blank document in the text editor.

9. Enter the HTML text exactly as shown in **Figure 9–3**.

FIGURE 9-3   lower1.html file

```
<html>

<head>
   <title>HTML and JavaScript</title>
</head>

<body>
   <div align="center">
     <h2>IMAGE LIST</h2>
     <table>
        <tr><td>1: LIONS.GIF</td></tr>
        <tr><td>2: TIGERS.GIF</td></tr>
        <tr><td>3: BEARS.GIF</td></tr>
        <tr><td>4: OHMY.GIF</td></tr>
     </table>
   </div>
</body>

</html>
```

10. Save your newly created file as **lower1.html** or **lower1.htm** in the same folder where you saved the files from the previous lessons.

11. Start your Web browser, and then open your **js-sixteen.html** or **js-sixteen.htm** file to view the file as a Web page. The Web page on your screen should look like the one shown in **Figure 9–4**.

FIGURE 9–4
Frame-based Web page

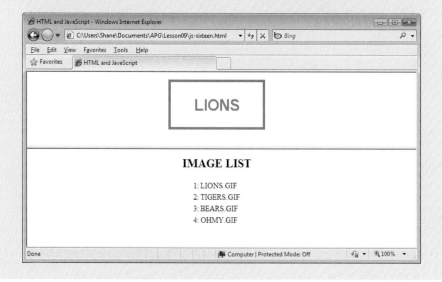

You should be familiar with the HTML code in this step-by-step because it contains nothing that was not previously presented in Lesson 4. But just to make sure that you have a good understanding of how this all works, it is important to review the most important concepts presented in these three HTML files.

The first file defines a frameset as it was initially presented in Lesson 4. This particular frameset contains two horizontal frames named *UpperFrame* and *LowerFrame*. The second file you created, **upper1.html**, loads and displays in the upper frame, and the third file, **lower1.html**, loads in the lower frame.

The second file is also simple, as it does nothing more than display an image that is horizontally centered on the screen. Note that the **name** attribute of this image is UpperImage. The **name** attribute is required in the file so that the image is accessible to JavaScript by name.

The third file defines a simple table that is also horizontally centered on the screen. The table contains four rows, and each row contains the name of an image file. For now, these filenames are nothing more than plain text, but they can be easily converted into hyperlinks. In fact, this is one of the tasks you perform in the next step-by-step.

Adding JavaScript Code to Your Frameset

Now that you have created a frame-based Web page to work with, you can make your frameset functional with JavaScript. The first thing you have to do is add a JavaScript function to the HTML document that is displayed in the lower frame. The purpose of this function is to change the image that is displayed in the upper frame document.

Once you define this function, you can convert the plain text filenames listed in the HTML table to hyperlinks. These links invoke the JavaScript function when the user clicks them in the Web page.

Step-by-Step 9.2

In this step-by-step, you modify the filename of the Web page displayed in the lower frame. You also add a JavaScript function to your lower frame document and create hyperlinks that invoke the new function.

1. Open Notepad, SimpleText, or your favorite text editor if it is not already open.

2. Click **File** on the menu bar, click **Open**, browse to the folder that contains the files for this book, click the **arrow** to display all of the file types, and then open the **js-sixteen.html** or **js-sixteen.htm** file you created in Step-by-Step 9.1.

3. Click **File** on the menu bar, click **Save As**, and then save the HTML file as **js-seventeen.html** or **js-seventeen.htm** in the same folder to preserve the js-sixteen.html file.

4. Change the name of the file to be displayed in the lower frame to **lower2.html**, as shown in this step and in **Figure 9–5**.

```
<frame name="LowerFrame" src="lower2.html">
```

FIGURE 9–5   js-seventeen.html file

```
<html>

<head>
  <title>HTML and JavaScript</title>
</head>

<frameset rows="150,*">
  <frame name="UpperFrame" src="upper1.html">
  <frame name="LowerFrame" src="lower2.html">
</frameset>

</html>
```

5. Save the changes to the **js-seventeen.html** file in the same folder where you saved the files from the previous step-by-step.

6. Click **File** on the menu bar, click **Open**, browse to the folder with your saved files, and then open the **lower1.html** or **lower1.htm** file you created in Step-by-Step 9.1 in your text editor.

7. Click **File** on the menu bar, click **Save As**, and then save the HTML file as **lower2.html** or **lower2.htm** in the same folder to preserve the lower1.html file.

8. Add a JavaScript function called `setImage(index)`, as shown in this step and in bold in **Figure 9–6**.

```
<script>
  function setImage(index)
  {
    if (index == 1)
    {
      parent.UpperFrame.document.UpperImage.
      src = "lions.gif";
    }
    if (index == 2)
    {

      parent.UpperFrame.document.UpperImage.
      src = "tigers.gif";

    }
```

```
                if (index == 3)

                {

                    parent.UpperFrame.document.UpperImage.
                    src = "bears.gif";
                }
                if (index == 4)
                {
              parent.UpperFrame.document.UpperImage.src
              = "ohmy.gif";
            }
            return;
        }
    </script>
```

9. Add <a></a> hyperlink tags to the table defined in the body of the lower2.html file, as shown in bold in this step and in **Figure 9–6**.

```
    <tr><td><a href="javascript:setImage(1)">1:
    LIONS.GIF</a></td></tr>
    <tr><td><a href="javascript:setImage(2)">2:
    TIGERS.GIF</a></td></tr>
    <tr><td><a href="javascript:setImage(3)">3:
    BEARS.GIF</a></td></tr>
    <tr><td><a href="javascript:setImage(4)">4:
    OHMY.GIF</a></td></tr>
```

FIGURE 9–6   lower2.html file

```
<html>
<head>
    <title>HTML and JavaScript</title>
    <script>
        function setImage(index)
        {
            if (index == 1)
            {
                parent.UpperFrame.document.UpperImage.src = "lions.gif";
            }
            if (index == 2)
            {
                parent.UpperFrame.document.UpperImage.src = "tigers.gif";
            }
            if (index == 3)
            {
```

Continued on next page ≫

FIGURE 9-6   lower2.html file

《 *Continued from previous page*

```
        parent.UpperFrame.document.UpperImage.src = "bears.gif";
      }
      if (index == 4)
      {
        parent.UpperFrame.document.UpperImage.src = "ohmy.gif";
      }
      return;
    }
  </script>
</head>

<body>
  <div align="center">
    <h2>IMAGE LIST</h2>
    <table>
      <tr><td><a href="javascript:setImage(1)">1: LIONS.GIF</a></td></tr>
      <tr><td><a href="javascript:setImage(2)">2: TIGERS.GIF</a></td></tr>
      <tr><td><a href="javascript:setImage(3)">3: BEARS.GIF</a></td></tr>
      <tr><td><a href="javascript:setImage(4)">4: OHMY.GIF</a></td></tr>
    </table>
  </div>
</body>

</html>
```

10. Save the changes to the file **lower2.html** or **lower2.htm** in the same folder.

11. Start your Web browser and then open the **js-seventeen.html** or **js-seventeen.htm** file to view the file as a Web page in the browser. The Web page on your screen should look like the one shown in **Figure 9–7**.

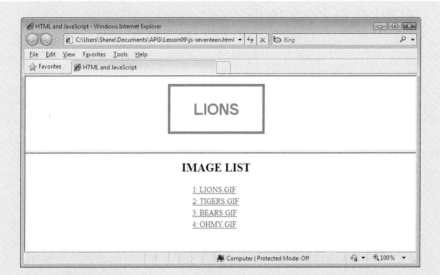

FIGURE 9–7
Web page with functional
hyperlinks

12. Click **LIONS.GIF**, click **TIGERS.GIF**, click **BEARS.GIF**, and then click **OHMY.GIF** to verify that the image in the upper frame changes appropriately when you click the hyperlinks in the lower frame.

13. If the links do not function correctly, review your files for accuracy and try again.

> **WARNING**
>
> If your browser displays the message, "To help protect your security, Internet Explorer has restricted this webpage from running scripts or ActiveX controls that could access your computer. Click here for options." click the message bar, click Allow Blocked Content, and then click Yes in the Security Warning dialog box.

Although this frame-based Web page does not look or behave much differently from the ones you created in Lesson 7, some important new concepts are at work here. Review the JavaScript in detail to make sure you understand it.

First, look at the JavaScript function called *setImage*. All JavaScript function definitions include a *parameter list*, which is a list of data items that the function needs to perform its intended action. All of the JavaScript functions you wrote in the past lessons have empty parameter lists, but this newest function contains one parameter called *index*. This parameter is used by the *setImage* function to determine which graphic file to use as the source for the upper frame image.

Another important concept you should understand is that the *index* parameter in the *setImage* function gets its value from one of the four hyperlinks defined in the lower frame. Notice that all four **href** attributes within the anchor tags contain calls to the same JavaScript function, but the parameter passed to that function is different for each graphic filename. By using the JavaScript *function parameter* to distinguish one hyperlink from another, it is not necessary to define four different functions. A function parameter is simply an object or data element that is accessed by an assigned name within the function. The parameter approach is efficient, especially when there are 10, 20, or 100 different hyperlinks, rather than just four.

One final note of significance is the use of the JavaScript *parent object* in the setImage() function. A **parent** object is a reserved word in JavaScript that refers to the parent frameset. The "Using the Parent/Child Relationship" section in this lesson further explains this relationship.

> **VOCABULARY**
> **parameter list**
> **function parameter**
> **parent object**

Creating a Frame-Based Slide Show

In Lesson 7, you created an electronic slide show that allows the user to change the image displayed on the screen by clicking hyperlinks or buttons. In this lesson, you create a frame-based Web page that performs essentially the same function. You learn how to write JavaScript code that makes this Web page functional. Begin by creating the basic frameset and the frames that it contains.

The HTML document that you use in the upper frame of the page you create in Step-by-Step 9.3 is the same one you used in the two previous step-by-steps (**upper1. html**), but the lower frame contains a new document with two control buttons. Initially, these buttons will not be functional, but you make them work later in the lesson.

Using the Parent/Child Relationship

If you refer back to the JavaScript functions you wrote to manipulate images, you should realize that the functions are defined in the same file as the images they access. However, in Step-by-Step 9.2, the **setImage()** function is defined in the **lower2.html** file, and the image it accesses is defined in the **upper1.html file**.

For a JavaScript function to access an object in a different file, the two files must be linked. In this particular example, the upper1.html and the lower2.html files are both contained within a common parent frameset, and this frameset can be referenced via the JavaScript object called **parent**. Keep in mind also that the frameset file defines two child frames, and these frames were given the names UpperFrame and LowerFrame. The upper frame contains an HTML document, and this document contains an image object called UpperImage (as defined in the upper1.html file in Figure 9–2). Putting all of this information together should help you understand exactly how the src property of the image object is set with the following JavaScript code:

```
parent.upperFrame.document.upperImage.src = "
<filename>";
```

Bear in mind also that image objects are not the only type of object that can be referenced across frames by JavaScript functions. The same technique can be used to access text field objects, drop-down list objects, button objects, and so on.

Step-by-Step 9.3

In this step-by-step, you create another frame-based Web page. The upper frame is the same as the Web page you used in the previous step-by-steps in this lesson, but you create a new HTML file for the lower frame.

1. Open Notepad, SimpleText, or your favorite text editor.

2. Click **File** on the menu bar, click **Open**, browse to the folder with your saved files, and then open the **js-seventeen.html** or **js-seventeen.htm** file you created in Step-by-Step 9.2.

3. Click **File** on the menu bar, click **Save As**, and then save the HTML file as **js-eighteen.html** or **js-eighteen.htm** in the same folder to preserve the js-seventeen.html file.

4. Change the name of the file to be displayed in the lower frame, as shown in this step and in **Figure 9–8**.

```
<frame name="LowerFrame" src="lower3.html">
```

FIGURE 9–8   js-eighteen.html file

```html
<html>

<head>
  <title>HTML and JavaScript</title>
</head>

<frameset rows="150,*">
  <frame name="UpperFrame" src="upper1.html">
  <frame name="LowerFrame" src="lower3.html">
</frameset>

</html>
```

5. Save the changes to the file **js-eighteen.html** or **js-eighteen.htm** in the same folder with the files from the previous lessons.

6. Click **File** on the menu bar, and then click **New** to create a new blank document in the text editor.

7. Enter the HTML text exactly as shown in **Figure 9–9**.

FIGURE 9–9   lower3.html file

```html
<html>

<head>
  <title>HTML and JavaScript</title>
</head>

<body>
  <div align="center">
    <h2>WELCOME</h2>
    <h3>to my</h3>
    <h3>Electronic Slide Show</h3>
    <p>
      <input type="button" value="Prev Image">
      <input type="button" value="Next Image">
    </p>
  </div>
</body>

</html>
```

8. Save your newly created file as **lower3.html** or **lower3.htm** in the same folder as the files for this lesson.

9. Start your Web browser and then open the **js-eighteen.html** or **js-eighteen.htm** file to view the file as a Web page in the browser. Your Web page on your screen should look like **Figure 9–10**.

FIGURE 9–10
Frame-based slide show Web page

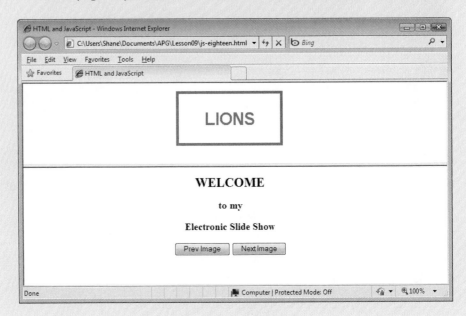

As was the case in Step-by-Step 9.1, the HTML code you just created contains nothing that was not already presented in previous lessons. The primary purpose of Step-by-Step 9.3 is to make sure you feel comfortable working with framesets and frames. The next step-by-step shows you how to make the *Prev Image* and *Next Image* buttons functional by using JavaScript events and functions.

TECHNOLOGY TIMELINE

The Progress of Programming Languages

Now that you have had an introduction to JavaScript, you might be interested in pursuing a career in programming. This is a good time to become a programmer because many advances have been made in programming languages. There is a long history of programming languages, each developed to make the task of programming progressively easier.

Machine language was one of the first ways programmers communicated with computers. Machine-language commands look like binary numbers. For example:

```
01010101
100001011 11101100
01001100
01001100
```

Machine language is a system computers can relate to. However, it's difficult for programmers to learn. Assembly language followed, which uses words as assembly commands that are then turned into machine-specific commands. Here is an example of assembly language:

```
PUSH BP
MOV BP,SP
DEC SP
DEC SP
```

Assembly language is also very difficult to learn, so an entire group of new languages emerged to make programming easier, including BASIC, FORTRAN, Pascal, and COBOL. A sample of Pascal code looks like this:

```
program AddIt;
var
i,  j,  k  :  integer;
begin
i   := 3;
j   := 2;
k  := i  +  j;
```

Pascal begins to look a bit more like what you have been learning in JavaScript. However, JavaScript is more like other, more highly developed languages, including C++, Visual Basic, and Java. Much of what you have learned while discovering JavaScript can be applied to these other languages. In fact, many concepts found in these higher-level languages will be very familiar to you.

Making Your Slide Show Buttons Functional

The primary purpose of the next step-by-step is to show you how to make the slide show buttons functional. Note that there is more than one way to accomplish this objective. In fact, when you are working with framesets, there are always multiple ways in which a particular problem can be solved.

Think back for a moment to the overall design of the frame-based Web page you created in Step-by-Step 9.2. In that example, you created a JavaScript function in the lower frame document that is invoked by hyperlinks in that same document but that accesses an image object in the upper frame document. In the next step-by-step, you take a slightly different approach. To be specific, you create two JavaScript functions in the upper frame document that access the image object in that same document but that are invoked by buttons contained in the lower frame document.

There are not necessarily any advantages or disadvantages to following the former approach, or to implementing JavaScript code using the latter technique. By learning different methods, you understand that you have various options available to you, and you can produce JavaScript solutions in different ways. In real-life programming situations, the method you choose is up to you.

Step-by-Step 9.4

In this step-by-step, you make the buttons of your electronic slide show functional. You accomplish this by modifying the HTML files displayed in the upper and lower frames of your frameset.

1. Open Notepad, SimpleText, or your favorite text editor if it is not already open.

2. Click **File** on the menu bar, click **Open**, browse to the folder with your saved files, and then open the **js-eighteen.html** or **js-eighteen.htm** file you created in Step-by-Step 9.3.

3. Click **File** on the menu bar, click **Save As**, and then save the HTML document as **js-nineteen.html** or **js-nineteen.htm** in the same folder to preserve the js-eighteen.html file.

4. Change the names of the files to be displayed in the upper and lower frames, as shown in bold in this step and in Figure 9-11.
   ```
   <frame name="UpperFrame" src="upper2.html">
   <frame name="LowerFrame" src="lower4.html">
   ```

FIGURE 9-11   js-nineteen.html file

```
<html>

<head>
  <title>HTML and JavaScript</title>
</head>

<frameset rows="150,*">
  <frame name="UpperFrame" src="upper2.html">
  <frame name="LowerFrame" src="lower4.html">
</frameset>

</html>
```

5. Save this modified file as **js-nineteen.html** to the same folder as the other files for this lesson.

6. Click **File** on the menu bar, click **Open**, browse to the folder with your saved files, and then open the **upper1.html** or **upper1.htm** file you created in Step-by-Step 9.1 in the text editor.

7. Click **File** on the menu bar, click **Save As**, and then save the HTML file as **upper2.html** or **upper2.htm** in the same folder to preserve the upper1.html file.

8. Add a `<script></script>` section to the header of your HTML file containing three JavaScript functions called `prevImage()`, `nextImage()`, and `startup()`, as shown in this step and in bold in **Figure 9–12**.

```
<script>
var imgArray = new Array(4);
var index = 0;

function prevImage()
{
  if (index > 0)
  {
    index--;
    document.UpperImage.src = imgArray[index].src;
  }
  return;
}

function nextImage()
{
  if (index < 3)
  {
    index++;
    document.UpperImage.src = imgArray[index].src;
  }
  return;
}

function startup()
{
  imgArray[0] = new Image;
  imgArray[0].src = "lions.gif";
  imgArray[1] = new Image;
  imgArray[1].src = "tigers.gif";
  imgArray[2] = new Image;
  imgArray[2].src = "bears.gif";
  imgArray[3] = new Image;
  imgArray[3].src = "ohmy.gif";
  return;
}
</script>
```

9. Add an onLoad event to the <body> tag of your HTML file, as shown in bold in this step and in **Figure 9–12**.

```
<body onLoad="startup()">
```

FIGURE 9–12   upper2.html file

```
<html>

<head>
<title>HTML and JavaScript</title>
<script>
var imgArray = new Array(4);
var index = 0;

function prevImage()
{
  if (index > 0)
  {
    index--;
    document.UpperImage.src = imgArray[index].src;
  }
  return;
}

function nextImage()
{
  if (index < 3)
  {
    index++;
    document.UpperImage.src = imgArray[index].src;
  }
  return;
}

function startup()
{
  imgArray[0] = new Image;
  imgArray[0].src = "lions.gif";
  imgArray[1] = new Image;
  imgArray[1].src = "tigers.gif";
```

Continued on next page 》

FIGURE 9–12   upper2.html file

《 *Continued from previous page*

```
    imgArray[2] = new Image;
    imgArray[2].src = "bears.gif";
    imgArray[3] = new Image;
    imgArray[3].src = "ohmy.gif";
    return;
}
</script>
</head>

<body onLoad="startup()">
  <div align="center">
    <img name="UpperImage" src="lions.gif">
  </div>
</body>

</html>
```

10. Save the changes to the file **upper2.html** or **upper2.htm** to the same folder.

11. Click **File** on the menu bar, click **Open**, browse to the folder with your saved files, and then open the **lower3.html** or **lower3.htm** file you created in Step-by-Step 9.3 in the text editor.

12. Click **File** on the menu bar, click **Save As**, and then save the HTML file as **lower4.html** or **lower4.htm** in the same folder to preserve the lower3.html file.

13. Add onClick events to the two <input> tags, as shown in bold in this step and in **Figure 9–13**.

```
<input type="button" value="Prev Image"
onClick="parent.UpperFrame.prevImage()">
<input type="button" value="Next Image"
onClick="parent.UpperFrame.nextImage()">
```

FIGURE 9–13   lower4.html file

```
<html>

<head>
  <title>HTML and JavaScript</title>
</head>

<body>
  <div align="center">
    <h2>WELCOME</h2>
    <h3>to my</h3>
    <h3>Electronic Slide Show</h3>
    <p>
      <input type="button" value="Prev Image"
      onClick="parent.UpperFrame.prevImage()">
      <input type="button" value="Next Image"
      onClick="parent.UpperFrame.nextImage()">
    </p>
  </div>
</body>

</html>
```

⊥— WARNING

If your browser displays the message, "To help protect your security, Internet Explorer has restricted this webpage from running scripts or ActiveX controls that could access your computer. Click here for options." click the message bar, click Allow Blocked Content, and then click Yes in the Security Warning dialog box.

14. Save the changes to the file **lower4.html** or **lower4.htm** to the same folder.

15. Start your Web browser, and then open the **js-nineteen.html** or **js-nineteen.htm** file to view it as a Web page in the browser. The resulting Web page should look like **Figure 9–14**.

16. Click the **Next Image button** three times, click the **Prev Image button** three times, click the **Next Image button**, and then click the **Prev Image button** to verify that the image in the upper frame changes appropriately when you click the buttons in the lower frame. (Please note that the images do not cycle back through the loop.)

FIGURE 9–14
Functional frame-based slide show

Begin your analysis of the previous step-by-step activity by taking a closer look at the new JavaScript code you added to the upper frame document.

First, you defined a four-element image array to contain the four graphics that make up the slide show. You also added two new JavaScript functions called *prevImage()* and *nextImage()* that change the image that is currently displayed in the upper frame and a *startup()* function to initialize the image array. This code is very similar to the JavaScript code you created in Lesson 7. You can refer to Lesson 7 (js-eight.html) if you need to review the details of defining, initializing, and accessing JavaScript arrays.

Next, you added an *onClick* event to each of the two buttons that were defined in the lower frame document. You should note that these *onClick* events will cause the Web browser to invoke the appropriate function in the upper frame document when its corresponding button is clicked. Once again, these JavaScript functions make use of the JavaScript **parent** object to access the parent frameset and the *UpperFrame* frame name to access the HTML document in the upper frame.

Creating a Top-Level JavaScript Function

As you learned in the previous step-by-steps, it is easy for one HTML document to access an object in another document if the two documents are contained within a common frameset. However, you should recognize that this process can get a little more complex if you are working within a Web page that contains nested framesets. To review nested framesets, refer back to frameset-2.html in Lesson 4.

If you have a frameset nested within a second frameset that is nested within a third frameset and so on, you can access any frame you want by developing the proper sequence of JavaScript **parent** objects. In other words, if an HTML document wants to access its parent frameset, it can do so by using the parent object. If that page needs to access the parent frameset of its own parent, it can use two instances of the JavaScript parent object. To access the frameset three levels up requires the use of three parent objects, and so forth. For example:

```
onClick="parent.parent.parent.someFrame.someFunction()"
```

The problem with this approach is that the JavaScript code gets long, confusing, and difficult to maintain if you make numerous references to the parent object. In many cases, you might find it much more convenient to place many JavaScript function definitions in the top-level frameset file, and then every HTML document—no matter how deeply it is nested within the Web page framework—can easily access these functions by using the JavaScript *top object*. The JavaScript keyword **top** will always refer to the highest-level frameset.

▶ **VOCABULARY**
top object

ETHICS IN TECHNOLOGY

You should recognize that JavaScript is a valuable tool. However, like any tool in the wrong hands, it can be used in a destructive manner. Unfortunately, many hackers have used JavaScript to create viruses that infect computers and cause considerable damage to computer data. Not only is this activity extremely illegal, it's also unethical and harmful to the important work people do on their computers. Think about it. What would you do if you knew that a friend of yours was writing JavaScript viruses and distributing them online?

Step-by-Step 9.5

In this step-by-step, you create a top-level JavaScript function and access that function from within lower-level documents. First, you convert the image object in the upper frame into a hyperlink that invokes the function. Then, you add a new button to the lower frame document that will also call the top-level function.

1. Open Notepad, SimpleText, or your favorite text editor if it is not already open.

2. Click **File** on the menu bar, click **Open**, browse to the folder with your saved files, and then open the file **js-nineteen.html** or **js-nineteen.htm** you created in Step-by-Step 9.4 in the text editor.

3. Click **File** on the menu bar, click **Save As**, and then save the file as **js-twenty.html** or **js-twenty.htm** to preserve the js-nineteen.html file.

4. Add a <script></script> section to the header of the file, as shown in bold in this step and in **Figure 9–15**.

```
<script>
function message()
{
  alert("We're off to see the wizard!");
  return;
}
</script>
```

5. Change the names of the HTML files to be displayed in the upper and lower frames, as shown in bold in this step and in Figure 9-15.

```
<frame name="UpperFrame" src="upper3.html">
<frame name="LowerFrame" src="lower5.html">
```

FIGURE 9–15   js-twenty.html file

```html
<html>

<head>
<title>HTML and JavaScript</title>
<script>
function message()
{
  alert("We're off to see the wizard!");
  return;
}
</script>
</head>

<frameset rows="150,*">
  <frame name="UpperFrame" src="upper3.html">
  <frame name="LowerFrame" src="lower5.html">
</frameset>

</html>
```

6. Save the changes to the **js-twenty.html** or **js-twenty.htm** file.

7. Click **File** on the menu bar, click **Open**, browse to the folder with your saved files, and then open the **upper2.html** or **upper2.htm** file you created in Step-by-Step 9.4 in the text editor.

8. Click **File** on the menu bar, click **Save As**, and then save the HTML file as **upper3.html** or **upper3.htm** in the same folder to preserve the upper2.html file.

9. Add a <a></a> hyperlink to the body of your HTML file, as shown in bold in this step and in Figure 9-16.

```html
<body onLoad="startup()">
  <div align="center">
    <a href="javascript:top.message()">
      <img name="UpperImage" src="lions.gif">
    </a>
  </div>
</body>
```

FIGURE 9–16   upper3.html file

```html
<html>

<head>
<title>HTML and JavaScript</title>
<script>
var imgArray = new Array(4);
var index = 0;

function prevImage()
{
  if (index > 0)
  {
    index--;
    document.UpperImage.src = imgArray[index].src;
  }
  return;
}

function nextImage()
{
  if (index < 3)
  {
    index++;
    document.UpperImage.src = imgArray[index].src;
  }
  return;
}

function startup()
{
  imgArray[0] = new Image;
  imgArray[0].src = "lions.gif";
  imgArray[1] = new Image;
  imgArray[1].src = "tigers.gif";
  imgArray[2] = new Image;
  imgArray[2].src = "bears.gif";
  imgArray[3] = new Image;
  imgArray[3].src = "ohmy.gif";
 return;
}
</script>
</head>
```

Continued on next page »

FIGURE 9–16   upper3.html file

《 *Continued from previous page*

```
<body onLoad="startup()">
  <div align="center">
    <a href="javascript:top.message()">
      <img name="UpperImage" src="lions.gif">
    </a>
  </div>
</body>

</html>
```

10. Save the changes to the file **upper3.html** or **upper3.htm** in the same folder as the other files for this lesson.

11. Click **File** on the menu bar, click **Open**, browse to the folder with your saved files, and then open the **lower4.html** or **lower4.htm** file you created in Step-by-Step 9.4 in the text editor.

12. Click **File** on the menu bar, click **Save As**, and then save the HTML file as **lower5.html** or **lower5.htm** in the same folder to preserve the lower4.html file.

13. Add a new button to the body of the HTML file, as shown in bold in this step and in **Figure 9–17**.

```
<body>
  <div align="center">
    <h2>WELCOME</h2>
    <h3>to my</h3>
    <h3>Electronic Slide Show</h3>
    <p>
      <input type="button" value="Prev Image"
       onClick="parent.UpperFrame.prevImage()">
      <input type="button" value="Show Message"
       onClick="top.message()">
      <input type="button" value="Next Image"
       onClick="parent.UpperFrame.nextImage()">
    </p>
  </div>
</body>
```

FIGURE 9–17   lower5.html file

```html
<html>

<head>
  <title>HTML and JavaScript</title>
</head>

<body>
  <div align="center">
    <h2>WELCOME</h2>
    <h3>to my</h3>
    <h3>Electronic Slide Show</h3>
    <p>
      <input type="button" value="Prev Image"
       onClick="parent.UpperFrame.prevImage()">
      <input type="button" value="Show Message" onClick="top.message()">
      <input type="button" value="Next Image"
       onClick="parent.UpperFrame.nextImage()">
    </p>
  </div>
</body>

</html>
```

14. Save the changes to the file **lower5.html** or **lower5.htm** to the same folder as the other files for this lesson.

15. Start your Web browser and open the **js-twenty.html** or **js-twenty.htm** file to view it as a Web page in the browser. The resulting Web page should look like the Web page shown in **Figure 9–18**.

FIGURE 9–18
Frame-based Web page with
top-level JavaScript function

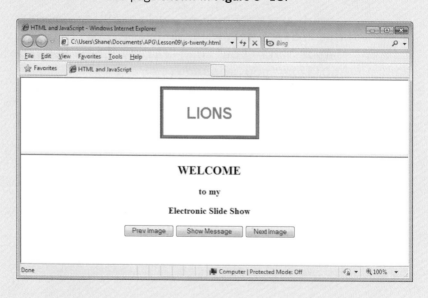

16. Click the image in the upper frame; the "We're off to see the wizard!" message box opens.

17. Click **OK** to close the message box, and then click the **Show Message button** in the lower frame to display the message again, as shown in **Figure 9–19**.

FIGURE 9–19
Web page after clicking the Show Message button

WARNING

If your browser displays the message, "To help protect your security, Internet Explorer has restricted this webpage from running scripts or ActiveX controls that could access your computer. Click here for options." click the message bar, click Allow Blocked Content, and then click Yes in the Security Warning dialog box.

It is helpful to examine the JavaScript function called *message()* that you added to the js-twenty.html file. There is nothing special about the function itself, which does nothing more than invoke the JavaScript *alert()* method to display its message. What is unusual about this function, however, is that it is contained in a frameset file rather than a standard HTML document. And because this particular frameset file happens to define the top-level frameset, this function becomes accessible to any lower-level document by using the JavaScript **top** object.

Further examine the code to review what you learned in the previous step-by-step. You converted the image in the upper frame document to a hyperlink which illustrates how a top-level function can be accessed from an image hyperlink. You added a new button to the lower frame document to illustrate that the same top-level function can be invoked by clicking a button and that this button can reside in a different HTML document than the image hyperlink.

The final concept you learned was that this top-level function, and any other JavaScript function for that matter, can be called from any HTML hyperlink (text or image) or by any JavaScript event. You can refer back to Lesson 7 if you need to review the names and usage of JavaScript events.

SUMMARY

In this lesson, you learned:

- How to create a JavaScript function with a parameter list.
- How to create JavaScript-enabled hyperlinks that affect frames.
- How to create JavaScript-enabled buttons that affect frames.
- How to create top-level JavaScript functions.

■ VOCABULARY REVIEW

Define the following terms:

child document   parameter list   parent object
function parameter   parent document   top object

■ REVIEW QUESTIONS

TRUE / FALSE

Circle T if the statement is true or F if the statement is false.

T   F   **1.**   Any Web page that contains a frameset is always composed of multiple files.

T   F   **2.**   The frameset file is known as the child document, and each frame file is known as a parent document.

T   F   **3.**   A parameter list is always part of a JavaScript function definition, even if the list is empty.

T   F   **4.**   A JavaScript function can be called with a JavaScript event, but not from a hyperlink.

T   F   **5.**   HTML hyperlinks defined in one frame can access JavaScript functions defined in a different frame.

T   F   **6.**   HTML buttons defined in one frame can access JavaScript functions defined in a different frame.

T   F   **7.**   JavaScript functions defined in one frame cannot access image objects defined in another frame.

T   F   **8.**   The JavaScript **parent** object can only be referenced once per statement.

T   F   **9.**   JavaScript functions can only be defined in frame files, not in frameset files.

T   F   **10.**   The JavaScript **top** object can be accessed by any frame file, regardless of how deeply nested the frame might be.

FILL IN THE BLANK

Complete the following sentences by writing the correct word or words in the blanks provided.

1. The frameset file is also known as a(n) _____ document.

2. The frame files contained within a frameset are known as _____ documents.

3. A(n) _____ list is a list of data items that a JavaScript function needs to perform its intended action.

4. The JavaScript _____ object can be used to access a frame's defining frameset file.

5. The _____ attribute of an HTML <a> tag can invoke a JavaScript function.

6. To be accessible by a JavaScript function, the HTML <img> tag must include a(n) _____ attribute.

7. The _____ event of an HTML button can be used to call a JavaScript function.

8. JavaScript _____ can be called from any HTML hyperlink or JavaScript event.

9. The JavaScript _____ object can be used to access the highest-level frameset.

10. Top-level JavaScript functions are defined in _____ files.

WRITTEN QUESTIONS

Write a short answer to each of the following questions:

1. What is the purpose of the parent document in a frameset?

2. How do you define and identify a child document in a frameset file?

3. What is the difference between the JavaScript **parent** object and the JavaScript **top** object?

4. Describe the usage of the JavaScript *onClick* event.

5. How do you define a top-level JavaScript function?

◼ PROJECTS

PROJECT 9–1: FROM 4 TO 6

Review the js-seventeen.html file you created for Step-by-Step 9.2. Demonstrate that you have mastered the concepts presented in this lesson by adding two more images to your image set. This means that you need to create or download two image files to accompany the existing four image files. Then, you need to modify the HTML code in the lower frame to display a six-row table in which rows five and six display the names of the two new image files.

Save your work as **Project 9-1.html** or **Project 9-1.htm**.

PROJECT 9–2: WEB PROJECT

Modify the frame-based Web page you created in Project 9-1 so that it is composed of three frames instead of two. Your new Web page should display a title in the upper frame, the images in the lower frame, and the hyperlinks in a navigation frame on the left. Make sure that you make the appropriate adjustments in the frameset file and in the HTML/JavaScript code in the child frame files.

Save your work as **Project 9-2.html** or **Project 9-2.htm**.

PROJECT 9–3: TEAMWORK PROJECT

Working within a team of three or four students, modify the frame-based Web page you created in Project 9-2 so that all of the JavaScript functions are defined in the parent frameset file. Also modify all of the hyperlinks and JavaScript events to use the **top** object rather than the **parent** object.

Save your work as **Project 9-3.html** or **Project 9-3.htm**.

■ CRITICAL THINKING

ACTIVITY 9–1: REFACTORING CODE

Professional programmers are often required to change the way that they have implemented their code. This is known as "refactoring" the code. **Code refactoring** is the process of changing a computer program's internal structure without modifying its external *functional* behavior or existing functionality to improve internal *quality attributes* of the software. In Step-by-Step 9.4, you were asked to create a Web page in which the HTML buttons in the lower frame access JavaScript functions defined in the upper frame. Refactor your code so that the JavaScript functions are defined in the lower frame, but the resulting Web page still functions the same as it did before you made the changes.

Save your work as **Activity 9-1.html** or **Activity 9-1.htm**.

ACTIVITY 9–2: REFACTOR AGAIN

Suppose that your supervisor at GreatApplications, Inc., wants you to modify (again) the HTML/JavaScript code you created for the previous activity (Activity 9-1). Now, he wants you to refactor your code so that all of the JavaScript functions are defined in the top-level frameset file. Make the appropriate changes and ensure that your resulting Web page still functions correctly.

Save your work as **Activity 9-2.html** or **Activity 9-2.htm**.

■ CAPSTONE SIMULATION

Think back to the electronic zoo that was described in the Teamwork Project of Lesson 6. GreatApplications, Inc., would now like you to create an electronic zoo that makes use of HTML frames and JavaScript. Your new Web page should display a navigation bar on the left containing a list of the animals in your e-Zoo. The right frame will display an appropriate title and a picture of whatever animal the user selects from your list. When the user clicks an animal hyperlink on the left, a JavaScript function will be invoked to change the image displayed on the right. Your completed Web page should look like the one shown in Figure 9-20.

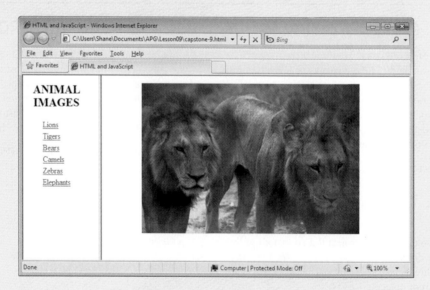

FIGURE 9–20   An electronic zoo with frames and JavaScript

Project Requirements:

- Your navigation bar (left side) should occupy about 20% of the screen width.

- Your navigation bar should contain an appropriate title and at least six animal hyperlinks.

- Your main page (right side) should display a picture of the currently selected animal.

- Neither your navigation bar nor your main Web page should contain a JavaScript function definition. Your JavaScript function should be defined in the parent (frameset) page.

- Use the JavaScript top object to access your JavaScript function.

- Save your work as **capstone-9.html** or **capstone-9.htm**.

LESSON 10

Using JavaScript with Styles

■ OBJECTIVES

Upon completion of this lesson, you should be able to:

- Define a simple frame-based style viewer.

- Make your style viewer functional.

- Define a simple frame-based document viewer.

- Make your document viewer functional.

- Create a dynamic style class viewer.

In Lesson 5, you learned how to create styles, cascading styles, Cascading Style Sheets (CSS), and style classes. In this lesson, you review some of these concepts and extend your knowledge by learning how to affect styles on a Web page dynamically with JavaScript. The programming techniques you use in this lesson are similar to those you use to alter images on a Web page. But in this lesson, you are not changing images; rather, you are changing the style components of an HTML document.

■ VOCABULARY

element

getElementById()

getElementsByTagName()

id

location

render

style

style viewer

Defining a Style Viewer

The HTML *style* attribute can be applied to virtually any HTML tag to describe how you want the Web browser to display that portion of the Web page. Although styles are by no means limited to text, applying a style to an HTML tag is one of the most common ways in which styles are applied. Whenever the browser displays text on the screen, there are always many style attributes that must be taken into account because they affect the appearance of the text. Suppose, for example, that you create a simple HTML document to display the phrase "Hello World Wide Web!" Before the browser can render this phrase, it must first determine the current font family, font size, font color, and other attributes. The term *render* simply means to display with the proper attributes applied.

Before you can write JavaScript code that affects the style of a Web page, you must first identify the HTML element that must be modified. An *element* in style terminology is just an HTML tag, and once you have identified the element you need to modify, you must make it accessible to JavaScript by assigning it an identifying name by means of the *id* attribute. This is basically the same as defining a variable in JavaScript code. An element's *id* functions much the same as a tag's *name* attribute that you used in previous lessons.

Step-by-Step 10.1

In this step-by-step, you create a simple HTML frameset. The left frame contains two drop-down list components to allow the user to select a foreground (text) color and a background (cell) color. It also contains a button for the user to click to apply the selected style to the style viewer defined in the right frame.

1. Open Notepad, SimpleText, or your favorite text editor.

2. Create a new blank document, if necessary.

3. Enter the HTML text exactly as shown in **Figure 10–1**.

FIGURE 10–1   js-twentyone.html file

```
<html>

<head>
<title>HTML and JavaScript</title>
</head>

<frameset cols="20%,*">
   <frame name="LeftFrame" src="left1.html">
   <frame name="RightFrame" src="right1.html">
</frameset>

</html>
```

4. Save your newly created file as **js-twentyone.html** or **js-twentyone.htm** in the same folder you saved the files from the previous lessons.

5. Click **File** on the menu bar, and then click **New** to create a new blank document.

6. Enter the HTML text exactly as shown in **Figure 10–2**.

FIGURE 10–2   left1.html file

```
<html>

<head>
<title>HTML and JavaScript</title>
</head>

<body bgcolor="#EFEFEF">
  <form name="StyleForm">
    <table align="center">
      <tr>
        <td align="center" height="40" valign="top">
          <b>STYLES</b>
        </td>
      </tr>
      <tr>
        <td>
          <p>
            <font size="2">Text Color:</font><br>
            <select name="TextColor">
              <option value="">- select -</option>
              <option value="black">Black</option>
              <option value="red">Red</option>
              <option value="green">Green</option>
              <option value="blue">Blue</option>
              <option value="white">White</option>
            </select>
          </p>
          <p>
            <font size="2">Cell Color:</font><br>
            <select name="CellColor">
              <option value="">- select -</option>
              <option value="black">Black</option>
              <option value="red">Red</option>
              <option value="green">Green</option>
              <option value="blue">Blue</option>
```

Continued on next page 》

FIGURE 10–2   left1.html file

《 *Continued from previous page*

```
                    <option value="white">White</option>
                </select>
            </p>
            <p>
                <input type="button" value="Apply Style">
            </p>
        </td>
    </tr>
    </table>
  </form>
</body>

</html>
```

7. Save your newly created file as **left1.html** or **left1.htm** in the same folder you saved the files from the previous lessons.

8. Click **File** on the menu bar, and then click **New** to create a new blank document in the text editor.

9. Enter the HTML text exactly as shown in **Figure 10–3**.

FIGURE 10–3   right1.html file

```
<html>

<head>
<title>HTML and JavaScript</title>
</head>

<body>
  <table align="center" border="1" bordercolor="black">
    <tr>
      <td align="center">
        <font size="3"><b>STYLE VIEWER</b></font>
      </td>
    </tr>
    <tr>
      <td align="center" height="100" width="400" style="background-
      color:white">
```

Continued on next page 》

FIGURE 10–3   right1.html file

《 *Continued from previous page*

```
    <div style="color:black">
       <font size="5">Hello World Wide Web!</font>
    <div>
      </td>
    </tr>
  </table>
</body>

</html>
```

10. Save your newly created file as **right1.html** or **right1.htm** in the same folder you saved the files from the previous lessons.

11. Start your Web browser and then open your **js-twentyone.html** or **js-twentyone.htm** file to view the file as a Web page. The Web page on your screen should look like the one shown in **Figure 10–4**.

FIGURE 10–4
Frame-based style viewer

As you can see, all of the elements in this frame-based Web page have been presented in previous lessons. You did not need to learn anything new to create this page. Nevertheless, take a few moments to identify those aspects of this Web page that are most critical before you move on to Step-by-Step 10.2.

The first file, **js-twentyone.html**, defines a simple frameset. This particular frameset contains two vertical frames named *LeftFrame* and *RightFrame*. The second file you created, **left1.html**, loads and displays in the left frame, and the third file, **right1.html**, is presented to the user in the right frame. Collectively, these pages define a *style viewer*, which is a simple tool that allows users to specify a style, apply the style, and then view the results.

▶ **VOCABULARY**
style viewer

The second file, **left1.html**, defines two drop-down selection controls that determine the color of the text in the style viewer and the background color of the table cell in which the text is displayed. Notice that the names of these two controls are *TextColor* and *CellColor*, respectively. This HTML file also includes a button labeled *Apply Style* that currently performs no action. This is addressed in Step-by-Step 10.2.

The third file, **right1.html**, defines a simple table that functions as a style viewer. The phrase displayed in the lower table cell is *Hello World Wide Web!* Notice that the **style** attribute of the table cell initially sets the background color to white. Likewise, the **style** attribute of the `<div>` tag that encapsulates the phrase sets the text color to black. These are the two style definitions that are modified in the next step-by-step to make the style viewer functional.

Making Your Style Viewer Functional

Whenever you add JavaScript functions to a frame-based Web page, you must decide in which file the JavaScript code should reside. This is always a matter of personal preference, but there are a few guidelines that help you keep your code as simple as possible. First, if you have a JavaScript event that occurs in one frame and the effect of the event is only seen within the same frame, then your JavaScript code should reside in the same frame file. This often eliminates the need to access the JavaScript objects **parent** and **top**. It should also eliminate the need to reference frame names such as *LeftFrame* and *RightFrame*.

However, if a JavaScript event occurs in one frame and affects an object or element in a different frame, then the placement of the JavaScript code is not so obvious. In many cases, the code can be kept to its simplest form if it is defined in the top-level frameset file. This is especially true if you are working with nested frames. Therefore, this is the convention used for the remainder of this lesson.

As was mentioned previously in this lesson, if you want to modify the style of a particular HTML element, it is necessary to assign an id to the element. This is done by adding an **id** attribute to the appropriate HTML tag. However, there is a corresponding JavaScript method called ***getElementById()*** that must be invoked for your JavaScript code to access it by id. This method accepts a single parameter that is, predictably, the id of the HTML element you want to access. The following step-by-step illustrates this principle as you add a top-level JavaScript function to make your simple style viewer functional.

▶ **VOCABULARY**
getElementById()

Step-by-Step 10.2

In this step-by-step, you modify all three files of your style viewer to make the *Apply Style* button functional. You add a top-level JavaScript function to your frameset file and make a few minor changes to the left and right frame files.

1. Open Notepad, SimpleText, or your favorite text editor if it is not already open.

2. Click **File** on the menu bar, click **Open**, browse to the folder that contains the files for this book, click the **arrow** to display all of the file types, and then open the **js-twentyone.html** or **js-twentyone.htm** file you created in Step-by-Step 10.1.

3. Click **File** on the menu bar, click **Save As**, and then save the HTML file as **js-twentytwo.html** or **js-twentytwo.htm** in the same folder to preserve the js-twentyone.html file.

4. Add a `<script></script>` section to the header of your frameset file, as shown in bold in this step and in **Figure 10–5**.

```
<script>
function apply_style()
{
  var textColor =
    LeftFrame.document.StyleForm.TextColor.
    value;
  var cellColor =
    LeftFrame.document.StyleForm.CellColor.
    value;
  var textElement =
    RightFrame.document.getElementById
    ("MessageText");
  var cellElement =
    RightFrame.document.getElementById
    ("MessageCell");
  textElement.style.color = textColor;
  cellElement.style.backgroundColor =
    cellColor;
  return;
}
</script>
```

5. Change the name of the files to be displayed in the left and right frames, as shown in bold in this step and in **Figure 10–5**.

```
<frame name="LeftFrame" src="left2.html">
<frame name="RightFrame" src="right2.html">
```

FIGURE 10–5 js-twentytwo.html file

```
<html>

<head>
<title>HTML and JavaScript</title>
<script>
function apply_style()
{
  var textColor = LeftFrame.document.StyleForm.TextColor.value;
  var cellColor = LeftFrame.document.StyleForm.CellColor.value;
  var textElement = RightFrame.document.getElementById("MessageText");
  var cellElement = RightFrame.document.getElementById("MessageCell");
  textElement.style.color = textColor;
```

Continued on next page 》

FIGURE 10–5   js-twentytwo.html file

« *Continued from previous page*

```
    cellElement.style.backgroundColor = cellColor;
    return;
}
</script>
</head>

<frameset cols="20%,*">
    <frame name="LeftFrame" src="left2.html">
    <frame name="RightFrame" src="right2.html">
</frameset>

</html>
```

6. Save the changes to the **js-twentytwo.html** file in the same folder you saved the files from the previous step-by-step.

7. Click **File** on the menu bar, click **Open**, browse to the folder with your saved files, and then open the **left1.html** or **left1.htm** file you created in Step-by-Step 10.1 in your text editor.

8. Click **File** on the menu bar, click **Save As**, and then save the HTML file as **left2.html** or **left2.htm** in the same folder to preserve the left1.html file.

9. Add a JavaScript *onClick* event to the Apply Style button, as shown in bold in this step and in **Figure 10–6**.

```
<input type="button" value="Apply Style"
onClick="top.apply_style()">
```

FIGURE 10–6   left2.html file

```
<html>

<head>
<title>HTML and JavaScript</title>
</head>

<body bgcolor="#EFEFEF">
    <form name="StyleForm">
        <table align="center">
            <tr>
                <td align="center" height="40" valign="top">
                    <b>STYLES</b>
```

Continued on next page »

FIGURE 10–6   left2.html file

《 *Continued from previous page*

```
              </td>
         </tr>
         <tr>
           <td>
             <p>
               <font size="2">Text Color:</font><br>
               <select name="TextColor">
                 <option value="">- select -</option>
                 <option value="black">Black</option>
                 <option value="red">Red</option>
                 <option value="green">Green</option>
                 <option value="blue">Blue</option>
                 <option value="white">White</option>
               </select>
             </p>
             <p>
               <font size="2">Cell Color:</font><br>
               <select name="CellColor">
                 <option value="">- select -</option>
                 <option value="black">Black</option>
                 <option value="red">Red</option>
                 <option value="green">Green</option>
                 <option value="blue">Blue</option>
                 <option value="white">White</option>
               </select>
             </p>
             <p>
               <input type="button" value="Apply Style"
               onClick="top.apply_style()">
             </p>
           </td>
         </tr>
       </table>
     </form>
  </body>

</html>
```

10. Save the changes to the file **left2.html** or **left2.htm** in the same folder.

11. Click **File** on the menu bar, click **Open**, browse to the folder with your saved files, and then open the **right1.html** or **right1.htm** file you created in Step-by-Step 10.1.

12. Click **File** on the menu bar, click **Save As**, and then save the HTML file as **right2.html** or **right2.htm** in the same folder to preserve the right1.html file.

13. Add **id** attributes to the `<td>` and `<div>` tags, as shown in bold in this step and in **Figure 10–7**.

```
<td id="MessageCell" align="center"
height="100" width="400"
 style="background-color:white">
  <div id="MessageText" style="color:black">
    <font size="5">Hello World Wide Web!</font>
  <div>
</td>
```

FIGURE 10–7   right2.html file

```
<html>

<head>
<title>HTML and JavaScript</title>
</head>

<body>
  <table align="center" border="1" bordercolor="black">
    <tr>
      <td align="center">
        <font size="3"><b>STYLE VIEWER</b></font>
      </td>
    </tr>
    <tr>
      <td id="MessageCell" align="center" height="100" width="400"
       style="background-color:white">
        <div id="MessageText" style="color:black">
          <font size="5">Hello World Wide Web!</font>
        <div>
      </td>
    </tr>
  </table>
</body>

</html>
```

14. Save the changes to the file **right2.html** or **right2.htm** in the same folder.

15. Start your Web browser and then open the **js-twentytwo.html** or **js-twentytwo.htm** file to view the file as a Web page in the browser. The Web page on your screen should look like the one shown in **Figure 10–8**.

FIGURE 10–8
Functional style viewer—default state

16. Click the **Text Color arrow** in the left pane, click **White** in the list, click the **Cell Color arrow**, click **Blue** in the list, and then click the **Apply Style button**. The Web page on your screen should look like the one shown in **Figure 10–9**.

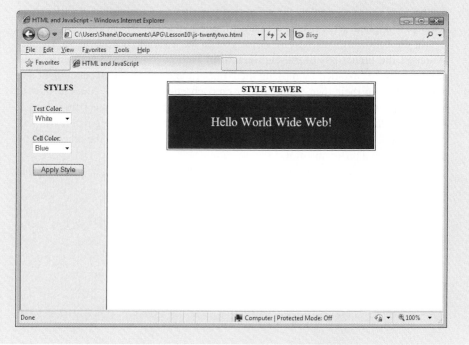

FIGURE 10–9
Functional style viewer—style applied

Obviously, the changes you made to the left and right frame files are very small, but they are necessary to support the top-level JavaScript function you added to the frameset file. The *onClick* event you added to the left frame invokes the function, and the **id** attributes you added to the right frame allow the function to access the **style** object of the appropriate HTML elements.

The most significant addition to the style viewer Web page is, of course, the JavaScript function itself, and it is important for you to understand what it does. First, it retrieves the text and cell color values that were selected by the user in the left frame. Next, it uses the *getElementById()* method to obtain references to two HTML elements. Specifically, it identifies the text string encapsulated by the `<div>` tag and the table cell defined by one of the `<td>` tags. And, finally, it uses these two references to set the appropriate style attributes of these elements. The end result is that the user can now select and apply different foreground and background colors to an active Web page.

Defining a Frame-Based Document Viewer

Consider for a moment the **eighteen.html** file you created at the end of Lesson 3. This HTML document contains hyperlinks near the top of the Web page that, when clicked, allow the user to jump to a specific location in the document. These locations correspond to the H2-level headers that are located throughout the document. In addition, this file contains a cascading style definition that causes all of the `<H2>` headers in the document to be displayed in a blue font rather than the default black color.

The hyperlinks and the cascading style definition in this Web page provide some useful functionality and visual organization. However, the design of the page contains some limitations. Suppose, for example, that you click one of the hyperlinks at the top of the page, and then you would like to click another link. The hyperlinks might no longer be displayed on the screen, so you cannot click them without returning to the top of the document first. Also, it might be nice to have the active H2 header highlighted in some way to distinguish it from the other H2 headers. But the cascading style definition affects all H2 headers in the same way, so they are all displayed in the same font at the same size with the same color. No distinguishing attribute is applied to the header you are currently viewing.

In the following two step-by-steps, you create a simple document viewer that addresses the limitations of the **eighteen.html** Web page design. The limitation of the hyperlinks is avoided by moving them out of the original HTML document and placing them in their own frame. This approach ensures that the links to the H2 headers are always accessible regardless of which document section is being viewed. In addition, the header of the active section is highlighted to distinguish it from all other headers. This is done by making the header a little larger than the others and by displaying it in a different color.

The first step in this process is to define a frame-based Web page, which is what you do in the following step-by-step activity.

TECHNOLOGY TIMELINE

Document Viewers

Many software publishing companies have developed and distributed document viewers over the past few decades. One good example of this is *Adobe Reader*, which has been available as a standalone and browser-based PDF document viewer for many years. This document viewer is much more sophisticated than the simple HTML/JavaScript viewer you create in this lesson. However, it does provide a very similar design. It displays a visual representation of a PDF document on the right side of your screen and a page navigation view of the document on the left side. When the user clicks a hyperlink on the left, the document on the right repositions to display the section of the document that corresponds to the link. These links are defined by the person who created the PDF document and, in most cases, represent a page outline or table of contents for the document. This same behavior is mimicked by your simple document viewer.

Step-by-Step 10.3

In this step-by-step, you create another frame-based Web page. The left frame contains an unordered list of section headers that correspond to H2 headers in the document displayed in the right frame. This document is very similar to the eighteen.html file you created in Lesson 3.

1. Open Notepad, SimpleText, or your favorite text editor, if it is not already open.

2. Click **File** on the menu bar, and then click **New** to create a new blank document in the text editor.

3. Enter the HTML text exactly as shown in **Figure 10–10**.

FIGURE 10–10   js-twentythree.html file

```
<html>

<head>
<title>HTML and JavaScript</title>
</head>

<frameset cols="20%,*">
  <frame name="LeftFrame" src="left3.html">
  <frame name="RightFrame" src="right3.html">
</frameset>

</html>
```

4. Save your newly created file as **js-twentythree.html** or **js-twentythree.htm** in the same folder you saved the files from the previous step-by-steps.

5. Click **File** on the menu bar, and then click **New** to create a new blank document.

6. Enter the HTML text exactly as shown in **Figure 10–11**.

FIGURE 10–11 left3.html file

```
<html>

<head>
<title>HTML and JavaScript</title>
</head>

<body>
  <p align="center">
    <b>HEADINGS</b>
  </p>
  <p>
    <li>Powerful Lines</li>
    <li>Web Resources</li>
    <li>Previous Pages</li>
    <li>Fancy Fonts</li>
    <li>Perfect Pictures</li>
    <li>Orderly Tables</li>
    <li>Extra Extras</li>
  </p>
</body>

</html>
```

7. Save your newly created file as **left3.html** or **left3.htm** in the same folder.

8. Click **File** on the menu bar, click **Open**, browse to the folder that contains the files for this book, click the arrow to display all of the file types, and then open the **eighteen.html** or **eighteen.htm** file you created in Step-by-Step 3.5.

9. Click **File** on the menu bar, click **Save As**, and then save the HTML file as **right3.html** or **right3.htm** in the same folder to preserve the eighteen.html file.

10. Drag to select each of the hypertext links from the body of the document, as shown in strikethrough in this step, and then press the **Delete key** to remove the hypertext links from the document. The resulting right3.html file should look like the one shown in **Figure 10–12**.

```
<a href="#powerful">Powerful Lines</a><br />
<a href="#hyperlinks">Hyperlinks to HTML and
JavaScript Sources</a><br />
<a href="#previous">Hyperlinks to Previously
Created Web Pages</a><br />
<a href="#fonts">Fancy Fonts</a><br />
<a href="#pictures">Perfect Pictures</a><br />
<a href="#tables">Orderly Tables</a><br />
<a href="#extras">Extraordinary Extras</a><br />
```

FIGURE 10–12   right3.html file

```html
<html>

<head>
<title>HTML and JavaScript</title>
<style type="text/css">
h1 {color:red}
h2 {color:blue}
h3 {color:purple}
p {color:black}
</style>
</head>

<body style="background-color:#E6E6FA">

<h1 style="text-align:center">Organizing Tags</h1>

<p>
   There are many ways to organize a Web page. This Web page will organize
   text, hypertext links, colors and fonts. You'll also demonstrate single
   spacing, double spacing, and the use of line breaks.
</p>

<p>
   This Web page will display how to organize Web pages in a number of ways
   using:
</p>
```

Continued on next page »

FIGURE 10–12   right3.html file

《 *Continued from previous page*

```
<hr />

<h2><a name="powerful">Powerful Lines</a></h2>
A Horizontal Rule that is 10 pixels high.
<hr style="height:10px" />

A Horizontal Rule 30 pixels high.
<hr style="height:30px" />

A Horizontal Rule width set at 50%.
<hr style="width:50%" />

A Horizontal Rule width set at 25% and height set at 20 pixels.
<hr style="width:25%;height:20px" />

A Horizontal Rule without attributes and values.
<hr />

<h2><a name="hyperlinks">Hyperlinks to HTML, XHTML and JavaScript
Sources</a></h2>
<a href="http://www.microsoft.com">Microsoft</a><br />
<a href="http://sites.google.com">Google</a><br />
<a href="http://www.mozilla.org">Mozilla</a><br />
<a href="http://www.facebook.com">Facebook</a><br />
<a href="http://www.w3.org">W3</a><br />
<a href="http://www.wikipedia.org">Wikipedia</a><br />
<hr />

<h2><a name="previous">Hyperlinks to Previously Created Web Pages</a>
</h2>
<a href="one.html">One</a><br />
<a href="two.html">Two</a><br />
<a href="three.html">Three</a><br />
<a href="four.html">Four</a><br />
<a href="five.html">Five</a><br />
<a href="six.html">Six</a><br />
<a href="seven.html">Seven</a><br />
<a href="eight.html">Eight</a><br />
<a href="nine.html">Nine</a><br />
<a href="ten.html">Ten</a><br />
<a href="eleven.html">Eleven</a><br />
<hr />
```

Continued on next page 》

FIGURE 10–12   right3.html file

《 Continued from previous page

```html
<h2><a name="fonts">Fancy Fonts</a></h2>
<h3>Font Style Samples</h3>
<p style="font-family:verdana">This is the Verdana font.</p>
<p style="font-family:times">This is the Times font.</p>
<p style="font-family:courier">This is the Courier font.</p>

<h3>Font Size Samples</h3>
<p style="font-size:150%">This is 150% normal size.</p>
<p style="font-size:100%">This is 100% normal size.</p>
<p style="font-size:75%">This is 75% normal size.</p>

<h3>Font Color Samples</h3>
<p style="color:red">This is Red.</p>
<p style="color:white">This is White.</p>
<p style="color:blue">This is Blue.</p>

<h3>Multiple Font Style Samples</h3>
<p style="font-family:verdana;font-size:110%;color:green">
   This is a sample of Verdana at 110% and colored green.
</p>
<p style="font-family:courier;font-size:140%;color:yellow">
   This is a sample of Courier at 140% and colored yellow.
</p>
<p style="font-family:arial;font-size:70%;color:orange">
   This is a sample of Arial at 70% and colored orange.
</p>
<hr />

<h2><a name="pictures">Perfect Pictures</a></h2>
<img src="levy.gif" />
<p><img src="levy.gif" align="right" height="50" width="50" /></p>
<img src="levy.gif" height="100" width="100" />
<img src="levy.gif" height="150" width="150" />
<img src="levy.gif" height="200" width="200" />
<p><img src="levy.gif" height="150" width="150" /></p>
<p><img src="levy.gif" height="200" width="200" /></p>
<hr />

<h2><a name="tables">Orderly Tables</a></h2>
<table border="5" cellpadding="10" align="center">
   <tr>
```

Continued on next page 》

FIGURE 10–12 right3.html file

《 *Continued from previous page*

```html
    <th>Images</th>
    <th>Colors</th>
    <th>Fonts</th>
  </tr>
  <tr>
    <td><img src="levy.gif" height="50" width="50"></td>
    <td bgcolor="red" align="center">Red</td>
    <td align="center"><font face="times" size="7" color="red">Times</td>
  </tr>
  <tr>
    <td><img src="levy.gif" height="75" width="50"></td>
    <td bgcolor="green" align="center">Green</td>
    <td align="center"><font face="courier" size="10"
color="green">Courier</td>
  </tr>
</table>
<hr />

<h2><a name="extras">Extraordinary Extras</a></h2>
<h3> Text Input Box </h3>
<form>
Enter your first name: <input type="text" size="25" /><br />
Enter your last name: <input type="text" size="30" /><br />
<input type="submit" />
</form>

<h3> Selection List Input </h3>
The favorite team is:<br />
<form>
<select>
<option>Chicago Bulls</option>
<option>Utah Jazz</option>
<option>Los Angeles Lakers</option>
<option>Cleveland Cavaliers</option>
<option>New Jersey Nets</option>
<option>Phoenix Suns</option>
</select><br />
<input type="submit" />
</form>

<h3> Radio Button Input </h3>
The best place to eat is:<br />
<form>
<input type="radio" name="best">Wendy's<br />
```

Continued on next page 》》

FIGURE 10–12   right3.html file

《 *Continued from previous page*

```
<input type="radio" name="best">Five Guys<br />
<input type="radio" name="best">Taco Bell<br />
<input type="radio" name="best">Burger King<br />
<input type="radio" name="best">Kentucky Fried Chicken<br />
<input type="submit" />
</form>

<h3> Checkbox Input </h3>
I like to eat:<br>
<form>
<input type="checkbox" />Hamburgers<br />
<input type="checkbox" />Tacos<br />
<input type="checkbox" />Chicken Strips<br />
<input type="checkbox" />Fries<br />
<input type="checkbox" />Hot Dogs<br />
<input type="submit"  />
</form>
<hr />

</body>

</html>
```

11. Save the changes to the **right3.html** or **right3.htm** file in the same folder.

12. Start your Web browser and then open the **js-twentythree.html** or **js-twentythree.htm** file to view the file as a Web page in the browser. The Web page on your screen should look like the one shown in **Figure 10–13**.

FIGURE 10–13
Frame-based document viewer

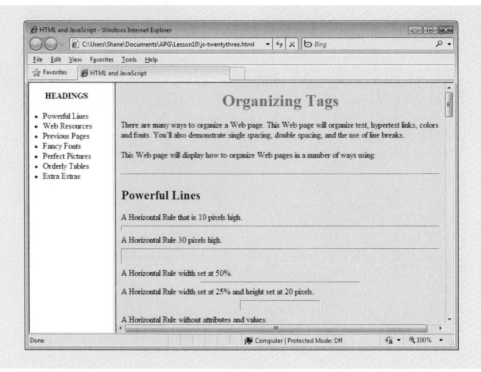

The basic organization of this Web page is the same as the one in Step-by-Step 10.1. The frameset file defines a simple left/right frame layout. The left frame contains an unordered list of the H2 headings that appear in the document displayed in the right frame. This is a common configuration for a simple document viewer.

Making Your Document Viewer Functional

The process of making a document viewer Web page functional is similar to making your style viewer functional. The first step is to add a top-level JavaScript function to your frameset file. This function performs the majority of the work required to locate a particular H2 heading and highlight it.

The JavaScript code in your js-twentytwo.html file makes use of the *getElementById()* method to identify and access the HTML elements that are modified. Similarly, your new function uses the JavaScript *getElementsByTagName()* method to reference an array of HTML elements to which a cascading style has been applied. It then determines which element is active and highlights it while the other elements are rendered in the default cascading style.

As was the case with the Web page created in Step-by-Step 10.2, the documents displayed in the left and right frames must be modified to support the main JavaScript function. The list of section headings in the left frame must be converted to hyperlinks to invoke the function. Also, the <h2> tags in the right-frame document must be modified to include **id** attributes. These attributes must match the **name** attributes in the corresponding <a> tags for the JavaScript code to function correctly.

▶ **VOCABULARY**
getElementsByTagName()

Step-by-Step 10.4

In this step-by-step, you modify all three files of your document viewer. You add a top-level JavaScript function to your frameset file and hyperlinks to the left-frame file. You also add **id** attributes to the right-frame file.

1. Open Notepad, SimpleText, or your favorite text editor.

2. Click **File** on the menu bar, click **Open**, browse to the folder that contains the files for this book, click the arrow to display all of the file types, and then open the **js-twentythree.html** or **js-twentythree.htm** file you created in Step-by-Step 10.3.

3. Click **File** on the menu bar, click **Save As**, and then save the HTML file as **js-twentyfour.html** or **js-twentyfour.htm** in the same folder to preserve the js-twentythree.html file.

4. Add a `<script></script>` section to the header of your frameset file, as shown in bold in this step and in **Figure 10–14**.

```
<script>
function locate(heading)
{
  var h2 =
    RightFrame.document.getElementsByTagName
    ("h2");
  var n = h2.length;
  for (i = 0; i < n; i++)
  {
    if (h2[i].id == heading)
    {
      h2[i].style.color = "red";
      h2[i].style.fontSize = "30";
    }
    else
    {
      h2[i].style.color = "blue";
      h2[i].style.fontSize = "24";
    }
  }
  var target = "right4.html#" + heading;
  RightFrame.document.location = target;
  return;
}
</script>
```

5. Change the name of the files to be displayed in the left and right frames, as shown in bold in this step and in **Figure 10–14**.

```
<frame name="LeftFrame" src="left4.html">
<frame name="RightFrame" src="right4.html">
```

FIGURE 10–14   js-twentyfour.html file

```
<html>

<head>
<title>HTML and JavaScript</title>
<script>
function locate(heading)
{
  var h2 = RightFrame.document.getElementsByTagName("h2");
  var n = h2.length;
  for (i = 0; i < n; i++)
  {
    if (h2[i].id == heading)
    {
      h2[i].style.color = "red";
      h2[i].style.fontSize = "30";
    }
    else
    {
      h2[i].style.color = "blue";
      h2[i].style.fontSize = "24";
    }
  }
  var target = "right4.html#" + heading;
  RightFrame.document.location = target;
  return;
}
</script>
</head>

<frameset cols="20%,*">
  <frame name="LeftFrame" src="left4.html">
  <frame name="RightFrame" src="right4.html">
</frameset>

</html>
```

6. Save the changes to the file js-twentyfour.html.

7. Click **File** on the menu bar, click **Open**, browse to the folder with your saved files, and then open the **left3.html** or **left3.htm** file you created in Step-by-Step 10.3.

8. Click **File** on the menu bar, click **Save As**, and then save the HTML file as **left4.html** or **left4.htm** in the same folder to preserve the left3.html file.

9. Add <a> hyperlink tags to the unordered list of headings, as shown in this step and in bold in **Figure 10–15**.

```
<li><a href="javascript:top.locate('powerful')">
  Powerful Lines</a></li>
<li><a href="javascript:top.locate
  ('hyperlinks')">Web Resources</a></li>
<li><a href="javascript:top.locate('previous')">
  Previous Pages</a></li>
<li><a href="javascript:top.locate('fonts')">
  FancyFonts</a></li>
<li><a href="javascript:top.locate('pictures')">
  Perfect Pictures</a></li>
<li><a href="javascript:top.locate('tables')">
  Orderly Tables</a></li>
<li><a href="javascript:top.locate('extras')">
  Extra Extras</a></li>
```

FIGURE 10–15   left4.html file

```
<html>

<head>
<title>HTML and JavaScript</title>
</head>

<body>
  <p align="center">
    <b>HEADINGS</b>
  </p>
  <p>
   <li><a href="javascript:top.locate('powerful')">Powerful Lines</a></li>
   <li><a href="javascript:top.locate('hyperlinks')">Web Resources</a></li>
   <li><a href="javascript:top.locate('previous')">Previous Pages</a></li>
   <li><a href="javascript:top.locate('fonts')">Fancy Fonts</a></li>
   <li><a href="javascript:top.locate('pictures')">Perfect Pictures</a></li>
   <li><a href="javascript:top.locate('tables')">Orderly Tables</a></li>
   <li><a href="javascript:top.locate('extras')">Extra Extras</a></li>
  </p>
</body>

</html>
```

10. Save the changes to the file **left4.html** or **left4.htm** in the same folder.

11. Click **File** on the menu bar, click **Open**, browse to the folder with your saved files, and then open the **right3.html** or **right3.htm** file you created in Step-by-Step 10.3.

12. Click **File** on the menu bar, click **Save As**, and then save the HTML file as **right4.html** or **right4.htm** in the same folder to preserve the right3.html file.

13. Add id attributes to the <h2> tags, as shown in bold in this step and in **Figure 10–16**.

```
.... skip code ....

<h2 id="powerful"><a name="powerful">Powerful
Lines</a></h2>

.... skip code ....

<h2 id="hyperlinks"><a
name="hyperlinks">Hyperlinks to HTML, XHTML and
   JavaScript Sources</a></h2>

.... skip code ....

<h2 id="previous"><a name="previous">Hyperlinks
to Previously Created Web Pages</a></h2>

.... skip code ....

<h2 id="fonts"><a name="fonts">Fancy Fonts</
a></h2>

.... skip code ....

<h2 id="pictures"><a name="pictures">Perfect
Pictures</a></h2>

.... skip code ....

<h2 id="tables"><a name="tables">Orderly
Tables</a></h2>

.... skip code ....

<h2 id="extras"><a name="extras">Extraordinary
Extras</a></h2>

.... skip code ....
```

FIGURE 10–16 right4.html file

```
<html>

<head>
<title>HTML and JavaScript</title>
<style type="text/css">
h1 {color:red}
h2 {color:blue}
h3 {color:purple}
p {color:black}
</style>
</head>

<body style="background-color:#E6E6FA">

<h1 style="text-align:center">Organizing Tags</h1>

<p>
  There are many ways to organize a Web page. This Web page will organize
  text, hypertext links, colors and fonts. You'll also demonstrate single
  spacing, double spacing, and the use of line breaks.
</p>

<p>
  This Web page will display how to organize Web pages in a number of ways
  using:
</p>

<hr />

<h2 id="powerful"><a name="powerful">Powerful Lines</a></h2>
A Horizontal Rule that is 10 pixels high.
<hr style="height:10px" />

A Horizontal Rule 30 pixels high.
<hr style="height:30px" />

A Horizontal Rule width set at 50%.
<hr style="width:50%" />

A Horizontal Rule width set at 25% and height set at 20 pixels.
<hr style="width:25%;height:20px" />
```

Continued on next page »

FIGURE 10–16   right4.html file

《 *Continued from previous page*

```
A Horizontal Rule without attributes and values.
<hr />

<h2 id="hyperlinks"><a name="hyperlinks">Hyperlinks to HTML, XHTML and
  JavaScript Sources</a></h2>
<a href="http://www.microsoft.com">Microsoft</a><br />
<a href="http://sites.google.com">Google</a><br />
<a href="http://www.mozilla.org">Mozilla</a><br />
<a href="http://www.facebook.com">Facebook</a><br />
<a href="http://www.w3.org">W3</a><br />
<a href="http://www.wikipedia.org">Wikipedia</a><br />
<hr />

<h2 id="previous"><a name="previous">Hyperlinks to Previously Created Web
  Pages</a></h2>
<a href="one.html">One</a><br />
<a href="two.html">Two</a><br />
<a href="three.html">Three</a><br />
<a href="four.html">Four</a><br />
<a href="five.html">Five</a><br />
<a href="six.html">Six</a><br />
<a href="seven.html">Seven</a><br />
<a href="eight.html">Eight</a><br />
<a href="nine.html">Nine</a><br />
<a href="ten.html">Ten</a><br />
<a href="eleven.html">Eleven</a><br />
<hr />

<h2 id="fonts"><a name="fonts">Fancy Fonts</a></h2>
<h3>Font Style Samples</h3>
<p style="font-family:verdana">This is the Verdana font.</p>
<p style="font-family:times">This is the Times font.</p>
<p style="font-family:courier">This is the Courier font.</p>

<h3>Font Size Samples</h3>
<p style="font-size:150%">This is 150% normal size.</p>
<p style="font-size:100%">This is 100% normal size.</p>
<p style="font-size:75%">This is 75% normal size.</p>

<h3>Font Color Samples</h3>
<p style="color:red">This is Red.</p>
<p style="color:white">This is White.</p>
<p style="color:blue">This is Blue.</p>
```

Continued on next page 》

FIGURE 10–16   right4.html file

« Continued from previous page

```html
<h3>Multiple Font Style Samples</h3>
<p style="font-family:verdana;font-size:110%;color:green">
  This is a sample of Verdana at 110% and colored green.
</p>
<p style="font-family:courier;font-size:140%;color:yellow">
  This is a sample of Courier at 140% and colored yellow.
</p>
<p style="font-family:arial;font-size:70%;color:orange">
  This is a sample of Arial at 70% and colored orange.
</p>
<hr />

<h2 id="pictures"><a name="pictures">Perfect Pictures</a></h2>
<img src="levy.gif" />
<p><img src="levy.gif" align="right" height="50" width="50" /></p>
<img src="levy.gif" height="100" width="100" />
<img src="levy.gif" height="150" width="150" />
<img src="levy.gif" height="200" width="200" />
<p><img src="levy.gif" height="150" width="150" /></p>
<p><img src="levy.gif" height="200" width="200" /></p>
<hr />

<h2 id="tables"><a name="tables">Orderly Tables</a></h2>
<table border="5" cellpadding="10" align="center">
  <tr>
    <th>Images</th>
    <th>Colors</th>
    <th>Fonts</th>
  </tr>
  <tr>
    <td><img src="levy.gif" height="50" width="50"></td>
    <td bgcolor="red" align="center">Red</td>
    <td align="center"><font face="times" size="7" color="red">Times</td>
  </tr>
  <tr>
    <td><img src="levy.gif" height="75" width="50"></td>
    <td bgcolor="green" align="center">Green</td>
    <td align="center"><font face="courier" size="10"
color="green">Courier</td>
  </tr>
</table>
<hr />
```

Continued on next page »

FIGURE 10–16   right4.html file

《 *Continued from previous page*

```html
<h2 id="extras"><a name="extras">Extraordinary Extras</a></h2>
<h3> Text Input Box </h3>
<form>
Enter your first name: <input type="text" size="25" /><br />
Enter your last name: <input type="text" size="30" /><br />
<input type="submit" />
</form>

<h3> Selection List Input </h3>
The favorite team is:<br />
<form>
<select>
<option>Chicago Bulls</option>
<option>Utah Jazz</option>
<option>Los Angeles Lakers</option>
<option>Cleveland Cavaliers</option>
<option>New Jersey Nets</option>
<option>Phoenix Suns</option>
</select><br />
<input type="submit" />
</form>

<h3> Radio Button Input </h3>
The best place to eat is:<br />
<form>
<input type="radio" name="best">Wendy's<br />
<input type="radio" name="best">Five Guys<br />
<input type="radio" name="best">Taco Bell<br />
<input type="radio" name="best">Burger King<br />
<input type="radio" name="best">Kentucky Fried Chicken<br />
<input type="submit" />
</form>

<h3> Checkbox Input </h3>
I like to eat:<br>
<form>
<input type="checkbox" />Hamburgers<br />
<input type="checkbox" />Tacos<br />
<input type="checkbox" />Chicken Strips<br />
<input type="checkbox" />Fries<br />
<input type="checkbox" />Hot Dogs<br />
<input type="submit"  />
</form>
<hr />

</body>

</html>
```

14. Save the changes to the file **right4.html** or **right4.htm** in the same folder.

15. Start your Web browser and then open the **js-twentyfour.html** or **js-twentyfour.htm** file to view the file as a Web page in the browser. The Web page on your screen should look like the one shown in **Figure 10–17**.

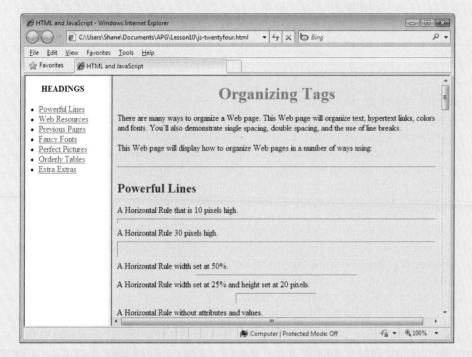

FIGURE 10–17
Functional document viewer—default state

16. Click the **Fancy Fonts** hyperlink in the left frame. Your Web page on your screen should look like **Figure 10–18**.

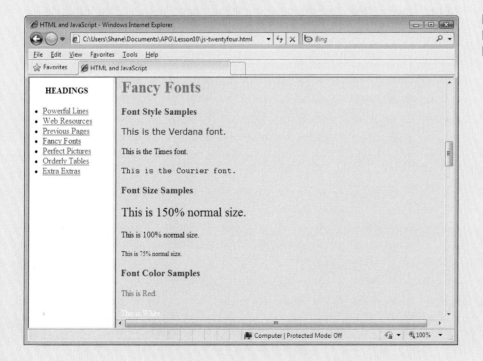

FIGURE 10–18
Functional document viewer—Fancy Fonts selected

The document in the left frame displays an unordered list of hyperlinks. When the user clicks a link, this page calls the top-level JavaScript function called *locate()*. It passes to the function a single parameter, which is the id of the <h2> tag to locate in the document displayed in the right frame.

The *locate()* JavaScript function first creates an array of all of the <h2> tag elements in the right-side document by using the *getElementsByTagName()* method. The function then tests each heading to see if it is the active one or not. If so, it sets the style of the heading to be red and 30 points in size. Otherwise, the heading is set to the default values of blue and 24 points in size. The function then sets the *location* property of the document object to correspond to the selected heading. The **location** property simply contains the URL of the current HTML document.

▶ **VOCABULARY**
location

Creating Dynamic Content with JavaScript Style Classes

The style manipulation techniques presented in the previous step-by-step exercises work well if you only need to change one or two style attributes. However, this approach becomes tedious if you need to change many different attributes at the same time. As a general rule, you need a line of JavaScript code for each style attribute you want to change. It would help to keep your JavaScript code simple if there was a way to change any number of style attributes with a single statement.

As it turns out, there is a way to do exactly that. Recall from Lesson 5 that it is possible to define many different style attributes in a style class within a Cascading Style Sheet. In fact, you can define any number of style classes within a CSS. The style **class** is then applied, by means of the class attribute, to an HTML element, and all of the attributes in the class take effect simultaneously. JavaScript can accomplish the same effect by changing the style class assigned to a Web page element. This is the technique you learn in the next step-by-step.

Step-by-Step 10.5

In this step-by-step, you create a simple Web page and a Cascading Style Sheet containing several style classes. The Web page displays a phrase with one style class, and then a JavaScript function repeatedly changes the appearance of the phrase by changing its assigned style class.

1. Open Notepad, SimpleText, or your favorite text editor if it is not already open.

2. Click **File** on the menu bar, and then click **New** to create a new blank document.

3. Enter the HTML text exactly as shown in **Figure 10–19**.

FIGURE 10–19   js-twentyfive.html file

```
<html>

<head>
<title>HTML and JavaScript</title>
<link href="js-twentyfive.css" rel="stylesheet" type="text/css"></link>
```

Continued on next page 》

FIGURE 10–19   js-twentyfive.html file

《 *Continued from previous page*

```
<script>
var index = 0;

function stylize()
{
  index++;
  if (index > 7) index = 1;
  var s = "myStyle" + index;
  var e = document.getElementById("MessageText");
  e.className = s;
  setTimeout("stylize()", 1500);
  return;
}
</script>
</head>

<body onLoad="stylize()">
  <table align="center" border="1" bordercolor="black">
    <tr>
      <td align="center">
        <font size="3"><b>STYLE CLASS VIEWER</b></font>
      </td>
    </tr>
    <tr>
      <td align="center" height="100" width="400">
        <div id="MessageText" class="myStyle1">
          Hello World Wide Web!
        <div>
      </td>
    </tr>
  </table>
</body>

</html>
```

4. Save your newly created file as **js-twentyfive.html** or **js-twentyfive.htm**
    in the same folder you saved the files from the previous step-by-steps.

5. Click **File** on the menu bar, and then click **New** to create a new blank
    document.

6. Enter the CSS text exactly as shown in **Figure 10–20**.

FIGURE 10–20   js-twentyfive.css file

```
.myStyle1 {color:black; font-size:12}
.myStyle2 {color:black; font-size:18}
.myStyle3 {color:black; font-size:24}
.myStyle4 {color:black; font-size:30}
.myStyle5 {color:red; font-size:30}
.myStyle6 {color:green; font-size:30}
.myStyle7 {color:blue; font-size:30}
```

7. Save your newly created file as **js-twentyfive.css** to the same folder.

8. Start your favorite Web browser and then open the **js-twentyfive.html** or **js-twentyfive.htm** file to view the file as a Web page in the browser. The Web page on your screen should look like the one shown in **Figure 10–21**.

FIGURE 10–21
Functional style class viewer—first state

WARNING

If your browser displays the message, "To help protect your security, Internet Explorer has restricted this webpage from running scripts or ActiveX controls that could access your computer. Click here for options." click the message bar, click Allow Blocked Content, and then click Yes in the Security Warning dialog box.

9. The Web page on your screen should look similar to the one shown in **Figure 10–22**. The appearance of the phrase "Hello World Wide Web" should begin to change size and color and continue to change in 1.5-second intervals until it eventually has the same styles as the Web page shown in **Figure 10–22**. The cycle then starts over and runs continuously.

FIGURE 10–22
Functional style class viewer—final state

To review, take a look at the Cascading Style Sheet you created for this step-by-step. It simply defines seven different style classes, each of which defines two style attributes. Specifically, each class defines a font size and a font color attribute.

Next, examine how your Web page makes use of the style classes. When the page is displayed initially, the style viewer renders the *Hello World Wide Web!* phrase in a black, 12-point font. Then, the *stylize()* JavaScript function is called, and the style viewer continuously renders the phrase in 1.5-second intervals using a different style class.

The *stylize()* function is similar in function to the *apply_style()* function you wrote for Step-by-Step 10.2. This function also uses the *getElementById()* method to access the HTML element it needs to modify. But in this case, the function changes the element's style class rather than a single style property. It then invokes the *setTimeout()* method to go to sleep for 1500 milliseconds (1.5 seconds), and then the *stylize()* function is called again. Each time the function is called, it generates a new class name and effectively changes multiple style attributes at the same time.

SUMMARY

In this lesson, you learned:

- How to define a simple frame-based style viewer.
- How to make your style viewer functional.
- How to define a simple frame-based document viewer.
- How to make your document viewer functional.
- How to create a simple style class viewer.

VOCABULARY REVIEW

Define the following terms:

element	id	style
getElementById()	location	style viewer
getElementsByTagName()	render	

REVIEW QUESTIONS

TRUE / FALSE

Circle T if the statement is true or F if the statement is false.

T   F   **1.**   The HTML style attribute can only be applied to a few HTML tags.

T   F   **2.**   The HTML id attribute allows JavaScript code to access HTML elements.

T   F   **3.**   The location of JavaScript functions is never a matter of personal preference.

T   F   **4.**   In some cases, placing JavaScript functions in the top-level frameset file can simplify your JavaScript code.

T   F   **5.**   It is sometimes a good idea to place hyperlinks in a different frame than the one containing the document that the hyperlinks affect.

T   F   **6.**   Once a cascading style has been applied to a document, it is no longer possible to modify the style attributes of the elements to which it was applied.

T   F   **7.**   It is not possible for hyperlinks to call top-level JavaScript functions.

T   F   **8.**   JavaScript code can access HTML controls, but not HTML elements (tags).

T   F   **9.**   Style classes can define multiple style attributes.

T   F   **10.**   Cascading Style Sheets can contain multiple style class definitions.

FILL IN THE BLANK

Complete the following sentences by writing the correct word or words in the blanks provided.

1. The term _____ means to display with the proper style attributes applied.

2. Another name for an HTML tag is an HTML _____.

3. The HTML _____ attribute can be applied to virtually every HTML tag.

4. The _____ attribute allows JavaScript code to access HTML tags.

5. The JavaScript _____ property contains the URL of the current document.

6. The _____ method allows JavaScript code to access an HTML tag by id.

7. The _____ method returns an array of HTML tags that match a specified name.

8. The JavaScript _____ object contains an HTML element's display properties.

9. The HTML _____ attribute can be used to specify multiple style attributes.

10. The JavaScript _____ method can be used to specify a delay interval.

WRITTEN QUESTIONS

Write a short answer to each of the following questions:

1. In general terms, describe the purpose of a style viewer.

2. Explain the relationship between the HTML **style** attribute and the JavaScript **style** object.

3. In general terms, describe the purpose of a document viewer.

4. What is the difference between the JavaScript methods *getElementById()* and *getElementsByTagName()*?

5. Explain the relationship between the HTML **class** attribute and the JavaScript **className** property.

■ PROJECTS

PROJECT 10-1: FORM VALIDATION

Review the frame-based Web page you created for Step-by-Step 10.2. What happens if the user clicks the Apply Style button without selecting a text color or a cell color? As it currently stands, the button performs no action. But suppose your manager at GreatApplications, Inc., wants you to change this behavior. Suppose he wants the style viewer to display a simple error message if the user fails to select valid text and cell colors. Can you do it? Change the top-level JavaScript function in your js-twentytwo.html file so that an appropriate alert is displayed.

Save your work as **Project 10-1.html** or **Project 10-1.htm**.

PROJECT 10-3: MORE STYLE CLASSES

The style class viewer you created in Step-by-Step 10.5 uses seven different style classes to render the phrase *Hello World Wide Web!* Demonstrate that you understand the concepts presented in this lesson by adding three more style classes to render the text in three new colors. You should recognize the fact that you must modify both the CSS file and the base HTML file to make your new viewer display the phrase in 10 different ways.

Save your work as **Project 10-3.html** or **Project 10-3.htm** and **Project 10-3.css**.

PROJECT 10-2: ITALIC HEADINGS

Your supervisor at GreatApplications, Inc., wants you to make a small modification to the document viewer you created in Step-by-Step 10.4. In addition to displaying the active heading in a 30-point red font, she would like to see it italicized. Given that the JavaScript style property that controls this display effect is called **fontStyle**, modify the top-level function in your js-twentyfour.html file so that it italicizes the active H2 heading. (And make sure that you do *not* italicize the other headings as well.)

Save your work as **Project 10-2.html** or **Project 10-2.htm**.

■ CRITICAL THINKING

ACTIVITY 10-1: DISAPPEARING TEXT

Review the frame-based Web page you created for Step-by-Step 10.2. What happens if the user clicks the *Apply Style* button after selecting a text color that matches the cell color? As it currently stands, this action causes the text to effectively "disappear." Suppose your manager at GreatApplications, Inc., wants you to make sure this does not happen. Suppose he wants the style viewer to display a simple error message if the user fails to select the same color for the text and the table cell. Can you do it? Change the top-level JavaScript function in your js-twentytwo.html file so that an appropriate alert is displayed.

Save your work as **Activity 10-1.html** or **Activity 10-1.htm**.

ACTIVITY 10-2: NEW H2 HEADERS

Your supervisor at GreatApplications, Inc., has changed her mind and now wants you to modify the document viewer you created in Project 10-2. Instead of an italic 30-point red font, she would like to see the H2 headers displayed in an underlined 32-point green font. Modify the top-level function in your Project 10-2.html file so that it functions in accordance with your supervisor's request.

Save your work as **Activity 10-2.html** or **Activity 10-2.htm**.

CAPSTONE SIMULATION

Demonstrate that you have mastered the concepts presented in this lesson by creating a new version of the style class viewer you created in Step-by-Step 10.5. In this new viewer, you must define at least 20 style classes that vary in font family, font size, and font color. Then, you must modify your JavaScript function so that it picks one of these style classes at random each time it is called. In addition, you need to create an array of at least five background colors, and your *stylize()* function selects one of these at random also. Use the knowledge you obtained in Step-by-Step 10.2 to set the table cell's background color, in addition to setting the foreground color of the text phrase. Refer to **Figure 10-23**.

FIGURE 10–23   Randomizing style class viewer

Project Requirements:

- Your CSS file must contain at least 20 style classes that define font family, size, and color.

- Your cell color array must contain at least five background colors.

- Your *stylize()* function must pick a style class at random.

- Your *stylize()* function must pick a cell color at random.

- Save your work as **capstone-10.html** or **capstone-10.htm** and **capstone-10.css**.

JavaScript Basics

JAVASCRIPT TAGS, METHODS, AND KEYWORDS SUMMARY

TAGS OR ATTRIBUTES	PURPOSE	LESSON
ad banner	A portion of a Web page reserved for advertisements.	7
alert("...")	A JavaScript method used to display an alert dialog box from within a JavaScript program.	6
array	A JavaScript variable that can contain multiple values.	7
binary code	The machine-readable code that is generated by compilers and interpreters.	6
check box	An input control commonly used to allow multiple selections within a group of options.	8
child document	A Web page displayed within one frame of a frameset.	9
compiler	A specialized piece of software that converts human-readable source code into binary code.	6
components	Web page input objects. Also known as controls.	8
condition	A programming comparison that must always evaluate to one of two conditions: true or false.	6
conditional statement	A JavaScript program statement that is only executed if the associated condition evaluates to true.	6
controls	Web page input objects. Also known as components.	8
cycling banner	A special ad banner that changes every few seconds.	7
data validation	The process of verifying user input in HTML forms.	8
decrement	Decrease the value of a variable by 1.	7

continued

TAGS OR ATTRIBUTES	PURPOSE	LESSON
document.write("...")	A JavaScript method used to write a string of text into the body of an HTML document.	6
element	Another term for an HTML tag.	10
else	A JavaScript keyword used to specify an alternative code block for an **if** statement. This keyword defines the action to take if a condition evaluates to false.	6
entity code	The code used to insert a special HTML character or symbol into a Web page.	7
event	A JavaScript behavior triggered either by a user action or a system action.	7
floating-point number	A number that contains a decimal point and a decimal portion. Also referred to as a real number.	7
function	A JavaScript keyword used to define a function.	7
function parameter	A data value passed to a JavaScript function.	9
getElementById()	A JavaScript method used to access the HTML element that has the specified id attribute.	10
getElementsByTagName()	A JavaScript method used to access an array of HTML elements that have the specified tag name.	10
hyperlink rollover	A visual action that occurs when the mouse pointer passes over a hyperlink.	7
id	A JavaScript attribute used to assign an id to an HTML tag.	10
if	A JavaScript keyword used to define a conditional statement block. The block is executed if the condition evaluates to true.	6
image rollover	A visual action that occurs when the mouse pointer passes over an image.	7
increment	Increase the value of a variable by 1.	7
index	A variable or constant used to identify a particular element within an array.	7
interpretation	The process of converting human-readable source code into machine-readable binary code on a line-by-line basis.	6
keywords	Special words that are reserved by the JavaScript language and may not be used as variable names, function names, etc.	6
location	A JavaScript property that contains the URL of the current Web page.	10
Math.random()	A JavaScript method used to generate a random number.	7
methods	Specialized functions that belong to predefined objects within the JavaScript language.	6

continued

TAGS OR ATTRIBUTES	PURPOSE	LESSON
objects	Collections of related methods and properties defined within the JavaScript language.	6
onAbort	A JavaScript event that fires when the user aborts the loading of a Web page.	7
onBlur	A JavaScript event that fires when a Web page control loses focus.	7
onChange	A JavaScript event that fires when the value of a Web page control changes.	7
onClick	A JavaScript event that fires when the user clicks the mouse button.	7
onError	A JavaScript event that fires when an error occurs.	7
onFocus	A JavaScript event that fires when a Web page control receives focus.	7
onLoad	A JavaScript event that fires when the browser finishes loading a Web page.	7
onMouseOut	A JavaScript event that fires when the mouse pointer moves off of a specified object.	7
onMouseOver	A JavaScript event that fires when the mouse pointer moves over a specified object.	7
onSelect	A JavaScript event that fires when the user selects (highlights) an object or control.	7
onSubmit	A JavaScript event that fires when the user submits an HTML form.	7
onUnload	A JavaScript event that fires when the browser unloads a Web page from memory.	7
operators	JavaScript symbols used to represent various mathematical operations such as addition, subtraction, multiplication, etc.	6
parameter list	A list of zero or more data values that are passed to JavaScript methods and functions.	6
parent	A JavaScript object used to access a parent document.	9
parent document	An HTML document that defines a frameset.	9
programming language	A computer language that is converted to binary code by means of a compiler.	6
properties	Values stored within JavaScript objects.	6
radio button	An input control commonly used to allow a single selection within a group of options. Also called option button.	8
real number	A number that contains a decimal point and a decimal portion. Also referred to as a floating-point number.	7
render	To display an object with the proper style attributes applied.	10

continued

TAGS OR ATTRIBUTES	PURPOSE	LESSON
<script></script>	HTML tags that define the beginning and ending of a section of JavaScript code.	6
scripting language	A computer language that is converted to binary code by means of an interpreter.	6
slide show	A series of images displayed in a specified sequence.	7
status line	The bottom line of the Web browser where status messages are displayed.	6
syntax	The grammar rules to which a programming language must adhere to compile or run correctly.	6
style	A collection of one or more display properties.	10
text field	An HTML control that accepts user input.	8
token	A JavaScript variable, object name, or constant.	6
top	A JavaScript object used to access the top-level parent document.	9
var	A JavaScript keyword used to declare a variable.	7
variable	A name assigned to a specific program value.	6
window.status	A JavaScript property used to access the browser status line.	6

■ REVIEW QUESTIONS

MATCHING

Match the correct term in the right column to its description in the left column.

1. The HTML tags used to denote the inclusion of embedded JavaScript code

2. The JavaScript keyword used to evaluate a condition

3. The JavaScript property used to access the Web browser status line

4. The JavaScript keyword used to define a function

5. The JavaScript method used to generate a random number

6. The JavaScript event that fires when a Web page is loaded

7. The HTML tag used to define various Web page controls

8. The process of verifying user input in an HTML form

9. The HTML input control that allows multiple selections within a group

10. A Web page displayed in one frame of a frameset

11. The JavaScript object used to access a frameset document

12. The JavaScript object used to access the top-level frameset

13. To display an object with the proper style attributes applied

14. A JavaScript method used to access a particular HTML tag with a particular id

15. A JavaScript method used to access all HTML tags of a particular type

A. child document

B. <input>

C. Math.random()

D. getElementsByTagName()

E. onLoad

F. function

G. data validation

H. check box

I. <script></script>

J. if

K. window.status

L. parent

M. top

N. render

O. getElementById()

WRITTEN QUESTIONS

Compose a brief answer to each of the following questions. Save the answers in a single document file named JavaScript Unit Summary.

1. Explain the difference between compiled and interpreted computer languages.

2. What is an array? What are the two main components of an array in JavaScript?

3. What is a function? Describe the JavaScript syntax to define a function.

4. Explain the difference between a parent document and a child document.

5. What is an HTML element? Identify two ways in which elements can be accessed by JavaScript.

■ CROSS-CURRICULAR PROJECTS

In this exercise, you will use HTML and JavaScript to create an online Web page quiz for learners in Language Arts, Science, Social Studies, Math, and a subject of your choice. Here's the trick—you have to create only one test form and then add different questions for each of the subjects later. In other words, create a master quiz and then change the questions for each subject area. Save each quiz separately so you will have five separate quizzes at the end of your effort.

Create an online quiz form that asks 10 questions. Combine HTML and JavaScript to create your master question-and-answer HTML/JavaScript document. Use a variety of question types: text fields, to allow short written answers; check boxes, to allow users to choose from a number of possible answers; and radio buttons, to allow users to select a single response from a list of alternatives. Use JavaScript to create a *Clear* button that will clear all of the answers from each quiz at the end of the test.

Revisit the sites you listed in the Unit 1 Review Cross-Curricular projects. Imagine that you are to visit each of the sites you recommended in those projects. Your job is to create a quiz that will test to see if users have truly visited the sites and learned something from the content found on those pages. Add questions to your master online quiz form for the following subject areas. Save each quiz separately.

LANGUAGE ARTS 2

Write 10 questions and insert them into your HTML/JavaScript quiz. Name this file **la-2.html** or **la-2.htm**.

SCIENCE 2

Write 10 questions and insert them into your HTML/JavaScript quiz. Name this file **sci-2.html** or **sci-2.htm**.

SOCIAL STUDIES 2

Write 10 questions and insert them into your HTML/JavaScript quiz. Name this file **ss-2.html** or **ss-2.htm**.

MATH 2

Write 10 questions and insert them into your HTML/JavaScript quiz. Name this file **m-2.html** or **m-2.htm**.

YOUR CHOICE OF SUBJECT 2

Write 10 questions and insert them into your HTML/JavaScript quiz. Name this file **mychoice-2.html** or **mychoice-2.htm**.

REVIEW PROJECTS

PROJECT 2–1: USING CSS TO CREATE AN EXCITING WEB PAGE

This is your chance to create a JavaScript project combining HTML and JavaScript to make something happen. For example, consider the hyperlinks in the left-hand navigation frame of Project 1-1 in the Unit 1 Review. Can you use the JavaScript *onMouseOver* event to display a brief description of each Web page in the browser status bar when the mouse pointer passes over it? What else can you create? Find a way to use your knowledge of Cascading Style Sheets, and incorporate a CSS file into your project. The CSS file can define the style of your text and background colors, hyperlinks, and table cells, as well as other elements. Save your work as **Project 2-1.html** or **Project 2-1.htm**.

PROJECT 2–2: IMPROVING JAVASCRIPT-ENABLED PAGES

It is time to show your handiwork to your peers, who have also created some innovative functionality with JavaScript in Project 2-1, in groups of three or four students. Demonstrate one of your HTML/JavaScript quizzes that you created for your Cross-Curricular projects.

If any team member is having problems making elements of his or her pages work, solve these problems as a team. Give suggestions to each other on how these JavaScript-enabled pages can be improved.

SIMULATION

JOB 2–1: RESEARCHING JAVASCRIPT-ENHANCED WEB SITES

Search the Web for five sites that use JavaScript in some way to enhance the Web site. List the sites and include a short sample of the JavaScript code used on each side in a single word-processing file named **Job 2-1**.

JOB 2–2: FINDING JAVASCRIPT RESOURCES

Do you want to learn more about JavaScript? Search the Web and see if there are any online tutorials that can help you learn more about implementing JavaScript in your Web pages. Learn at least one new technique and create a Web page that includes your newly learned JavaScript code. Save your work as **Job 2-2**.

■ SUMMARY PROJECT

In this unit, you learned how to manipulate images with JavaScript. You also learned how to use JavaScript to validate Web forms and to apply styles, cascading styles, and style classes. Now you can demonstrate that you have mastered these concepts by creating a Web page that implements image processing, form validation, and styles.

GreatApplications, Inc., would like to start selling computer systems over the Internet, and they need you to create an online order form for them. Your order form should allow customers to select different types of computer cases, monitors, and printers. As customers make their selections, the total system price should be updated. The order form should also allow customers to enter their name, shipping address, phone number, and e-mail address. The entire form should be validated before being submitted to GreatApplications. When the order form is complete, it should look similar to the one in Figure U2–1. Name your completed project **unit2-summary.html** or **unit2-summary.htm**.

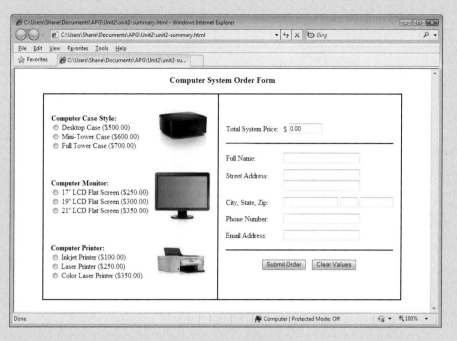

FIGURE U2–1   Computer system order form

PROJECT REQUIREMENTS

- Give your order form an appropriate title.

- Give the customer at least three choices of case styles, monitors, and printers.

- Display a 125 × 125 pixel image of the customer's selections.

- You may download your computer component images from the Internet. Please avoid downloading copyrighted images.

- The total system price should update automatically when the customer makes a selection. But the customer should not be able to update the price manually. (This means the text field should be read-only.)

- When the customer clicks the Submit Order button, a JavaScript function should validate the order form. All fields are required except the second line of the Address field.

- If any field of the order form fails its validation check, an appropriate error message should be displayed.

- If the order form passes all validation checks, an "order submitted" message should be displayed.

- If the user clicks the Clear Values button, a JavaScript function should clear the entire form (and reset the total system price to $0.00).

- Use a CSS file to define the style attributes of the order form.

■ PORTFOLIO CHECKLIST

Include the following files from this unit in your student portfolio:

_____   JavaScript Unit Summary Questions

_____   Language Arts 2

_____   Science 2

_____   Social Studies 2

_____   Math 2

_____   Your Choice of Subject 2

_____   Project 2-1

_____   Project 2-2

_____   Job 2-1

_____   Job 2-2

_____   Summary Project

GLOSSARY

A

active   The state of a hyperlink when it has focus (mouse button clicked).

ad banner   See *cycling banner*.

angle brackets   HTML tags appear in pairs and are enclosed in angle brackets < >. The brackets can be found on the comma (,) and period (.) keys on the keyboard.

app   An application generally created as a relatively small object, usually small and targeted in scope and purpose, that can run online and on computers, handhelds, and cell phones.

array   A collection of similar objects that are accessed by a variable name and an index. When you give several controls the same name, they are considered an array of objects. The array is required to have an index value that will always start with zero and increase for each element in the array.

attribute   Tags, such as <body>, used to enhance an HTML tag by assigning different types of values to change the appearance of the Web page's body or background.

B

binary code   The machine-readable version of a script or program.

border attribute   Used within the <frameset> tag to define the width of frame separators.

buttons   Input controls that are defined with the type="button" attribute within the input tag.

C

.css   The file extension normally applied to Cascading Style Sheets files.

Cascading Style Sheets (CSS)   An HTML enhancement that describes how Web pages should look. Used to efficiently bring unity and similar styles to Web sites.

check box   An input control that allows the user to select any or all of the listed options from a set of options.

child document   An HTML frame file that is part of a frameset.

cols attribute   Defines widths of vertical frames (with pixel or percentage values).

compiler   A highly specialized piece of software that takes a programming language that humans can understand and converts it into a language that computers can understand.

components   See *controls*.

condition   Made up of two tokens and a relational operator. A conditional statement tells the browser that if this condition is met or true, perform this function; if not or false (else), perform a different function.

controls/components   An interactive object with a JavaScript form. Controls or components must be given a name so they can be referenced within the JavaScript code.

cross-frame interaction   Action performed when an action in one frame affects the appearance of a different frame. All of the frames that make up a Web page can communicate with each other by means of JavaScript functions.

CSS files   Another way to refer to Cascading Style Sheets.

cycling banner   Several graphics are displayed one after another with a pause between images. The graphics scroll on either a fixed or random order. Also called an ad banner.

D

data validation   The process of checking user input data to make sure it is complete and accurate.

decrement   To subtract one member from a value; decreasing the value of a variable by 1.

depreciation   When a tag is downgraded or made obsolete.

E

element   An HTML tag.

entity code   An HTML code that represents a special symbol on a Web page.

event   The operating system's response to the occurrence of a specific condition.

F

Flash   A high-impact multimedia creation tool for the creation of Web page content.

floating-point number   See *real number*.

fonts   The style of letters that determines the appearance of text in Web documents. Fonts have three attributes that can be changed: size, style, and color of text.

frame   A rectangular area, a subset of a browser's screen, capable of displaying a Web page that is separate from other frames on the screen.

frame separator   Semithick line displayed between frames.

frameset   Allows the definition of a set of rectangular areas on a Web page called frames where each frame is capable of displaying a different Web page.

function   A piece of JavaScript that can be called upon to perform certain tasks. Functions are written by the programmer and can contain any number of JavaScript statements, including calls to other functions or methods.

Function parameter   An efficient way to pass a parameter to a function, especially if there are 10, 20, or 100 different parameters.

G

Gadget   See *app*.

getElementById()   JavaScript method that returns the HTML element that matches a specified ID.

getElementsByTagName()   JavaScript method that returns an array of HTML elements that matches a specified tag name.

GIF   An acronym for Graphics Interchange Format. GIF files are compact in size and are one of two popular graphic formats used in Web documents. The extension, .gif, helps to tell the Web browser that these files are pictures, not Web documents.

Graphics   Pictures that can be placed in Web documents.

Graphics Interchange Format   Compact graphics, also called GIFs, that are small enough in size to use in Web documents.

H

hexadecimal   Digits that operate on a base-16 number system rather than the base-10 number system; use the letters A, B, C, D, E, and F along with the numbers 0–9 to create 16 different digits.

home page   The main Web page for a corporation, individual, or organization. A home page is often the first page you see when you start your Web browser.

hover   The state of a hyperlink when the mouse pointer is over it.

HTML   An acronym for Hypertext Markup Language. See *Hypertext Markup Language*.

HTML page   An HTML page, or HTML document, is any document created in HTML that can be displayed on the World Wide Web.

HTTP   An acronym that stands for Hypertext Transfer Protocol. On the location line in your Web browser, this is often seen in the following format: *http://www.cengage.com.*

Hyperlink rollover   An image that changes when the mouse pointer clicks on or moves over a hyperlink graphic.

Hyperlinks   Allows users to click on a specific spot in a Web document and have it link to another page they've created, to another Web page on the World Wide Web, to another document on the same computer, to a document residing on any Web server on the Internet, or to another spot within the current document.

Hypertext links   See *Hyperlinks*.

Hypertext Markup Language   Tags created within a Web document that give instructions to a Web browser. These instructions determine the look and feel of a Web document on the Internet.

Hypertext Transfer Protocol   The type of digital language that Web servers use to communicate with Web browsers. A protocol is a communications system that is used to transfer data over networks.

I

id   HTML attribute used to assign an ID to a tag.

image   A term used to refer to a graphic in a Web document. The letters *img* are part of the HTML tag used to determine attributes of an image on the World Wide Web.

image rollover   The appearance of an image changes when the mouse pointer moves over the image.

increment   To add one number to a value.

index A variable that usually has the value of zero assigned to it. The index variable is used to access information about the array.

Internet Explorer A major Web browser used to view information on the World Wide Web. Internet Explorer was created by Microsoft Corporation.

interpretation A term used by programmers to describe the line-by-line conversion process that occurs automatically at run time or when the Web browser launches the JavaScript commands that are enabled in the Web document.

J

Java A programming language that creates programs called applets. Applets can be added to Web documents using tags similar to HTML text.

JavaScript More powerful than HTML, JavaScript allows Web page developers to add programming features to a Web document without having to know a programming language.

Joint Photographic Experts Group Compact graphics called JPEGs that are small enough in size to use in Web documents.

JPG or JPEG An acronym for Joint Photographic Experts Group. JPEGs are picture files that are compact in size and are one of two popular graphic formats used in Web documents.

K

keywords A word that is recognized by the programming language as part of its language. A keyword, like *if*, *else*, or *return*, cannot be used as a variable.

L

landing page A targeted welcome page used by Web advertisers.

left-hand navigation A narrow left-hand frame that contains hyperlinks that can be used to navigate a Web site.

location JavaScript property that contains the URL of the current Web page.

look and feel Another term for appearance and behavior of a Web page.

M

methods Specialized functions within the JavaScript object that call upon the services of the object. A method is invoked after you enter the name of the object, followed by a period.

Mosaic The first Web browser that allowed pictures and sound to accompany text on a Web page. Mosaic was created in 1992 at the University of Illinois.

N

name attribute Used with the <frame> tag as a frame identifier.

navigation bar A series of hypertext links, usually organized horizontally or vertically on a Web page or in a frame. Used to navigate a Web site.

nested frameset A term programmers use to describe a structure, keyword, or tag that contains one or more additional instances of the same item.

Netscape Navigator An early popular Web browser used on the Internet. Created in 1994, it allowed powerful features such as animated graphics into a Web document.

noresize attribute Used with the <frame> tag to prevent users from changing the size of a frame.

normal The state of a hyperlink when the mouse pointer is not over it and it has not been clicked.

O

objects Invisible entities that have a defined set of capabilities. Encapsulated collections of related methods and properties.

operators Specialized symbols placed between two tokens in a conditional statement that define a relationship between the two.

option button An input control that allows the user to select just one option from a set of options. Also called radio button.

P

parameter list A list of information that provides a programming method what it needs to perform a specific function correctly.

parent document An HTML frameset file.

parent object For a JavaScript function to access an object in a different file, the two files must be linked. The "parent" frameset can be referenced via a JavaScript object. The frameset file defines "child" frames, and these frames are given names.

pixel An individual tiny dot of light inside a computer monitor.

Portable Network Graphics An image file format saved with the .png file extension. Also called PNG.

programming language A language that has to be converted from a human-readable format into machine-readable format. This process is accomplished by using a compiler to complete the operation.

properties Objects that programmers access to obtain information about the object; elements of JavaScript objects that contain information about the object.

R

radio button An input control that allows the user to select just one option from a set of options. Also called option button.

real number A real number that has a decimal portion. Also called floating-point number.

render Display an HTML object or element with style attributes applied.

return value Whenever a function is called, its name is replaced by the value it returns.

S

<script> and </script> tags The beginning and ending tags that are necessary in a Web document for a JavaScript statement to be executed. All JavaScript code must be placed within the beginning and ending tags.

scripting language A language that does not have to be run through a compiler for it to be understood. Web browsers take the human-readable format and convert it into machine-readable format "on the fly."

slide show A collection of images that change when the user clicks on the image.

src attribute Used within the <frame> tag to specify the filename of the source HTML page.

standards Publically agreed-upon rules or guidelines that are agreed to within the HTML, CSS, XML, XHTML, and other communities that guide browser and Web page design, development, and functionality.

status line The area of the screen that displays various messages at the bottom of the browser's window that can be accessed from within a JavaScript program.

style An attribute applied to any particular tag within an HTML file that affects the way HTML elements are displayed.

style class A named collection of style attributes that can be applied to an HTML tag.

style sheets Another way to refer to Cascading Style Sheets.

style viewer A simple tool that allows users to specify a style, apply the style, and then view the results.

syntax The rules of grammar for a scripting language.

T

table cell The box in which you can place text and graphics to keep a Web document organized. Each cell can have different attributes applied to text, can have a different background color, or can contain a different graphic.

tags Code that marks Web page elements, interpreted by Web browsers.

target attribute Used within the <a> tag to identify the frame in which the target Web page is displayed.

text field An input control that allows someone to type a string value into a specific location on a Web page.

title bar The topmost bar in an open window or a frame used at the top of the Web page; provides a constant title for a Web site.

token Either a variable name or a literal constant, used within condition statements, which is followed by a relational operator. A JavaScript condition will always consist of two tokens.

top object JavaScript functions can be defined in the top-level frameset file, no matter how deeply it is nested within the Web page framework. These functions can be accessed by using a JavaScript "top" object.

U

Uniform Resource Locator (URL) The Internet addressing scheme that defines the route, or path, to a file or program. The URL is used as the initial access to an online resource.

V

value Used to define attributes. For example, in the tag <body bgcolor=red>, red is a value used to define the background color attribute in a body tag.

variable A name that is assigned to a literal value or to an object. Once assigned, that name can be used throughout the HTML document to refer to that particular value or object.

visited The state of a hyperlink when it has been clicked at least once.

VRML An acronym for Virtual Reality Markup Language. A language used on the World Wide Web that allows people to view and search three-dimensional landscapes and models.

W

Web browser   Software that allows users to interface with different operating systems and view information on the World Wide Web. It allows Web page developers to have JavaScript compiled and interpreted "on the fly."

Web page   Any page created in HTML that can be placed on the World Wide Web.

Web site   Includes a series of Web pages that can be linked to other Web sites on the Internet. Web sites are stored on Web servers.

Webmaster   A person assigned to create and maintain Web pages for a Web site.

welcome page   An introduction page to a Web site. A welcome page often includes the Web page owner's e-mail address and name.

X

XHTML   Acronym for Extensible Hypertext Markup Language, which is a merger between XML and HTML.

XML   Acronym for Extensible Markup Language and provides formatting and data-sharing standards for use on online pages.

INDEX

Note: Page numbers in boldface indicate discussion of key terms.